MY CONFESSION

My Confession

Recollections of a Rogue

Samuel E. Chamberlain

ISBN: 9798859869701

WWW.DISSIDENTREVIEW.COM
[@Dissident_Rev on X]

Cover art by Clay Cottingham
[@Southern_Arch on X]

Edited & Compiled by Alaric
[@0xAlaric on X]

TABLE OF CONTENTS

The following manuscript was written by Samuel Chamberlain between 1855 and 1861.

It details his life prior to, during, and after his service in the Mexican-American War of 1846-48.

It requires no further introduction.

BATTLE OF
BUENA VISTA

The sun rose bright and clear from behind the "Sierra Free" on the morning of the 23rd of February 1847. It shone on a scene well calculated to stir ones blood to a fever heat with warlike enthusiasm and make a coward brave. I doubt if the "Sun of Austerlitz" shone on a more brilliant spectacle than the one before us. Twenty thousand men clad in new uniforms, belts as white as snow, brasses and arms burnished untill they glittered in the sunbeams like gold and silver. Their Cavalry some six thousand in number was magnificent, these richly caparisoned cavaliers, in uniforms of blue faced with red, with waving plumes and glittering weapons advanced towards us as if they would ride down our little band, and finish the battle at one blow. They formed line facing us, and then their Infantry moved forward in line of battle and formed on the left of the cavalry. Their band consolidated in front of the line, was we to be treated to Corps Dress Parade! It look like it. Soon a procession of ecclesiastical dignitaries with all the gorgeous paraphernalia of the Catholic Church, advanced along the lines, preceded by the bands praying a solemn Anthem, the Infantry knelt down, the Cavalry lowered their lances, and uncovered and their colors drooped as they passed down the line. This ceremony offered a striking contrast to the condition of things in our lines there was not a Chaplain in our army! The Priest retired, a smoke arose from a battery about a mile and a half off, and a thirty two pound solid shot plumped in to the road near the pass and the conflict commenced. The skirmish in the mountain opened lively. The enemy showed great activity along their whole line, their heavy guns keeping up a continuous fire on our right but without effect. With the exception of our skirmishers in the mountain, not a shot was fired from our line. Gen. Wool seeing that Marshal was being pressed hard by the overwhelming force of Mexicans, sent three companies of the 2nd Ill. vols under Maj Trail, to their assistance. During the night the foe had dragged a howitzer up the mountain, and opened with this on our riflemen, but as our men were well sheltered behind rocks it did not do much harm. While this was going on a heavy column of Infantry and Cavalry, moved up the Luis road against our right and charged on the pass. Capt. Washington, poured into their ranks such a rapid fire of shell and canister, that whole lines seem to sink at every disch-

A page from the original, handwritten manuscript

I

I LEAVE HOME

THE day was cold and drear in December, 1844, when I bid good-by to my friends at the Worcester Depot, in the good city of Boston, and embarked on the train for Norwich en route for the great West. I was in my sixteenth year, full of life, yet felt sad and downhearted enough at leaving home for years if not forever. What a change the last few months had made in my prospect for life! From a promising member of the Baptist Church in Bowdoin Square, and a prospective Theological Student at the Northampton Institute, I was now, to quote the language of the Rev. R.W. Cushman, of the above Church, "worse than the Devil!"

What had produced this change? Who was to blame? Well I confess I was to blame, I was the cause. I had been strictly brought up under religious influences, my reading confined to the Bible, and the usual books of a Sabbath School Library, and at fourteen I considered it my duty to become a member of the Church. At fifteen I unfortunately for my religious career joined the Junior Class at Sheridan's Gymnasium, on Washington Street, and here under the tender instructions of "Belcher" Kay and "Prof." Joe Long in sparring, and "Monsieur" Huri in the stick and small sword, I soon developed into a muscular Christian. And alas, such is the pernicious influence of the ungodly that one night in a set-to with the Professor, when I succeeded in getting one in on his "nob," I felt more elated than if I had just been ordained over a flourishing Church. Then I got hold of Scott's immortal works. What a glorious new world opened before me, how I devoured their pages and oh how I longed to emulate his heroes! I took pride in all athletic exercises and was anxious for a chance to use my strength and skill in defense of oppressed beauty.

One Sunday on my way to Church I was insulted by a rough, and on my remonstrating with him for using profane language on the Holy Sabbath, he with a fearful oath struck at me. Now while I was ready to forgive the sinner for his insult to me, I felt it was my Christian duty to punish him for his blasphemy. With my right I neatly stopped his blow, and landed a stinger on his "potato trap" with my left "duke," drawing the "Claret" and "sending him to the grass." The Rowdy got up and ran down Chardon Street, and I turned to cross over, when I saw one of our good Deacons with his two lovely daughters passing. From their looks I knew they had witnessed the little unpleasantness. This alarmed me at first, but when I caught sight of a merry twinkle in the good Deacon's eyes and an admiring glance from the young Ladies, I felt safe.

Other members had seen the incident, and the matter was brought before the Church. I was cited before a committee, where I somewhat astonished the worthies by my plea that "I consciously believed that I had acted as a good Christian should act, and for the interest of the Church!" My good friends appeared for me and I was cleared of all sinful intention in this wholesome rebuke to a sinner.

Without egotism I must confess, however painful it may be to my feelings, that I had always been rather a favorite with the young Sisters, but this little affair gave the darlings such inflated ideas of my prowess that I was in great demand as an escort for them home on Prayer Meeting nights, monthly concerts, etc. Among the many beautiful girls, there were two who were allowed by all to be pre-eminent, yet of different styles. One, a splendid brunette with magnificent black eyes and hair, Miss Annah D—a, was all the world to me. The other, a blue-eyed beauty with the face of an Angel, was a most arrant coquette, Miss Caroline W—, who caused more heart burning among the pious young brethren, than all the rest of the Sisters united. Our worthy minister's son, Austin S. Cushman, was the favorite one, yet she would flirt in the most angelic manner with many others. The minister took sides with his son and gave me a severe lecture for going home with the flirt, though there was a perfect understanding between her, Miss Annah, and myself. I did not take him very kindly and by too free expression of my thoughts made him my enemy.

My lessons at the Gymnasium continued, and I there formed new associates who were not exactly of the same religious principles as those of Bowdoin Square Church, but good fellows nevertheless.

My religious record was culminating to a crisis, and soon the bolt fell. One night at Singing School the Singing master, David Paine, who was also Organist for the Church, was ungentlemanly enough to call out the name of my adored one, for whispering!! The sensitive, high-toned beauty, overcome at the painful insult, burst into tears. I first rushed to her assistance, but finding the Sisters were assisting her, I turned on the inhuman author of her woe, and declared "that no gentleman would thus insult a lady."

His answer was to order me to leave the Vestry and School! On my declining to do so, he proceeded to put me out. Shades of Belcher Kay forbid! "Harry of the Wynd," Ivanhoe, Don

Quixote, inspire me to meet this shameless oppressor of girls' rights! He clinched me, and then all the long pent-up Knight errantry and the Seven Champions of Christendom, consolidated in me, burst, and Paine lay prostrate, bleeding, almost annihilated. The tears of my loved one was revenged in blood.

But the end was not yet. I had struck a most romantic attitude and exclaimed "Time!" when I was beset by foes, and though I fought like another Black Knight yet I was overcome by numbers and dragged out. My Lady Love brought out my personal effects, and we retreated to her paternal mansion. Her governor thanked me warmly for resenting the insult to his darling, and that night in the hall my beautiful brunette vow'd to be mine and mine alone forever. So with swelled face, black ear and cut lip, I returned her vows, and home in a most blissful dream of happiness.

This was too glaring an act of mine to let pass and I was again summoned before the outraged Church. Some of my friends, the good Deacon Wilbur, Calvin Haven and a few others, worked hard defending me but I was expelled, and then my good Shepherd, Rev. R.W. Cushman, pronounced me "worse than the Devil." Coming from such authority, what an excellent character for a boy not yet sixteen!

One consolation was left me, the love of my beautiful brunette, my own Queen of Hearts. I called at her house. She received me coldly, but explained that though she still loved me and always should, yet her parents had forbid her seeing me after this interview, and she must respect their wishes, and she vow'd that though she would obey them in this, she would never marry another.

Thus I lost confidence in woman's love, and faith in religion, and went forth shunned as if I was another Cain.

I had at this time formed the acquaintance of Bob Jones, scenic artist at the National Theatre, which was now seeing its palmy days, and of his lovely daughter Fanny, danseuse, who was all the rage of the City Bloods. I was soon good friends with the charming Fanny and was her regular escort home from the Theatre; she was as charming in mind as in person, in character above suspicion. I found myself a general favorite with all outside the Church—with the "pugs" I was looked upon as a promising future member, the Thespians found in me a useful friend, the Bohemians of the Press were beholden to me for many a sensational item, and the Ladies—well I was a boy of a man's proportion, muscles like steel, not bad looking, and very modest!

I felt unhappy, reckless, and tried in the pleasures of my new life to forget the old, yet amid all the sensual enjoyments of the times, I often felt contrite and sighed for my former career, and then one kind word would have reclaimed me, but that word was never spoken. In December, 1844, I made up my mind to go West and hunt up an Uncle of mine, one Adam Chamberlain, who lived somewhere in Illinois. So after this long digression I go back to where I started in the cars bound for Norwich, with a sinking pain at heart.

The train left the Worcester Depot at 4 o'clock and it seemed to me as if I had left behind all that was worth living for. All the world was before me, but it had no allurements for me. Oh, how I longed to be back as I was a year before! If I could only live my life over again, I thought, and I not yet sixteen.

As we dashed across the Back Bay, the snow commenced to fall, and the would-be hero fell fast asleep.

At Norwich I awoke and embarked on the Steamer *John W. Richmond* for New York. The Sound was full of floating ice, which with a heavy snowstorm made the passage anything but a pleasant one. Several times we run onto huge cakes of ice, jarring the Boat from stem to stern. The bell was kept ringing, the steam whistle shrieking, the Ladies would rush out of their State Rooms in fright; there was but little sleeping on the Boat that night.

In New York I took a "Cab" for the Jersey Ferry, rode up one street and down another and found myself close to the pier from where I started, the Ferry being the next Ship. For this little experience in New York style, the cabby only charged me the sum of two dollars! I thought it dear at fifty cents, and said that was all that I would give. He threatened to keep my trunk, whereupon I caught hold of one handle as he hung on to the other. As he pulled back, I gave a shove, when in order to save himself from falling he let go, and I gained the Ferry Boat in safety.

That night I stopped in Baltimore and then took the cars for Cumberland via Harpers Ferry. Owing to some six inches of snow on the track our progress was very slow even with the assistance of an extra engine. We arrived at Harpers Ferry about noon; the dinner bells of the Hotels were ringing, and the conductors shouted, "Twenty minutes for dinner." The men rushed for the dining rooms, paying fifty cents for the fare. The Landlord was a long time carving and serving, and not more than half a dozen had commenced to eat when the engine bell rung; the cry was "all aboard." This "trick upon travelers" was too palpable to pass, even with me, and when a jolly red-faced old gentleman cried out, "Help yourselves gentlemen!" I obeyed orders with a hearty good will, by sequestering a roast chicken and an apple Pie. In spite of the remonstrance of the out-flanked Landlord, the table was relieved of all its eatables, and we ate our dinner in the cars with our lady passengers to grace the feast, and a right jolly time we had of it. I shared my plunder with two elderly Ladies, who contributed by producing a well filled lunch box and a pocket companion of good brandy.

We reached Cumberland at dark; a glowing fire in the Parlor and a hot supper set us all to rights and prepared us for a cold night's ride in the mountains, this being the Terminus of the B.&O.R.R. Although there was two foot of snow on the ground the Stages that run to Wheeling were on wheels, without buffalo robes, nothing but straw to keep our limbs from freezing; the Thermometer was down to 0°.

I secured a back seat, and the center one, with a man on one side and a lady on the other. I offered the latter my seat as being warmer but it was declined. It was so dark inside that I could form no idea whether she was old or young, handsome or ugly, but I was certain she was not one of my brandy drinking acquaintances of the dinner, as they had concluded to stop in Cumberland overnight, and when we left they were at their fourth glass of hot Peach and Honey.

Wrapping myself up in my fur lined overcoat I tried to sleep, but it was so bitter cold I could not rest. I would drop into an uneasy slumber, disturbed by horrid dreams, and would awake numb with cold. The miserable night ended at last, and when the early dawn gave us light I gave an anxious look at my bowers. The right one was a two hundred and fifty pound Negro, his breath a villainous compound of whiskey, tobacco and onions. I gave him a shove, when a gentle sigh drew my attention to my left. By Venus! What a contrast! A young and lovely girl, richly and warmly clothed in velvets and furs, was reclining her head on my shoulder, fast asleep. I got rid of my Sable friend on my right, and devoted my whole attention to my friend on my left. I found it necessary, to preserve her equilibrium, to put my arm around her, and we passed over many a mile when a sudden jolt awoke the beauty, who looked at me with surprise and apologized for the freedom she took in using my shoulder, and I for being so familiar as to have my arm where it was, as I deem'd it necessary to keep her from falling. We were soon chatting away as if we had been acquainted all our lives, but then it don't take long to be intimate when the parties have slept together!

She informed me she was the daughter of the late Senator Fulton of Arkansas, who died recently in Washington; his remains had been shipped from New York for New Orleans. She said that she had been three terms to the Georgetown Female Seminary, and was now on her way home with a gentleman, her guardian, who she pointed out—the red faced old gentleman who gave orders to secure our dinner at Harpers Ferry. She was a great talker, and her eyes that were jet black, how they would sparkle, dance and flash as she run on! How fast her questions came! Before we stopped to Breakfast I knew her whole history, and she as much of mine as I chose to tell. She was sorry I was a Yankee, but when I assured her that I had never made a wooden Nutmeg or peddled a wooden Clock in my life she thought better of me. She was some three years older than myself and when she found this out, she commenced to patronize me, most fearfully.

After a hearty Breakfast, of bacon and eggs, broiled chicken, corn and wheat bread, butter, honey and coffee, we again started on our way. I made an objection to having his Sable majesty ride inside, but I was verdant to Southern customs. A young Virginian, the master of the Negro, got into a rage and swore, "that the boy was worth twelve hundred dollars, and doggone his buttons if he would allow him to catch his death a cold for all the cursed Yankees that ever wore Store Clothes."

I did not object to his care for his property but the contemptuous allusion to myself rather excited me. I felt as if Plymouth Rock, Bunker Hill and the Frog Pond weighed on my shoulders. I had taken this representative of the Southern

Chivalry by the collar when the voice of my beauty made me recollect that there was ladies present. What a little tempest she was! She declared that the Negro should not ride in the coach! that his master was a mean white, that if the Negro caught cold and died she would pay for him, but ride in the same coach he should not. Her guardian laughed at the rage of his ward, when her violent rage subsided in hysterical tears. But her point was gained, the Virginian, with a savage look at me, took passage with his chattel in another coach.

We had the back seat all to ourselves, and as her jolly old Guard gave her a heavy lap robe, we got along very comfortably. Coming to a long steep hill, most of the passengers got out to walk; there being a strong crust on the snow, the walking was excellent. She gave me an introduction to Mr. Wyman, her guardian. At first he was as crusty as the snow, but gradually thawed and produced a bottle of Cordial, and after we each took a drink, he showed more cordiality. He soon got tired, left us and resumed his seat in the coach. Her ladyship's tongue ran faster than ever. She described her home. The imaginary home of Claude Melotte paled before her description of her Paradise on the Arkansas, of the Cotton fields, the hundred slaves and she the sole heiress of all. During this walk she often said, "It's too bad you are a Yankee; how I wish you were a Southerner."

The day passed pleasantly enough, walking up hills and riding down, with a glorious dinner and supper at wayside Inns. At the place where we got supper, Mr. Wyman purchased a heavy quilt for his fiery little charge, and when we took our seats for another night's ride, we were well prepared for it. With our furs, robe and quilt, the back seat all to ourselves, and pressed in each other's arms, we thought the weather had wonderfully moderated; we felt no cold, in fact we were all in a glow, and if our lips did meet in blissful kisses, it could not be wondered at. We at last fell asleep and did not awake until the Stage drew up at the door of the United States Hotel in Wheeling at 3 o'clock in the morning. The passengers were so numb and cramped with cold that most of them had to be carried into the Hotel.

Mr. Wyman, the guardian, was undeniably drunk. I am sorry to record it, but the truth compels me to make the statement. His bottle was empty. He tried to sing, made a failure, and sank into a chair and was soon asleep. I booked the names, had him carried up to his room, and returned to look after my fair charge. The office room was crowded as other Stages had arrived, a glorious soft coal fire blazed up in an open grate, the jovial Landlord and assistants were busy attending to the various calls and concocting mysterious hot drinks. Colored Servants were carrying trunks and showing the sleepy ones to their rooms.

My charmer was seated in an easy chair, her eyes fixed on the glowing coals, and as I watched her brilliant features lit up by fire I thought I never saw a more charming girl, and my loyalty to my loved one at home was seriously tried. When a colored girl came to show her her room, I assisted her to rise, when with a silly laugh she said to my astonishment, "Don't leave me, love, come with me." I saw that she had a touch of the same complaint that troubled her guardian; in fact she had taken too much strong hot whiskey Punch, and the heat of the room sent it to her head. To avoid a scene I went with her and the girl to her room door, and then I was obliged to tear myself away.

Next morning Miss Fulton did not make her appearance at the Breakfast Table, but that afternoon we walked out and she was as loving as ever. The Ohio River was frozen up solid; no Boats had passed for a week. The town was full of strangers, the Hotels crowded, the price of board gone up, and no signs of a thaw.

Some few days after this I and my enchantress took a long walk on the Hills. She was more quiet than usual, and after walking on some time in silence, she remarked, "We are going back to Baltimore in a few days. You will accompany us of course!"

I hesitated and her eyes blazed up with sudden fury and she broke out with, "You must and shall come! I always have my own way and I say you shall go with me and live with me!" and threw her arms around me and sobbed like a child.

Somehow this violent exhibition of passion killed all my tender feelings for her and I tried to make her understand that it was impossible, that I must go on to Illinois, that I was a mere boy not sixteen, poor and without friends, with nothing but his own strength to fight the battles of life, while she was a young lady of nineteen, rich and with a host of friends; the thing was not possible. I might as well have reasoned with a whirlwind. She fairly raved, declared I did not love her, then she would call me a "mean Yankee" and say she "hated me, her Guard'y should kill me," and the next moment declare she would marry me and go on to Illinois with me.

I almost consented; visions of returning to Boston with a rich heiress as my wife, the sensation it would make, flittered before me. I really liked the girl, I blamed myself for the part I had taken, but I thought of the one so dear to me at home, of my desire to go into and see the World. With my arm around her waist I led her to a seat and then after long and tender conversation I solemnly swore that I would join her as soon as I could after visiting Illinois. She became satisfied, we vowed eternal love and constancy, ratified our engagement with many a kiss, and I intended fully to keep my contract to the letter and spirit. But, *l'homme propose, et Dieu dispose.*

Two days after, they started back to Baltimore to proceed from there by the Southern route. Our parting took place in the privacy of her own room, and we considered ourselves Man and Wife. As she rode away I regretted that I had not gone with them. I had Paradise open before me and I had refused to enter. I was perfectly miserable, and mad with myself. I wrote as agreed on to Baltimore, stated all my feelings and regrets, and five days after I got three loving and tender epistles, but not in answer as she had not received mine yet.

II

A FIRE, A FIGHT, &
A FLIGHT

ABOUT the middle of January King Sirius relinquished his grip on the river and a Boat from Pittsburgh made its appearance, a stern wheeler or "Wheelbarrow" as they are called on the western waters. The river was full of floating ice and our wheel got badly damaged, rendering our passage slow and tedious, eight days being spent in the passage to Cincinnati. I was delayed ten days more before there was a Boat for St. Louis, from where I took passage on the Alton packet *Tioga*.

It was a Saturday night when we reached Alton, a plank was run out, and a fearful voice told me to jump! I stood on the plank hesitating, when the same rough voice exclaimed, "Come, don't stop all night! Jump." Seeing the faint glim of a light far below, I sprang into the darkness and landed in three foot of the Illinois mud. I looked up; the Boat had already cast off and was moving away in the blackness, her furnace fires shining on the figures of men on the boiler deck, clothing them in bright red.

I seemed hopelessly stuck when a light flashed before my eyes, a hand was laid on my shoulder and a voice enquired, "Franklin Sir?" I said "yes," was hauled out, and found my trunk on a wheelbarrow high up on the bank in charge of another man. My friend with the lantern assisted me along, for I carried so much real estate on my boots I could not have walked without his support.

No other unfortunate having landed, I was the sole prize cast ashore so the porters of the Franklin House crowed considerable over the less fortunate ones of the Eagle and Alton Hotels. Words led to blows and poor me, covered with mud, cold, wet, and hungry, had to set down on the wheelbarrow, which was as muddy as myself, while the Altonites fought it out. It was about 9 P.M., quite dark, no light but the one lantern, which had been given to me at the commencement of the fray. The inhabitants came pouring out, dogs rushed through the street, barking and fighting, oaths and curses fill'd the air. I became uneasy at this slight misunderstanding and when a red-headed offender came to me I could resist the temptation no longer, but launched out with my left, caught him under the ear, sending him to mud. Somehow the fight stopped as if this was all that they had been waiting for; we were victors.

The landlord of the Franklin House informed me that my uncle, Adam Chamberlain, lived some five miles back from the town at a place called Monticello on Skerrett's Prairie. I remained here all night, had my clothes and boots cleaned of mud and to my surprise the appreciating Landlord refused any pay! "No," he said, "the man that can lick Jim Melchor at one blow can stop with me a month, and not cost him a red."

I got full directions how to find my uncle's place, and after breakfast I started. I called at the Post Office, found twelve letters from my adored one, nine from home. I went up what is called the Coal Branch and after getting into the woods I sat down on a log and opened my letters. They were dated from various places, the last three from her home. How glowing with the warm language of love and devotion their pages were! But the last one contained a sentence I could not understand; it read, "I sometimes think our acquaintance was but a blissful dream! yet so happy, so full of ecstatic joy that I would never wish to awake. You should have married me there. You should be here with me. Here is your place! Am I not your wife in the sight of God! Come at once or I am lost to you forever!"

I read this over and over again; its contents half crazed me! What could I do? I was almost out of money! I resolved to tell my uncle a part of my story, obtain a loan sufficient to carry me through, and fly to rejoin my treasure.

I proceeded on, following the Branch for a guide, and soon came to a clearing of some two hundred acres with a large Barn painted red, a small log house and numerous outbuildings. I knew at once this was my Uncle's farm. I knocked but received no answer, the latch string was out so I pulled and went in; no one was present to bid me welcome. The house was built of hewn logs, neatly fitted together; there was three rooms on the ground floor and everything was neat and in excellent order. I went out and took a survey of the grounds, the huge frame Barn, with cattle, horses, sheep, hogs and numerous fowl. There was a fine peach orchard, Smoke house, and various buildings for storage. Returning to the house, I found a file of the Saint Louis Republican, read until I fell asleep, and did not awake until late in the afternoon and found the family, returned from Church, standing around me. After I made myself known I was received I thought very coolly.

My Uncle was a man of some forty five, quite gray with Avarice speaking out from every line of his sharp Yankee face.

When I saw this my heart felt like lead; it killed all thoughts of a loan. The family consisted of Uncle and Wife, two boys and one girl. The oldest boy, Augustavus, was a year and a half older than myself, and was as rough a cub as ever went unlicked.

Uncle owed my family $500 and after supper I stated my case and asked for a part of the debt, due for years. He denied it *toto*. I then requested a loan sufficient to go to Arkansas with, offering any interest he might ask. He only laughed at me and insulted my poverty. Oh Grace! how I repented then in agony at not taking your advice. I went to bed and cried myself to sleep.

My Uncle made me an offer to remain with him until I was twenty-one—five years. I was to work on the farm six months, the other six attend the Academy in Upper Alton, and when I was free he was to give me eighty acres and some stock. I said nothing but mentally resolved to be in Arkansas if I could raise the money—how I did not hardly care, for go I must. In two weeks I had, no matter how, some dollars and had made up my mind to start by the next Boat, when I received a letter that destroyed all my hopes. Grace wrote that she was to be married in May and start for Europe! She said she loved me as dear and fondly as ever, that it was all my own fault, and in the next line said she hated me and before she consented to be the wife of the man she was to marrying she had told him all and he had sworn to kill me on sight! What a change in two months! But my dream was over.

Monticello Seminary was a large building built of Limestone on Skerrett's Prairie, about two miles from Uncle's house. In this delightful institution there was in residence some forty young ladies, the daughters of wealthy Missourians and Kentuckians. The only church service in the neighborhood was in the school room of the building which I attended

16

regular every Sunday. I had quieted down at sixteen, all the joy and romance of Me departed as I thought forever.

I now went to work in a listless, mechanical sort of a way. The farming implements seemed to lose all their strength and durability in my hands. Axes, hoes, pitchforks &c, broke, carts and wagons came apart or smashed up in the most unaccountable manner, to Uncle's great grief and indignation! Finding my experimental farming did not pay, my Uncle asked me to break to the saddle some colts of which he had a large number. If I succeeded I could have my choice for my own! Though I knew that he was in hopes that I would get my neck broke, yet I accepted the offer with joy. I always was a dear lover of Horses and I entered heartily into my new employment and the gloomy condition of my mind was gradually dispelled by the healthy exercise. I was more or less on horseback every day, riding around the country having a good time generally.

One day as I approached the Seminary I observed a black smoke pouring out the glass observatory on the roof. I dash'd up to the building and found all was confusion. The principal was absent, there was no man about the place. The teachers with a few of the oldest pupils were at work removing some of the lighter furniture and trunks out of the house; dense smoke filled the Halls and staircases; the frightened inmates thought the whole house was on fire. I cried out that the fire was in the roof and seeing a row of Fire Buckets hanging in the Hall, I threw them down, rushed with two to the well, filled them, and run up the Stairs, asking one of the teachers to see they were all filled and brought up. The door leading to the observatory was opened, the smoke rolling out thick and fast, a fire blazing. I recommended opening the doors and windows below to get rid of the suffocating smoke, forming a line of girls to pass Buckets, putting the stout servant girls at the well to man the windlass. All this was done, water came freely and after a fifteen minutes' battle, the fire was conquered.

I remained to supper at the Seminary. The principal had returned, the fire was discussed; how it originated no one could surmise. I suggested that it might have been caused by the rays of the sun, the glass of the dome bringing them to a focus as a sun-glass. We adjourned to the scene of the fire and found in the heavy glass plate a "bull's eye," which was undoubtedly the cause of the mischief. A fine astronomical instrument badly injured, some Books and papers destroyed, and the woodwork somewhat burnt was the extent of the damage.

This acquaintance, commenced amidst fire and water, soon ripened into warm friendships and, as the season advanced and the walking became good, some of the girls would walk over to our house, when I would escort them home through the woods. All this was very pleasant, but Uncle did not like it. He, with an eye to business, wished for his Gus to do the gallanting, and took care to inform them that I was a poor relative, depending on him for support.

About this time Uncle committed an act of meanness that would have shamed an Indian. I done considerable work about the place, and I always fed the Cattle before going to bed. One night I had put the lantern down on the Barn floor and climbed up on the haymow to throw down some hay when a heavy groan coming apparently from under my feet saluted my ears. With pitchfork poised to stab, I cried out, "Who's there?" A dark something rose up out of the hay and a trembling Negro voice begged me not to hurt him. I made him descend the ladder and at the point of the pitchfork marched him into the house. He proved to be a runaway slave from Missouri. Aunt got him a hearty supper, Uncle took him back to the Barn to sleep and promised to take him some distance north next night. He remained hid all next day, and at dark Uncle with Gus hitched up a mare to a covered wagon and started off with the fugitive.

I felt that I had done my uncle injustice; that there was a kind spot in his heart. I supposed he was taking the poor fellow towards Canada and liberty. But this renegade Yankee and hypocritical Church member had gained the confidence of the trembling slave, found out his owner and was driving through the American "Bottom" to cross over to Saint Louis and deliver the man who had ate bread and salt under his roof to the mercies of his master, to stripes and torture, receiving $500 of blood money for his treachery! This I found out by overhearing the father and son disputing about the division of the blood money. I felt bad for the part I had taken in the affair, and my good Aunt suffered greatly in mind at the atrocious act of her husband. She was a kind motherly woman, but lived in constant fear of the tyrant who never spoke one word of kindness, but always found fault with everything she done.

With all my amusements I performed a great deal of hard work on the farm. I ploughed, planted, made fences, mauled rails, and I convinced my guardian that there was some good in me. I grew hearty and ruddy, and in the glory of my strength I felt anxious for somebody to pitch into, and this gratification I soon had. I had finished ploughing a lot, had put up my horses and was going towards the house when Gus ordered me to go and do some job about the Barn. I was surprised at this unusual assumption of authority, but discovered the cause in the appearance of several of the young ladies from Monticello. The Cub evidently wanted the coast clear for his own advancement. I went in, washed, and as the girls had come to spend the evening with Aunt (so they said) I went in for a good time generally.

19

During our frolicking Gus hung around and made himself very disagreeable by his insulting remarks, but we gave as little notice to him as possible. Two of the plumpest of the girls, with sleeves tucked up. Aunt's aprons on, were helping that good old soul prepare Supper, laughing and chatting like the madcaps that they were. I with three had been milking, and was coming into the yard in front of the house where Uncle was seated smoking, when the Cub called me a "d—d Beggar." I deposited the milk in the house and walked out again when the fool renewed the insult and struck me. Quick as a flash my left shot out, catching him on the breast and sending him to the ground with a heavy thud. A scream from all the girls made me look round just in time. My precious uncle was rushing on me with an uplifted axe. To avoid the blow, wrench the murderous weapon from his hands, with a blow from my fist to lay him beside his motionless son, was but the work of a moment. I felt all on fire. With one foot on his chest I brandished the axe to brain him, the girls shrieked and some fainted, when my better nature prevailed and throwing the horrid weapon away I sat down on a log and cried like a child.

Aunt helped up her husband and son and they disappeared in the house, while the girls crowded around me. Cousin Elizabeth brought out the girls' things and we started for the Seminary. I stayed there all night and in the morning Timothy Turner, Post Master, rode over to Uncle's, got my Trunk and one hundred dollars, the price, as Uncle said, for my Colt. Bidding farewell to all my dear friends, I drove to Alton, where I embarked on the Luella for Saint Louis.

A Cousin of mine from Ohio, Bradley Chamberlain, I found here in business as Agent for Laflins Powder Co. I obtained employment driving a light wagon making deliveries of gunpowder to the Steam Boats. I remained here but a few weeks, then with one hundred and fifty dollars in my pocket I was off for New Orleans. I had at this time acquired a fondness for strong drink and on the Boat down I drank freely; in New Orleans I indulged in all kinds of dissipation, and my money was soon gone. I now led a precarious life for several months. I had befriended a French girl who kept a Coffee Stand in the French market and she insisted on my sharing her bed and board, when I could not do better.

I became acquainted with a Gentleman, the Warden of the Penitentiary at Baton Rouge, who made me an offer to do the clerical duty of that establishment. I accompanied him to Baton Rouge, which lays about one hundred miles above New Orleans. My duty was easy, with good pay and excellent board, and I made up my mind that I was all right at last and done my best to give satisfaction to my employer, and I succeeded.

I had a fine saddle horse placed at my disposal, and when the weather permitted I took horseback excursions into the interior.

One day I was riding up the river on the Levee when I saw a horsewoman approaching at speed, on a road at right angles with the embankment. A cry for help reached me; the lady's horse was running away, direct for the river! Driving spurs into my steed, I dashed on, and fortunately reached her just as her frightened horse struck the levee. I caught her around the waist with my right arm, when being overbalanced I fell to the ground dragging her with me. At the same moment her horse plunged into the swollen Mississippi.

The lady, or rather girl, was not hurt, but was quite frightened and faintish. She soon recovered her self-possession and poured forth her thanks in the prettiest manner possible. She was very "petite," a brunette, with such eyelashes! so long! so black! how they made my heart thump as her eyes glanced from under them! I was about to pour forth my joy in being instrumental in saving so much loveliness when a little old gentleman rode up, sprang off his horse and clasped the girl in his arms, talking with the greatest volubility in French. He then thanked me in English for saving his *wife*!

His wife! That beautiful fairy-like being wedded to that old dried-up man of sixty! Impossible! They both noticed the look of astonishment and disgust that I could not prevent, and while the richest crimson suffused her cheeks, a look of bitter hatred spread over his apelike features.

The next day as I was engaged at the landing a servant rode up to me and handed me a note. It was from the Mistress instead of the Master. She wished to see her preserver (so she called me) and described a cabin where she would meet me at 5 P.M. I was punctual at the rendezvous; an old Negress came out of the cabin and telling me to go in, led my horse away. I entered and was clasped in the arms of the impulsive little beauty, who was more like a child than a wife.

When she became calmer, she gave me her history. Her married name was Stella Laboyce. She was the only child of wealthy Creole parents, and she had remained in a Convent in New Orleans until she was seventeen, when she was taken home and Old Laboyce was introduced to her as her future husband. Being pleased to be released from the restrictions of Convent life, and being totally ignorant of the true relations of married life, she had wedded in joy, but to awake to the sad reality of being the slave to the capricious whims of an old lustful tyrant.

Poor little Bird! We were both young, loving and passionate, and that humble hut became a Paradise to us. Before we parted we made arrangements to meet at the same place as often as we could; for three months we were as happy as mortals can be in this world. Old Laboyce appeared to have forgotten my existence. We formed a plan to elope to the North, and without waiting for the tie to be severed that bound her to Laboyce we would marry and be happy for life!

What foolish blissful dreams! One afternoon I was busy at the lower landing when my employer, Mr. Hays, rode up and gave me the startling information that old Laboyce had been at the Penitentiary with a half a dozen armed men inquiring after the "Yank," and swearing to have his life. Hays gave me his horse and a pocket Derringer, and told me to put for some steamboat landing below. I was off none too soon, for the old Frenchman and his riders caught sight of me, and with fierce cries increased their speed. Taking the Lower Levee road, I soon lost sight of my pursuers; the smoke stacks of a steamer appeared over the trees—she was at a small wharf wooding up. I rode down to her just as they were casting off, turned my horse loose, and sprang aboard as she left the shore.

I found myself on the *White Cloud*, one of the great "bragboats" of the Mississippi, and bound for Saint Louis. We soon came in sight of my pursuers, who waved a handkerchief and hailed us. Fortunately a huge Steamer came puffing around a bend, making for us. The captain recognized her as a new boat— the Saint Anthony—built expressly to beat the White Cloud. Instead of stopping, our fires were increased, black smoke rolled out of the chimneys and we dash'd through the water at great speed. Our opponent replied with her steam whistle in notes of defiance and vast volumes of dense smoke; it became a race and we flew by Baton Rouge with the *Saint Anthony* half a mile astern.

My mind was no longer on the race, but on her whom I was so cowardly deserting. Now I could see the huge cypress tree near the hut where we had enjoyed so many happy hours. Oh, how I wished that Stella was the companion of my flight! How I regretted that I had not eloped with her before the denouement took place! But such thoughts were idle, I felt we were separated forever.

We gradually dropped the *Saint Anthony*, and in four days and a half we lay at the levee at Saint Louis.

The Franklin House in Alton, Illinois. It was later used as Lincoln's campaign headquarters, and subsequently renamed the Lincoln Hotel.

III

MUTINY OF THE ALTON GUARDS

I LEFT Saint Louis on the *Luella* for Alton and arrived there on the 20th of May, 1846. The town was in a blaze of excitement caused by the news that General Taylor was surrounded by the Mexican Troops on the Rio Grande. General Gaines, commanding at New Orleans, had issued a call for fifty thousand volunteers, four thousand from Illinois. Drums were beating all over town and two hours after I landed I enlisted. I went with the crowd hurrahing and drinking whiskey until after several days we numbered one hundred strong.

Our company, the Alton Guards, elected our own officers, as did all the other volunteers. The election was held in a ten pin alley! I was ambitious and wanted a commission. I worked hard for it, drilling the men in Scott's tactics—thanks to orderly Sergeant Hall and Captain N.A. Thompson of the City Guard in Boston, I was tolerably proficient in the manual and evolutions— spent my money freely on whiskey, defeated a Major Ward of Texas in fencing, and expected to get the First Lieutenancy. A staff officer of Governor Ford called the meeting to order, when a large red-faced man mounted the bar and delivered the following speech.

"Fellow citizens! I am Peter Goff, the Butcher of Middletown! I am! I am the man that shot that sneaking, white-livered Yankee abolitionist s—n of a b—h, Lovejoy! I did! I want to be your Captain, I do; and I will serve the yellow bellied Mexicans the same. I will! I have treated you to fifty dollars worth of whiskey, I have, and when elected Captain I will spend fifty more, I will!"

It is needless to state he was elected almost unanimously. My opponent for the First Lieutenancy was one James W. Baker. I found I had no chance to win—my money was all gone—but I made a spread eagle speech, with plenty of the "Halls of Montezuma" and "Golden Jesus's" of Mexico, but alas, the "Suckers" preferred whiskey present to Jesus's in the future. The Company organized as follows: Captain, Peter Goff; 1st Lieutenant, James Baker; 2nd Lieutenants, Edward Fletcher and Rodney Ferguson. Captain Goff appointed me the drill Sergeant.

We were quartered in an unfinished Church, on a hill overlooking the town. The Company was composed of the floating population of a Mississippi River town, wild reckless fellows, excellent material for soldiers, but requiring strict discipline to curb their lawless spirits. The officers, as might be expected, proved totally incompetent, took no care of their command, but spent their time in drinking and gambling. I sought to do my duty in drilling the men but receiving no support from my superiors, I was obliged to give it up.

I was so disgusted with the debauchery around me that I quit drinking and renewed my acquaintance with my fair friends at the Monticello Seminary. I heard often from my uncle's family, yet I did not call on them.

Volunteers continued to arrive, and soon the complement was full. Four Regiments was organized—1st Reg't, Colonel John J. Hardin, 2nd Reg't, Colonel Bissell, Lieutenant Colonel James L.D. Morrison, Major Xerxes F. Trail; 4th Reg't, Colonel Floyd; 4th Reg't, Colonel E.D. Baker. We moved into camp in June; it was laid out in a beautiful grove in Upper Alton. We were uniformed as each company selected and strange grotesque costumes now filled the Camp. Ours, Co. A, 2nd Regiment, made choice of jacket and pants of blue mixed Kentucky jeans with yellow stripes across the breast like a Dragoon Bugler. By permission I had mine made with dark blue cloth, with only my Sergeant's chevrons, and it was quite a neat affair.

Captain Goff seldom made an appearance in Camp, and then he was generally drunk and abusive. One day he came down the company Street raving drunk; he knocked down two privates and then meeting Lieutenant Fletcher, to show he was not impartial, sent him to grass. The men secured the maniac. He was knocked down, tied and a guard placed over him. The other officers interfered, but they were driven out of Camp.

I had taken no part in the outbreak and was seated on a log when a committee of the malcontents tendered me the command of the mutineers! This dangerous honor I declined, but they insisted, and yielding on their promising implicit obedience to my orders, I became the captain of a hundred half drunken desperadoes. We had drawn that morning several thousand rounds of Ball and Buck cartridge for target practice; this I issued at once, and was making a speech when Colonel Bissell rode up and ordered the release of Captain Goff. The unruly dogs only hooted him for his pains and he rode off with threats of dire revenge.

I had formed the company to march to town when I saw two companies of Rifles advancing in line on our quarters. I sent out a few skirmishers to halt them and if they continued to advance, to fire on them. I had all the axes kept busy chopping down trees to form Barricades and made quite formidable preparation for a vigorous defense when word was brought that a body of horsemen was approaching on the Alton road. I went out to reconnoiter and recognized Colonels Bissell, Hardin and Morrison and two Generals who proved to be Generals John E. Wool and Shields with Governor Ford. As no troops accompanied them, I was satisfied there would be no fighting, that diplomacy and negotiation was now the order of the day.

I hurried back to my command and to their astonishment ordered them to "fall in" outside the Barricade. They done so promptly. I dressed the ranks, commanded "present arms," which was neatly done, just as the cavalcade rode up. General Wool returned the salute, asked "who was the ringleader?" I replied I had that honor. The General gave us a lecture on the foolishness of our émeute, said we deserved death but by the intercession of His Excellency Governor Ford he would pardon us if we returned to duty with promises of good behavior for the future.

Goff came forward and apologized; my command gave him three cheers! The thoughts of his whiskey made the hearts of the mutineers soften, and I really believe that if he gave the word the Suckers would have bayoneted me on the spot, so volatile is the popularity of a mob.

General Wool enquired of Captain Goff who had planned the Barricades. I was designated as the Engineer. The Captain evidently wished to do me what harm he could. General Wool asked my name, age, where born etc. He appeared surprised on learning I was not yet seventeen and made some remark to

32

the gentlemen around him at which all laughed. He then said to me, "My man, if you don't get shot for insubordination, you will, if you live and see service, rise in the profession."

Captain Goff now took command, marched the company back to their parade ground, made them a speech in which the egotistical "I" and the all powerful word "whiskey" formed the groundwork, and ordered a barrel of the article into Camp as a Peace offering. The men made themselves hoarse in cheering the valiant Captain, who so well understood and appreciated the natures of his reliable command. I was blamed for all the trouble, broke of my warrant and reduced to the ranks, and this was the end of the Mutiny of the Guards.

The time came to depart for Mexico; about the middle of July, six companies of the Second Illinois Regiment, with General Wool and staff, embarked on the steamer Convoy for New Orleans. Two other boats, the Hannibal and Big Missouri, both crowded with volunteers, went with us. Our passage down the River proved very pleasant though our accommodations were somewhat limited. My mind wandered in bright dreams of glory and renown in that region of romance, the land of Cortez and Montezuma. We landed and went into Camp at Chalmette, the scene of the famed Battle of New Orleans, some seven miles below the City.

Our Regiment's quarters was near the Live Oak, under which tradition states General Packingham died.

This Camp was one great scene of drunkenness and debauchery; officers as well as the men seemed to defy all military restraint and vie with each other who would commit the greatest excesses. Though I indulged freely when off duty, yet I believed in keeping up some discipline while on, and so disgusted I became with the state of things that I resolved to enlist in the Regular Army as soon as I could. I visited the City and hunted up my accommodating Coffee Girl of the French Market, who appeared right glad to see me, and was as complacent as ever.

One night I visited with others a gaming establishment on St. Charles Street, and won quite an amount of money. I started for Camp in company of an old Regular, one Brown; we had drank freely at my expense and made the night hideous with Bacchanalian songs as we headed down the Levee. It was past midnight, very dark, with a cold mist on the River. Old Brown lagged behind on the slippery path and I supposed he was some distance in my rear, when something seemed to fall on me, and I fell crushed to the ground.

Stunned, bewildered, almost senseless, I still retained consciousness enough to be aware that I was being dragged down the bank toward the river. What had happened? Where was my companion? These thoughts flashed in my mind, when the painful fact that Brown himself was my assailant became only too evident. The old rascal evidently thought I was dead, for he laid me on the bank, partly resting in the water, while he proceeded coolly to search my pockets.

I lay still, feeling weak and faint, yet collecting all the energy and life left in me for a struggle for existence. He emptied my pockets and stooped to lift me into the water, when with a grip like death I grasped with both hands his throat, while my teeth fastened on his nose so desperately that they met. He struggled to throw me off, but though I was in a dreamy languid state and my head had a heavy roaring noise like a cataract in it, my hold could not be shaken off. His efforts were terrible, but all in vain; my grasp was immovable, like the embrace of a corpse.

Brown, ignorant and superstitious, really imagined that such was the case, that the victim was trying to drag its murderer with it into the dark flood. When my muscles relaxed, he fell down in a swoon! I staggered to my feet and dashed some water on my head, which seemed all stoved in, it felt so soft and mashy. I was afraid I had received my death wound, and this idea made me determined that my destroyer should keep me company. I drew my Bayonet and went for him. He had begun to recover and yelled with affright. I plunged at him with my weapon which penetrated his neck pinning him to the ground. I thought he was finished and then hope sprang up that I might recover, and I wished I had not gone so far. I pulled out the Bayonet and was glad to find the villain was alive; the weapon had passed through the thick muscles of the neck without touching a vital part, making a painful but not a serious wound.

I made him give back my money, we repaired damages as well as we could, and started for Chalmette. I compelled him to go ahead, and kept my Bayonet in hand. We reached Camp at daylight, told a story of a row, and were sent to the Hospital.

A few days later, the Alton Guards embarked on the Brig *T. Street* for Port La Vaca, Matagorda Bay, in Texas. It was a fearful passage to me. I still suffered extremely from the injuries in my head; the heat was excessive, with no awnings to the deck, which was densely crowded, with the volunteers in an open state of mutiny brought on from the unlimited indulgence in strong drink obtained by broaching the Cargo, which consisted of sutlers' goods.

We landed and went into Camp on a low prairie, twelve miles from La Vaca. The ground was covered with water, it seemed to rain all the time, and the mumps, the measles and the Scarlet Fever broke out among the troops. There was a great scarcity of doctors, hospital tents and medical attendants, and many of the men died here.

General Wool with what men could march pushed on for San Antonio, one hundred and sixty miles in the interior. Though I was in the Hospital, threatened with brain fever, I put out and joined the marching column. How I kept up I don't know; weak, emaciated, I struggled on; anything was better than staying behind in the Hospital, where men were dying every hour. My would-be murderer Brown stayed with me and assisted me every way in his power. Although I harbored a suspicion that he only sought an opportunity of giving me my quietus yet I let him have his own way, giving him to understand however that Lieutenant Ferguson was carrying all my money.

The marching was severe in the extreme; the low land extended seventy miles covered with water and grass three foot high. One day I gave up and lay down and I really wished to die. Nothing appeared real. The dark murky sky, the grass and trees all seemed to whirl and tip over in the most remarkable manner. Lieutenant Colonel Don Morrison rode up and seeing how I was, dismounted, placed me in the Saddle, and proceeded on with me until we overtook the wagons, when I was placed in one and in that way reached San Antonio.

General Wool displayed great energy now in breaking into proper military discipline the rough material sent him for soldiers. The sick were examined and all reported unfit for the long march before us received their discharge. I was one of these, and received mileage back to Alton, Illinois. This, with what money I had in the hands of Lieutenant Ferguson, amounted to nearly three hundred dollars, quite a little fortune in this part of the world.

IV

LIFE IN THE LONE STAR STATE

AFTER my discharge I went to board in town and with good quarters, fine air and excellent food I gained fast. A gambler named Jim Scott roomed with me, and very kindly volunteered to teach me all the tricks of the trade. The mysteries of faro, monte and poker, games of "short" cards and "waxed" cards became clear to me by his skillful instruction, and I proved a promising pupil.

One evening I with Scotty sauntered into the Bexar Exchange, a noted drinking and gambling Saloon. The Bar room was crowded with volunteers, regulars, Texan Rangers, a few Delaware Indians and Mexicans. The Rangers were the Scouts of our Army and a more reckless, devil-may-care looking set, it would be impossible to find this side of the Infernal Regions. Some wore buckskin shirts, black with grease and blood, some wore red shirts, their trousers thrust into their high boots; all were armed with Revolvers and huge Bowie Knives. Take them altogether, with their uncouth costumes, bearded faces, lean and brawny forms, fierce wild eyes and swaggering manners, they were fit representatives of the outlaws which made up the population of the Lone Star State.

Scotty joined in a four-handed game of Poker, and I sauntered from table to table, watching with interest. Oaths and cigar smoke filled the air, knives were drawn but no blood was spilt as friends would interfere before the disputants came to blows. At one small table sat two men playing Eukre for the drinks. One, who was quietly playing his hand in a mild timid way utterly at variance with his hardened desperate appearance, was short and thick set, his face bronzed by exposure to the hue of an Indian, with eyes deeply sunken and bloodshot, and coarse black hair hanging in snakelike locks down his back. His costume was that of a Mexican herdman, made of leather, with a Mexican blanket thrown over his shoulder. His opponent was a tall reckless, good looking young Ranger, dressed in a red shirt and buckskin leggins. A dispute arose, the short ruffian threw a glass of liquor in the tall one's face, who sprang to his feet, drew his revolver, and placing the muzzle against the breast of the thrower, swore with fearful oaths "that if he did not apologize he would blow a hole through him a Rabbit could jump through!"

The threatened man did not move from his seat, but replied, "Shoot and be d—d, but if you miss, John Glanton won't miss you!" When he mentioned his name, a look of fear passed over the Ranger's face; he pulled the trigger, but only the cap exploded! Quick as a flash Glanton sprang up, a huge Bowie knife flashed in the candlelight, and the tall powerful young Ranger fell with a sickening thud to the floor a corpse, his neck cut half through. Glanton jumped over the table and placing one foot on his victim said,

"Strangers! Do you wish to take up this fight? If so step out, if not we'll drink." As no one seemed disposed to accept the challenge, all hands went with him to the Bar and touched glasses with him. The warm body was carried out, sawdust was sprinkled over the bloodstained floor, Glanton carefully wiped his knife on the leather sleeve of his jacket, and matters in the Bexar Exchange resumed their usual course.

I enquired about Glanton, for whom somehow I felt a sort of admiration, in spite of my horror at his bloody deed, and learned he was a famous Indian fighter and desperado of the frontier, the hero of many bloody personal encounters with the outlaws of the border.

I thought in a society so dangerous I should go armed, and purchased myself a Bowie Knife with a nine-inch blade warranted to cut through bone without turning the edge. A few days later I had trouble with Scotty about the division of some money we had won at a three handed game of Poker with a commissary clerk, in which, to keep up appearances, I lost all my money to Scotty, along with the clerk. When I asked for a settlement, Scotty denied all partnership and swore he had won not only the clerk's, but my money in a fair game, and this when I had "rung in the cold deck" that fleeced us both!

There was only one way in Texas in '46 to settle misunderstandings of this nature. We went for each other, and he very foolishly ran onto the point of my "Arkansas toothpick" and was badly cut for his want of judgement. I was seized by the guard, old Spanish irons were placed on me, and I was thrust into the "Callaboose," a room about twenty feet square, inhabited by a very select society of Indians, Texans, Horsethieves, Murderers and the vilest characters of the lawless frontier.

The horrors of the Old Spanish Jail in San Antonio were more terrible than any scene in the Inferno of Dante. How long I remained here I never knew; it seemed years, though it could have been but a few days. I was covered with vermin, the heavy rusty irons wore the flesh of my ankles in which the lice burrowed, my jacket was stolen, and my shirt I tore into strips to bind around the irons to keep them from chafing! The place was outrageously filthy, the air hot and pestiferous, food scant and poor, with water unfit even for washing. The awful blasphemy of the wretches incarcerated with me, their horrid bestial orgies too revolting for belief, drove me in my weak state insane.

Fortunately for me Scotty recovered and declined to appear against me, so I was turned loose, with nothing on but my pants, and wild with my sufferings. I can faintly remember flying, I thought pursued by Demons, and then came darkness and oblivion.

From this I awoke with a most delicious sense of comfort and freedom from pain. I was in a nice soft clean bed and an old lady was sitting close knitting beside an open window through which came a sweet fresh breeze. Hearing me stir, she left the room crying out, "Carl! Carl!" and a young man entered the room. He congratulated me on the recovery of my reason and informed me that I was in his house in Castroville, thirty miles from San Antonio, that I had been found by a farmer three weeks before, lying near the road entirely nude and insensible. My host was a Doctor, Carl Ritter by name, a member of the German settlement at Castroville.

Dr. Ritter had altered to fit me a suit of his clothes, made of fine German broadcloth, and they well became me. This family placed me under the greatest obligations by their extreme kindness. Katherine Ritter, the Doctor's sister, was not over sixteen, innocent and confiding, and I soon knew that she had given me unsolicited her first pure love. She seemed to consider she had an exclusive right to me, that in fact I was her property. I was afraid to hurt her feelings, yet honor forbid my returning her constant care.

One night after the family was all in bed I was awakened by having sweet soft lips pressed to mine and found Miss Ritter by my side, her arms around me. She was in her night dress and as the night was very warm I was lying on the outside of the bed. She cried and whispered to me in German language the most loving entreaties. Her kisses and thrilling embraces aroused all my amorous passions, and unconsciously the unsophisticated girl became almost delirious with hitherto unknown desires! What a trial for one's principles of honor! The temptation of Saint Anthony was not a circumstance to mine! Nature guided her in her innocence to seek relief to her distressed condition, and I not only had my own passions to fight, but the most provoking manipulations from this charming girl, who knew no wrong in following the teachings of Dame Nature. But I resisted and triumphed and the honor of the house of Ritter suffered not at my hands. Poor Katherine, at daylight left my room, weak and exhausted, and though still a virgin, yet no longer innocent in mind, and more in love than ever.

I started early next morning for San Antonio, where I reported to Regular Army headquarters and enlisted for the war in Company E, First U.S. Dragoons, Captain Enoch Steen commanding.

General Wool's division consisted of the 1st and 2nd Illinois Volunteers under Colonel J.J. Hardin and Colonel William H. Bissell; Major Bonneville's battalion of the 6th U.S. Infantry; the Arkansas Cavalry under Colonel Yell; Captain Washington's battery of light artillery; and Colonel William S. Harney's Dragoons, in which I served, and a "spy company" of Texan Rangers, the whole numbering about 3,000 men and officers.

The Dragoons encamped near the Mission of Concepcion. We were officered as follows; Co. E—Captain, Enoch Steen; 1st Lieutenant, Daniel H. Rucker; 2nd Lieutenant, Abraham Buford. Co. A—Captain, William Eustis, with Lieutenants Carleton, Whittlesey and Conts. I was now placed under a drill Sergeant, and was put through in the "School of the Soldier" in the riding school and in Carbine and Sabre exercise. I recovered my health and strength very rapidly and gained a love for the life of a Dragoon.

One day Colonel Harney ordered the old Mission to be cleaned out, intending to use it to store forage for his command. A large detail of Dragoons well provided with shovels and brooms commenced to clean out the nave of the Church. The floor was covered to the depth of two foot with the excrement of Bats. While some of the detail were at work, others provided themselves with torches to explore the subterranean vaults and passages under the building and said to connect with the Fortress of the Alamo.

Behind where the Altar formerly stood, a flight of stone steps descended into the dark and gloomy place. It was one mass of Bats! They hung on the walls and arched roof in clusters like bees when swarming, the floor was covered, and yielded under the step like a bog. Out of sport some of the Dragoons fired their Pistols into the living squirming mass, when like a tornado the Bats flew out of the passage, extinguishing the torches but fortunately carrying the men out of the vault with them. The party in the Church rushed for the door in the wildest alarm and though some were knocked down and badly frightened, all got outside in safety. The little wing'd animals poured out of the great door for two hours, making their way to the Mission of San Jose, six miles below, their column being so dense as to resemble a suspension bridge! Thousands lay in the church and on the ground dead and dying from the crush. The stench in the Mission prevented its being used.

One evening there was to be a Mexican "Fandango" at San Jose. Several of us obtained a pass until reveille from our company commander, and I took it to Major Benjamin L. Beall, 2nd Dragoons Officer of the Day, to be countersigned. He was a short red-faced-and-nosed man, and looked the Major all over; it was evident that nature intended him for that position and nothing else. He was known in the army as "Old Brilliant," and from his unusual brilliant appearance at this time I judged that the influence of old Rye had something to do with it. The jolly Major signed the pass and remarked, "Report to me at the Guard Tent at Tattoo." Accordingly at that time half a dozen of Uncle Sam's Bold Dragoons drew up in line in front of the guard quarters, when the Major soon joined us with the 2nd Dragoon Band. Old Brilliant was a little more so and carried with him a number One Camp Kelly, for a Drum.

We started down the bank of the San Antonio, a jolly party enough. The Major went down several times before we reached the ford, but he still held on to the Camp Kettle. The water was a good three feet deep at the ford and running like a mill race. We stripped but the fat Major would wade through without undressing, got swept away and it was with difficulty we saved him. But alas, the Camp Kettle was lost!

The arrival at the ballroom of so distinguished a party rather surprised the "Greasers" but they soon recovered and we were cordially invited to participate in the festivity. The Major dashed into a Waltz with a dark skinned white robed Señorita, on whom he certainly produced an impression. I will long remember that night of wild fun and unlicensed debauchery, wine and *aguardiente* (brandy) cheap and abundant, the women fine shaped, with black flashing eyes, and very accommodating!

For hours the Fandango was all fun and frolic, the Major's voice could be heard, "brilliant! by G——d, Brilliant," until at daylight we started for Concepcion, all pretty well intoxicated with love and liquor. As we approached Camp, we saw to our dismay Colonel Harney at the Guard Tents. We expected to be roughed, and were not disappointed. Those who knew Harney can appreciate the scene. To all that was said by Harney, our Major had only one reply: "Brilliant Fandango, brilliant! By G——d, brilliant girls. Colonel! Brilliant night!" Harney placed him under arrest and we were confined to quarters for twenty four hours.

V

THE MARCH TO THE RIO GRANDE

GENERAL WOOL'S Division left San Antonio for Mexico on September 25. The command made quite an imposing appearance as they marched through the Grand Plaza of San Antonio, which was crowded with a motley assembly of wild looking Texans, Mexicans in their everlasting blankets, Negro Slaves, a sprinkling of Lipan Indians in full dress of paint and feathers, white women, squaws and señoritas.

We encamped the first night at Castroville. I had hardly dismounted when I was embraced by my dear friend Carl Ritter, who to my astonishment informed me that his sister, the lovesick Katherine, was married!! Inconstancy, thy name art woman! That evening she with her husband and Carl called on me, and obtaining permission I went home with the happy couple. Her husband was a stupid Dutchman, who went off with Carl to visit the Camp after supper, leaving me to entertain the Bride of a week. We soon walked out in the beautiful moonlight and ascended a slight elevation behind the house and seated ourselves beneath the trees. The Dragoon Band was playing and we could see many a soldier arm in arm with white-robed village maidens, strolling under the shade of the sheltering woods. Katherine lay reclining in my arms, her arms pressed around me as of old, and I—well, my nature is too volcanic to play the Joseph too often! We reveled in bliss and happiness, until prudence warned us to return to the house. The complaisant gentleman had not yet returned, so we walked toward the Camp to meet them, and bid fond farewell while the Band was playing "The Girl I Left Behind Me."

Good-by, sweet Kate and Castroville, forever!

Our march after we left the German settlements was through a barren waste, scant grass, and water only found in the beds of rivers. We crossed the Nueces, Medina and Frio Rivers, making about twenty five miles per day, our camping ground being governed by the juxtaposition of wood and water.

As we approached the Rio Grande, horsemen appeared on the distant hills. Our guide, Dan Henrie, pronounced them Comanches, and our long straggling column was closed up, flankers thrown out and ammunition issued. During this day only small parties appeared, but the next day a force of several hundred savage looking horsemen came charging towards us, uttering their frightful yells and brandishing long lances. They certainly made a most gallant appearance, and reminded me of the description in *The Talisman* of the reception the Saracens gave to him of the Lion-Heart.

The main body remained about half a mile off, displaying their feats of horsemanship, while a dozen of their principal Chiefs dashed up to General Wool, lance in rest, until within a few paces, when the points were lowered, their horses pulled back on their haunches, and there they stood as motionless as so many bronze equestrian statues. Our little General, under the impulse of the moment, backed his horse. This seemed to tickle these red devils, who against all my previous ideas of Indians, roared with laughter. The head one, an old wolfish greasy cuss known as Santana, rode up to General Wool, held out his hand and said, "How de do, budder." The General shook hands, when the Chief gave him such a squeeze that the General's face showed signs of pain. This caused the redskins to yell in derision.

Colonel Harney offered his band to Santana who with a grin took it and gave it another fancy grip, but the old rascal had got hold of the wrong man; the Colonel's grip was like that of a vise. Harder and harder his hand closed on the Indian, until he writhed in pain and gave vent to his agony in a fearful howl. I believe that the bones of his hand were crushed. The other redskins looked astonished and gazed on Harney with amazement.

One of the Chiefs now made a harangue in Spanish, which was interpreted to General Wool. It was to the effect that they, the Comanches, were good friends to us but enemies of the Texans, that they were great warriors who would kill a heap of Mexicans and wanted arms, ammunition and pay for Scalps. General Wool replied that he would not give them arms, and if he caught them committing outrages on the defenseless inhabitants of Mexico he would hang them.

At this reply their actions were very insulting. Two Dragoons threw themselves on old Santana, dragged him from his Pony, tied him up to a Gun Carriage and gave him a sound flogging with a mule whip! When released he mounted in silence, and withdrew with his awe-stricken warriors. Soon, in a long file, they were out of sight.

The night before we reached the Rio Grande I was detailed for Picket duty and was posted some three miles from Camp on one of the low hills that covered the prairie land. At sundown General Wool with his escort rode out to my post, visiting the picket line. He ordered me to another place, a low plain further out, and rode on. I moved on to the place pointed out, when my horse exhibited much fear, snorting and plunging in affright; an infernal din broke out all around me, yaps, hoots and yells saluted my ears from all sides! It was now quite dark and strange shapes flew around my head, and crawled on the ground at my horse's feet.

I was at first considerable alarmed but a scene in one of Cooper's novels came to my mind and I knew I was stationed in a prairie dog town. The prairie dog, so called from the short yelping sound which it utters, is a pretty animal about sixteen inches long. They settle in communities and are exceedingly prolific and their town sometimes covers many acres. They burrow in the ground; the earth removed is piled up in little mounds at the entrance to their burrows. The little animals are not suffered to remain unmolested; the owl and the deadly prairie rattlesnake take forcible possession of their snug warm houses and beyond doubt live on the young pups. The instinct of my horse told him that the honeycombed ground, full of rattlesnakes, was dangerous, and the affrightened inhabitants had resented our intrusion in their various ways. The prairie wolf and coyote haunt the towns for food and their howls and dismal cries were added to the chorus that had alarmed me.

I moved slowly out from the dangerous neighborhood and sought to regain my former position, but the night was so dark that I was quite lost. I had been hours on my post and wondered why I had not been relieved. I dismounted and holding my horse by the bridle sat down in the grass, when moving objects on a distant ridge attracted my attention. A long column of horsemen were moving noiseless across the hill. They were in single file, the muzzle of each horse close to the croup of the one that preceded him; on they passed as silent as specters. Comanches on the march! Soon a carbine shot followed by others showed me the position of the picket line, the dark horsemen disappeared as by magic and, mounting, I was soon with the picket guard who had been withdrawn a mile nearer Camp. The Indians gave no further trouble to the command.

We reached the Rio Grande opposite the Mexican town of Presidio del Rio Grande. No enemy appeared to dispute our crossing, though the Camp was full of rumors that a Brigade of Lancers with terrible Batteries lay hid in the dense woods that covered the Mexican side of the river, and that we were to be allowed to cross and then the entire army of "Greasers" would fall on us and no quarter to be given! General Wool was busy preparing to effect what is considered the most difficult of all military operations: the *passage of a deep river in the face of the enemy*, for all believed the other bank would be desperately defended.

When all was ready Washington's Battery took position to shell the other bank, and at the blast of a Bugle three hundred Dragoons, with Harney at their head, dashed into the swift stream and made for the opposite bank. Our horses were soon swimming, and the current was so rapid that we were carried downstream some 300 yards before we effected a landing. The passage was witnessed by the entire army which lined the Texan bank; all expected to see us fired on every moment, and when they saw us safe over their enthusiasm broke out in prolonged cheers.

We form'd as fast as we landed, advanced as skirmishers for a mile, when the towers of the Presidio appeared in sight, but no signs of the foe. A strong picket was thrown out in the form of a semicircle, the flanks resting on the river. The Infantry crossed next on a pontoon bridge of wagon beds; a stout picket rope was stretched across and hauled taut by purchase, the

Pontoons fastened to this, and in a short time the command was over, without loss!

The Army encamped on the bank that night—October 12— and next day General Shields and General Joe Lane with two regiments of Indiana Volunteers overtook us. We marched through the Town, a miserable tumble-down place, built of "adobe" or unburnt brick which seemed to be about to return to its original material, the mud that filled the streets. The Presidio, or Soldiers' quarters, an old Church, with its clumsy tower cracked and threatening to fall on the "greasers" who crowded its huge doors to see "*Los Gringos*" pass, and about one hundred hovels made up the Town of Presidio del Rio Grande. We passed through droves of donkeys, pigs, goats, no-haired dogs and chickens and encamped some three miles beyond the place on the bank of an irrigation canal. Next morning the Camp was alarmed by the rapid discharge of firearms and the ringing of Bells in town. The "long roll" beat, "Boot and Saddle," sounded, a line of battle was formed with Artillery in position, a strong line of skirmishers cautiously advanced on the place, and found that it was only some Saint's day!

Resuming our undisputed march, we passed two swift rivers and the "cities" of Nava, San Fernando and Santa Rosa.

Crossing the Rio Grande

VI

MY FIRST SCOUT

GENERAL WOOL had been ordered to march to the important City of Chihuahua, by a route marked with red ink, on a map sent him by the sapient head of the War Department, Marcy. Unfortunately for the success of this wise scheme to capture a place once taken by seven Apaches, there lay in the way of the proposed route several high ranges of mountains that a goat could not climb, and that it would take weeks to flank, through deserts without water. General Wool decided to communicate with his superior. General Taylor, and Lieutenant Carleton, Co. A, 1st Dragoons, with six men, was detailed to carry the dispatches to the Hero of the battles of Palo Alto and Resaca de la Palma.

Thanks to my excellent horse and the favoritism of our worthy 1st/Sgt. Charles Hardy, I was detailed on this (to me) pleasant duty. With four days' rations of coffee and sugar in our haversacks—for the rest we were expected to live on the country—we left at dark to pass through two hundred miles of enemy territory, and this without a guide.

Taking a Mule trail, we pushed rapidly forward most of the night. Carleton was an "Old Prairie Tramper" and kept our course well by the stars. At early dawn, seeing the white walls of a *rancho* a short distance from the road, we made for it, and were inside the gate or *zaguan* before the sleepy "greasers" made their appearance. They were rather astonished and somewhat alarmed at their early visitors, and the size of our horses filled them with amazement and admiration. One of our men was stationed on the *azotea* or roof of the Chapel and no one was allowed to leave the place. The horses were unsaddled and well rubbed down, watered and fed with barley obtained in the place. The men in the rancho were an ill-looking set of cutthroats, and gave us glances of hatred, but the women, the young ones especially, were kind and gave us some excellent cooked beans, *frijoles*.

An old man gave the Lieutenant to understand that a large body of Soldiers had passed to the eastward the day before; this was good news for us as they were dressed in American uniforms. We saddled up, and taking a supply of barley in our forage bags and some jerked beef for our own use, we were off again at sunrise.

This day and the next passed without any incident of note. The following day our route lay through a low level country different in every respect from any I had ever seen before. Cactus in a hundred varieties, with the white leaved wild olive, covered the ground in all directions; away off to our right sharp blue peaked mountains rose grandly in the clear air. I enjoyed this march exceedingly; I had fully recovered from my severe injuries and sickness, I felt no fatigue and my appetite was truly wonderful. The road was broad and good, with the chapperal rising on both sides like a wall. In the forenoon we reached a hacienda belonging, it was said, to General Mariano Arista, and done ample justice to the good fare found there.

We had not left the hacienda two miles behind when the report of a Carbine from our advance guard of one man caused us to draw sabre. He made his appearance coming back at speed, and close on his rear came a crowd of fierce guerillars yelling like devils. I must confess that my first thought was to turn and run for it, but the quick command of Carleton to "Charge and give them your sabres!" caused me to go in with the rest, though my heart was up in my throat choking me. I parried a lance thrust, a black savage face was before me for an instant, my horse crushed another underfoot, then another, and I came out of the dust surprised to find myself alive and unhurt. Carleton and my companions were all safe; not a man or horse touched, our entire loss was confined to a few forage sacks and one Carbine.

This was my maiden charge, and I believe I acquitted myself with credit. True, there was no blood on my Sabre, but there was plenty on my spurs. My good steed Soldan had done all the fighting and had done it well.

Our road led us into the dry bed of an arroyo flanked on each side by huge boulders. We were passing a clump of dead cottonwood trees when the Lieutenant, who was in advance, held up his hand in warning. Right in our path, not a hundred yards distant, was a Lancer stationed with his back to us! He was so intently watching a cloud of dust rising towards the distant mountains that he was unaware of our presence.

Carleton drove his spurs into his horse, and followed by the rest, was on him before he could run. Our prisoner was a guerillar, clothed entirely in leather, well mounted on a small but wiry mustang. He was armed with a lance, a *lazo*, two huge pistols, a short gun and a sword! He was badly frightened and gave us to understand that it was the army of "Los Barbarians del Norte" that raised the dust and that they were then only twelve miles off. Tying him on his horse by his own *lazo*, we moved on and in about two hours, emerging from the trail into a broad road, we encountered our rear Guard at a place called Ramas, on the Camargo and Monterey road.

Two days later we were at General Taylor's main camp outside of Monterey, in a most beautiful grove of live oak and pecan trees, the woods of San Domingo, call'd by our army Walnut Springs. This was a most delightful place to encamp an army. Huge shade trees covered many acres of good hard sod while springs of the coldest water gushed out of the ground, and run in crystal streams through the grove, affording an abundant supply of excellent water for man and beast.

Here we heard confirmed the terms of the capitulation which was granted by General Taylor to the beaten Mexicans after the capture of Monterey in September. What a disgrace to American Amis! Everything most advantageous to the Mexicans and injurious to the United States. The Mexican infantry were allowed to retain their arms, the Cavalry their horses, the Artillery, one field battery of six guns, with 21 rounds to a gun! The U.S. troops were not to advance beyond the Rinconada Pass, and there should be armistice for eight weeks! When in another hour's fighting we could have had them all unconditional prisoners, and used nothing but our steel!

"Old Rough and Ready" committed a great blunder, with no justifiable excuse. Ben McCulloch's Texan Rangers were still loud in their expressions of indignation, threats were made against General Taylor, and the old hero deem'd it necessary to double the Dragoon guard around his Headquarters.

EDITOR'S NOTE

(from the 1956 edition)

"Here, the sequence of events in Chamberlain's journal becomes confused. In the interests of clarity the publishers have accordingly omitted several pages. Apparently young Sam spent about two weeks with General Taylor's army at Walnut Springs, during which time he visited Monterey and made numerous sketches depicting the recent fighting for the city. He also, it appears, did his share of roistering, for he rejoined General Wools army— probably early in November—lashed to his saddle, suffering from a severe head wound and a bad case of what he called 'mania-a-potu.'

General Wool had by this time advanced as far as the Mexican town of Monclova, some 200 miles south of the Rio Grande, and was there awaiting expiration of the armistice."

Sam's entry into Monclova

VII

EXPERIENCES ON PICKET DUTY

THE city of Monclova, in the State of Coahuila, was built in the year 1687 as a stronghold against the French, who threatened the Spanish possessions from Louisiana. It was formerly the Capital of the State and contains about four thousand inhabitants who I judge obtain a precarious living by murder and robbery; the women appeared to be all of the most common character and the men, regular assassins.

When not on duty, I went into town day and night, armed with a Bowie Knife and the chamber of my Hall's Carbine, visited the Fandangos and gambling rooms, danced, gambled, drank wine and Mezcal, made love to the Señoritas and with many a gold *onza* in my pockets staggered into camp at reveille, all safe, while many a poor fellow's body would be found horridly mutilated, stripped and thrown into a ditch to be devoured by the Coyotes and Buzzards.

The disgraceful armistice granted by General Taylor proved a severe blow to Wool's Division; with inadequate rations we were to remain here over three weeks, surrounded by a hostile population and the most demoralizing influences. The volunteers growled, and finally the two Illinois Regiments broke out in open mutiny, and started on their way back to the Rio Grande. The Regulars by order of General Wool promptly suppressed this and they confined themselves to muttered threats.

At this time the guard duty at Camp was done in a very negligent and reprehensible manner. I often saw two sentinels meet at the ends of their post, stick their muskets in the ground by the Bayonets, set themselves and indulge in a game of "Old Sledge" or Eukre. Others with a dusky Señorita for a companion would leave their post and retire to some inviting shade, and in love dalliance contrive to pass their two hours quite pleasantly! And this in a country filled with prowling bands of Guerillars, who recognized no treaties or laws.

When I first enlisted I resolved to discharge all duty prompt and faithful, and when off Duty, I considered I had the right to enjoy myself as I deem'd proper.

One day when I was on General Wool's guard, he with his staff rode into town to dine. As we approached the guard line a "Sucker" on post was seated on the ground with a roguish looking Señorita, engaged in eating *frijoles* and *pan de maiz*. The sentinel coolly eyed the cavalcade, and with no thoughts of rising to salute, he remarked, "Good day General, hot riding out I reckon."

The General thundered out, "Call the officer of the guard!"

The man just raised himself on his elbow and drawled out, "Lieutenant Woodson, come here right quick, post nine, for the old General wants you!" He then turned to his companion with a self-satisfied air, as if he had discharged his duty in the most exemplary manner.

The officer of the guard made his appearance without belt or sword, coat unbuttoned and a straw hat on. The General gave him a severe reprimand for his own appearance as well as the unsoldierlike conduct of the guard, whereupon the officer broke out, "Jake Strout, yer ain't worth shucks. If you don't git right up and salute the General, I'll drive yer gal away, doggone if I don't."

The gallant sentinel riled up at this and replied "that if the General wanted saluting the Lieutenant might do it, he wan't agoing to do anything of the kind."

General Wool cut them short by telling the officer to follow him down to the main entrance where the 6th U.S. Infantry were on guard. "Come," he said, "and I will show you how guard duty should be done."

The first "Boy in Blue" we came to was a six foot Irishman who was bent in the most extraordinary manner, near double. "What! What's the matter my man?" cried the General as the "mick" faced to the front and presented, without straightening in the least.

He replied, "The General will excuse me but ever since I have ate corn, I have been troubled with a goneness and a bastely appetite, and faith I believe I am turning into a horse and will be on all fours before long."

The General without waiting to hear more dashed off for town.

Picket Guard duty with scouting and Foraging kept the Dragoons pretty well employed. This suited me, anything but lying in Camp which was hot, dusty and without shade. Our details for Pickets, which were for twenty-four hours, were mounted with one day's rations for man and horse. One favorite post with me was a place about nine miles from

Monclova on the Parras road. Here on a "mesa" or table land, well shaded with Mesquite trees, we formed our "reserves" and with one Vidette thrown out we would unsaddle, spread our blankets in the shade, play cards, spin yarns, drink mezcal and *vino*, and have a good time generally.

From our position, we had a fine view of the country in our front for more than twenty miles, while we were completely hid by the welcome shade trees. Here I have listened to thrilling stories of Napoleon's campaigns, related by an old cavalryman of fifty years' service who had served in Italy, Egypt and in the Russian campaign, and at the age of seventy was still a vigorous soldier in the United States service. Then some son of the Emerald Isle would relate stirring tales of adventures by land and sea under the cross of Saint George, in the Indies fighting the Sikhs or at the Cape Colony against the wild Kaffers; or some old Dragoon, whose soldierlike appearance and re-enlistment stripes told the veteran, would tell of bloody encounters with savage beasts and still more savage Indians in the Everglades of Florida and in the Pawnee country.

One day while on picket here, with all the guard listening to the adventures of a comrade, one of the party called our attention to a cloud of dust rising out of the valley towards Parras. The glint of steel amidst the dust told of armed troops, and of course enemies. Our vidette had been so interested in the story that he had neglected his duty, and the column must have been in sight for some time. Corporal Cory was in command, and convened a hurried council of war; our horses were led out of sight.

I suggested to our worthy Corporal the propriety of sending one man on foot down the hill to the road, keeping well out of sight in the chapperal, to find out what it amounted to, and to come back and report. Rash youth! My plan was adopted, and the grim Corporal said that as I had proposed the plan I should have the honor of executing it.

I would have been glad to have been excused from this duty, but knowing I was in for it, I resolved to discharge it to the best of my ability. I left my Sabre on my saddle, and advising the corporal to fall back on the Infantry pickets, in case I fired (as I should only do so in case of discovery), I, Carbine in hand, started on my disagreeable mission. Dodging from bush to bush I reached the road some half a mile ahead of the advancing column, where I crawled under a clump of mesquite and yuccas, close to the road.

Soon I heard voices mingled with the jingle of spurs and the clatter of Sabres, and some twenty horseman came in sight, at a walk. Their leather jackets, high glazed hats, proclaimed them "Guerillars" or "Salteadores," and black savage-looking rascals they were. Mounted on small, active mustangs, armed with Escopettes, Pistols, Sabres, and murderous looking Lances, with their national weapon, the *lazo*, coiled at their Saddle bow, they presented quite a formidable appearance, but to my mind over-armed. They were laughing and chatting, all smoking the corn husk *cigarittos*, showing conclusively that they were not aware of the close vicinity of some of the hated invaders. I could feel my heart beat as if it would break through my ribs; as they passed me, so close that I could have touched some of their horses, I noticed that they had nothing ready for use, most of their arms being lashed to the saddles.

The dust they raised in passing almost suffocated me to death, and I was well buried by it. Next came a long pack Mule train, and a villainous no-haired dog smelt around me and commenced to bark! I thought I was gone up sure, but fortunately my tormentor soon trotted on.

When all had passed I started back for the hill and reported what I had seen, estimating their number at about one hundred armed men besides the *arreadores* or muleteers. Corporal Cory was more perplexed than ever; he finally concluded to send word to the Infantry pickets and Camp. We thought that this must be an enemy Convoy of provisions, collected in this part of the country occupied by us, and on its way to their Camp.

I told Cory that I considered it plainly our duty to attack and hinder their advance until reinforcements reached us, but the Corporal was not equal for the emergency, and we done nothing. Nearly an hour passed, when we saw a small body of horsemen on the road towards Monclova. On coming up it proved to be twelve men and Sergeant Jack Miller of the 2nd Dragoons, who, being out on a scout, had met our courier, who gave information of the foe, when they came on to see for themselves. I gave Sergeant Miller full particulars in regards to their arms, way of marching and gratuitously gave my opinion "that we could lick them out of their boots."

Miller was for attacking them at once, but Cory objected on account of the disparity of numbers, and the distance from Camp in case of repulse. Miller replied, "Corporal, if you are afraid you had better return to Camp, but I shall beat up their column as soon as possible!"

We all agreed to stick by the brave Sergeant. Cory after some words with me, in which my words were anything but complimentary, went growling with us. Across the country we went to avoid raising a dust, while the cloud that rolled up in the distance served as a guide to our course. A sharp trot for an hour brought us near their rear guard, when we slung Carbines. Jack Miller said, "No firing, men! If twenty Dragoons can't whip a hundred greasers with the Sabre, I'll join the Doughboys, and carry a fence rail all my life."

We took the gallop and were soon on them. They were riding in the same careless manner as when I watched them and we were within twenty yards before they discovered us and their danger. With the charging shout of the Dragoons, we rode them down, horse and man. Some tried to get at their weapons, but a few cuts from our Sabres stopped all resistance, and the rear guard was ours.

To secure their horses and arms, make the prisoners lie down in a pile, was but the work of a minute; leaving four men to guard them with cocked Carbines, we dashed on. Overtaking the Mule train we passed it like a whirlwind and found the advance and main force drawn up in line to receive us, but instead of meeting our charge with a counter charge with their Lances, they opened fire with their Escopettes. We struck them at full speed. They made some resistance with the Lance, but our keen blades and powerful horses cut down and overthrew all opposition. Many tried to escape, a few succeeded; the greater part surrendered at discretion. The fruits of our victory summed up as follows: of the Enemy, 6 Killed; 13 Wounded; 70 prisoners, with horses, equipment, and Arms; and 360 pack mules, loaded with beans, corn, mezcal and powder. We had only one man and three horses, slightly wounded.

As this neat affair took place on the bank of the Arroyo de los Palmos, Sergeant Miller gave it that name.

In the attack on the main body, I had found myself alongside of a black-whiskered chap who lunged at me with his lance. I parried it and gave him a right cut across the face, which added neither to his beauty or health. I gave another a front cut which took effect on his high sombrero, driving it like an extinguisher down over his face, bringing him to the ground.

Collecting our prisoners, we lashed the wounded to the Pack Saddles, left the dead as they lay, and started back for Monclova in the following order of march. Four Dragoons, on the advance, then the pack mules; next the prisoners in a column of fours, their horses lashed together by lassos; flankers on both sides; and the rear guard, all the Dragoons, earning their Carbines at an Advance. At the reserve we found a new picket guard sent out to relieve us, and Yell's Arkansas regiment of Cavalry, ordered out by General Wool on receiving Corporal Cory's dispatch.

On seeing us the "Rackensackers" broke ranks, and surrounded us yelling and whooping like Indians. Their officers had no control over them, and only our bold front saved our defenseless prisoners from being massacred by these brave chivalric sons of the South. Finding they could not butcher our charge, they went off at a jump to find other victims. Woe to the cripples and sick women who fell in their way, for their cruelty was only exceeded by their insubordination.

After a half hour's rest, having our wounded seen to, we started again, passed the Infantry pickets, reached the town, and passed through the Grand Plaza while the garrison were out on Dress Parade.

I felt so satisfied of my share of the achievement that I expected to be promoted to a Lance Corporal at least, but rather wilted when Corporal Cory came and confined me in the Guard House, by order of Captain Steen, Cory having reported me for using disrespectful language to him! Thus were all my dreams of ambition and glory vanished in the snug quarters of Company Q.

The command was inspected next day by Colonel Harney. When he came to the guard house, I with other prisoners was paraded on the left of the guard. The Colonel asked the prisoners what they were confined for. Two recruits replied, "For nothing, Colonel."

"Nothing? G—d d—n you, nothing! Lieutenant Buford, tie the d——d sons of b——s up by the thumbs for two hours! The next time you come here, come for something!"

My turn came next. Knowing my customer, I replied, "For acting the man in the guerillar fight of yesterday and calling Corporal Cory a d——d coward."

Harney said, "You did, did you? Release this desperate fellow before he injures any of you."

I was released and sent to my company, but alas! such was the perversity of my cruel fate that the same day Corporal Cory insisted on running his face against my hand (which happened to be closed at the time) and in consequence the stupid fellow's eyes got in mourning, and his face resembled a raw beef steak! And he blamed me for it! Again I was quartered in Company Q. I was taken up to Captain Steen's tent; Cory related his story and I mine. Sergeant Miller sent for a Dragoon who corroborated mine, and gave me great credit for the part I took in the whole affair. I was released, Cory was reduced to the ranks and Lieutenant Buford, who was detached to drill the Arkansas Cavalry, had me detailed for his orderly and I acted as "Fugleman" for that regiment in the Carbine and Sabre exercise. During the remainder of the time we lay at Monclova I had the best of times, and I enjoyed my life greatly.

It was while we were here encamped that I acquired the name by which I thereafter became known. It happened in this fashion. One day when I with several comrades were in town on a pass, we visited a confectionery shop to purchase some *dulces* (sweet-meats). A number of ugly "greasers" were present engaged in a favorite pastime of theirs, the game of *Peloncillo*.

A small cake of the brown sugar of the country in the shape of a sugarloaf is placed on a block, little end up, and for the sum of two "clacko" (about three cents) one is allowed to cut at it with a Sabre; if two ounces are sliced off, the Sugar, worth six; cents, is his, if not he loses. As the cake is as hard as a rock the percentage is largely in favor of the dealer.

We were bantered into trying our hand and my comrades selected me to represent the U.S. Dragoons in this international affair. I accepted the post of honor on condition of being allowed to use my own Sabre instead of the clumsy machete of the shop. After some grumbling the terms were granted, and a wiry-looking "greaser" took up a heavy cutlass and commenced the game. In a dozen trials he cut off the allotted amount seven times.

It was now my turn and my first three attempts were decided failures, and our swarthy opponents grinned in delight and my companions looked blue! But I felt confident, my eye was true, wrist firm and my Sabre as keen as a razor. I cut the remaining nine almost in halves, and we demanded that the little game should continue. In spite of the remonstrance of the astonished shopkeeper, I kept on until three dozen of the sugar cakes were ours.

The Mexicans cried out, "*Que Diablo Peloncillo Juan!*" (What a devil peloncillo John is!) My comrades caught at the nickname and "Peloncillo Jack" it was to everybody and everywhere except on the company books.

VIII

MARCH TO PARRAS

ON November 13 the disgraceful armistice came to an end at last, and on the 24th General Wool, leaving four volunteer companies to garrison Monclova, started with the remainder of his Division for Parras, some 180 miles to the southwest. The men of Wool's command had formed so many acquaintances with the dark eyed, passionate daughters of Monclova that the Provost Guard were obliged to drive them back as they followed us up by hundreds, some on foot, some on Ponies and Donkeys, and some even in primitive oxcarts.

The first day we marched only nine miles, and encamped at a *ganado* or cattle ranch. During the evening a violent tornado visited us and played the Old Harry with things generally; tents were blown away, loaded wagons upset, our horses stampeded, while the air was filled with clouds of dust, in spite of the rain, which descended in torrents. Next morning the sun shone bright and clear, and we having righted matters resumed our march which was very severe on the Infantry, as the day was hot, and the road dusty. The chapperal rose like a wall on each side of the road, confining the dust to the tract and nearly suffocating the poor devils of footmen. About twenty miles was considered a good day's march, though the distance we made depended on the water, which was scarce and poor, often containing large portions of minerals, and sometimes was hot and boiling.

On this march I often contrasted the great difference there was between the Regular and the Volunteers, and I came to the conclusion that the Dragoons were far superior in materials to any other arm of the service. No man of any spirit and ambition would join the "Doughboys" and go afoot, when he could ride a fine horse and wear spurs like a gentleman. In our Squadron were broken down Lawyers, Actors and men of the world. Soldiers who had served under Napoleon, Polish Lancers, French Cuirassiers, Hungarian Hussars, Irishmen who had left the Queen's service to swear allegiance to Uncle Sam and wear the blue.

Our officers were all graduates of West Point, and at the worst, were gentlemen of intelligence and education, often harsh and tyrannical, yet they took pride in having their men well clothed, and fed, in making them contented and reconciled to their lot. The volunteer officers on the other hand would tie up a man one day, drink and play cards with him the next, and excuse their favorites from drill and guard duty, in short, most of them were totally incompetent, and a disgrace to their profession. The two companies of "Quincy Rifles" in the First Illinois Regiment, under the command of the brothers Morgan, and a company of "German Rifles" raised in Texas, and commanded by Captain Connors, an old Dragoon Sergeant, were an exception to this rule.

One day while our Squadron was the rear guard, I noticed a poor ragged fellow seated beside the road, looking completely used up. He was emptying the gravel from his shoes, as Colonel Hardin rode up and inquired "who gave him leave to fall out?" He replied "no one, but his feet was so badly galled that he was obliged to stop to clear his shoes." Hardin who was a Deacon in the Presbyterian Church at home swore "that if he did not instantly move on he would put a file of bayonets on his back." He got up and hobbled on, giving his "Christian" commander a look of revenge as he passed.

On this march I was constantly reminded of scenes in Don Quixote, in fact the costumes, customs and buildings are all borrowed from Old Spain, with but little change. The Barbers Basin, the skins of wine, quaint old inns, with fun-loving *dulcineas*, exist in all their purity here! The scenery as we approached Parras was grand and often magnificent, high craggy mountains, deep canons, wild fearful passes which a dozen determined men could have defended against our army for hours.

Little or no resistance was offered to our advance. The Guerillars contented themselves in hanging around our flanks and rear and they served to keep our column well closed up. Woe to the unfortunate soldier who straggled behind. He was lassoed, stripped naked, and dragged through clumps of cactus until his body was full of needle-like thorns; then, his privates cut off and crammed into his mouth, he was left to die in the solitude of the chapperal or to be eaten alive by vultures and coyotes. Such were the daily acts of the Guerillars.

Paso el Diablo is a strange freak of nature, a pass or canyon through the Sierra Madre, about nine miles north of the City of Parras. The pass was evidently of volcanic origin; vast rocks lay piled up in Titanic heaps of the most grotesque shapes, with layers of pumice stone in different places. It was expected this place would be strongly defended, and General Wool dispatched Colonel Yell's regiment of Arkansas Cavalry to seize and hold it, if possible. They found the place undefended, and they encamped here until the Division came up. It was a wild fearful looking place, and I wondered, as we defiled through its narrow limits between the overhanging rocky walls, at the criminal apathy of the Mexican authorities. Ten men with crowbars by one hour's work could have rendered it impassable for days. But no obstacles were thrown in our way and our army, with its immense trains of wagons, passed through in safety and encamped at the Hacienda el Abuja, five miles beyond.

I afterwards heard a tradition connected with the Pass which I call the Legend of San Patricio and the Devil.

His Satanic Majesty, while roaming around the world seeking whom he might devour, came to Parras to tempt a certain holy *padre*, Patricio by name, who bore the reputation of being a saint of the first water. The devil offered the holy Father long life and the sole proprietorship of a gold mine, in exchange for his soul. San Patricio accepted the bargain on two conditions: first, that the Devil should do the mining, second, that the gold should be sprinkled with Holy Water! His Satanic Majesty, who was undoubtedly fuddled on the rich Parras wine, agreed to the terms, and in the company of the good *padre* proceeded to this part of the Sierra Madre and commenced operations. A shaft was sunk, and gold soon reached and large quantities thrown out. The good Father threw on the Holy Water, with so much zeal that some of it flew into the pit and fell on the satanic miner! The effect was wonderful! With a howl of baffled rage and infernal malice, the Devil sprang through the mountain to his subterranean abode, leaving the saintly Father in possession of his soul, gold and long life, and Parras with a new pass through the mountains, shortening the route from Monterey two hundred miles.

If any heretic doubts this true legend of the Holy Church, let them go to the city of Parras in the State of Coahuila, visit the church of San Patricio and find one fat Father Guies, who related this to me, and he can hear it from the good man's holy lips, and many other legends of like undoubted veracity, and be shown a painting of questionable merit portraying the Saint throwing on the holy water, and the Devil with a tail many miles long bursting through the mountain, surrounded with red and blue flames.

IX

A DUEL IN A BEDROOM

THE City of Parras, which we reached the next day, contains about fifteen thousand inhabitants, and is delightfully situated on a plain at the foot of a high mountain. The climate is unsurpassed in the world; the air is so pure that flies and mosquitoes are unknown; pears, grapes, pomegranates, olives and melons of all kinds grow in abundance and of the best quality. Wheat, Corn, oats and Barley fields cover the plains while the wine and Brandy is famed all over Mexico. The city contains a Citadel and is usually garrisoned by some three hundred men as a protection against the Lipans and Comanches, but all of the Mexican soldiers had departed before we arrived.

I enjoyed myself in this place to my full capacity. I was in town every day making sketches for the officers, and I met with various adventures. The women of Parras possess more than their share of beauty. Some have skins as fair as our own New England girls, with such enchanting glorious eyes! and black glossy hair! What little feet and hands and divinely graceful shapes! Often mothers at thirteen, grandmothers at thirty, they become fearful old hags at forty.

I became acquainted with a family named Velasco which contained twin sisters so very handsome as to be known as "*El dos hermosas hermanas*" (the two beautiful sisters). Both were so faultlessly lovely that I could not make up my mind which to admire the most. When looking into the lovelit eyes of Nina, I was ready to vow eternal allegiance to her, the next moment when listening to the sweet melody of Rosita's songs, I felt as if I was her slave forever, and ended by swearing love to both.

The girls took great interest in my rough sketches and I tried my hand at taking their portraits, but seeing how impossible it was to do justice to their beauty I gave it up in despair. The beauties delighted to curl my long hair and would spend hours in fixing it to suit their tastes. But on my return to Camp I would find that I was guilty of abducting many of the inhabitants of the place, for alas! my charmers like all Mexicans raised large stocks of *piojos* (lice), not only for home consumption, but for distribution among their friends.

I was still on duty as orderly to Lieutenant Abe Buford, but my service was through by nine A.M. and having a standing pass I spent most of my time in town with my fair friends, escorting them to Fandangos or the Theatre, made them presents, and we were well known at all the places of amusement in Parras. But then an incident occurred that put an end to my enchantment. One morning I stopped at the *casa* of Velasco to make an early call. I fastened my horse in the patio and entered the sleeping apartment of the young ladies with the freedom of an old friend of the house. This was a great mistake of mine—I should have sent in my card! My two charmers were in bed, but not alone! The black shaggy head of a Mexican lay on the pillow between the raven tresses of Rosita and Nina!

I recognized the invader as one Antonio, a renegade who acted as guide to our army. Overcome with my emotions, I was about to retire with becoming modesty when the voluptuous rascal sprang up and drawing a machete from under his pillow, and wrapping his blanket around his left arm, rushed on me like some wild beast. The fastidious young ladies, instead of fainting or screaming, sat up in bed and cried *"Bravo! Bravo! bueno Antonio! matar! matar el grande pendejo!"* (Bravo! Bravo! good Antonio! kill! kill the big fool!)

What charming creatures! I drew my sabre and came to guard in an instant. He was as active as a cat, and I found I had all I could attend to in keeping his ugly knife from getting between my ribs, while all my cuts and points were received on his confounded blanket. More than once his knife glided over my guard, cutting my jacket. I could hear the gentle Nina say, *"Anda! Anda! mia dulce, mia alma!"* (Quick! quick! my sweet, my soul!) while Rosita in her most dulcet tones murmured, *"Antonio, mia amor, punga el gringo, que la cama!"* (Antonio, my love, stick the foreigner and come to bed!)

How cheering to myself were the words of the darlings! But I did not lose heart, and finally succeeded in giving my antagonist an ugly slash across one of his bare legs, causing him to drop his knife, when I gave him a point in a part that made him howl with agony, and would cause him to lose the regards of the *"dos margaritas."*

Leaving the villain on the floor bleeding profusely, I made a graceful exit, and returned to camp, thoroughly disgusted with the fickleness of womankind, Mexican Señoritas in particular.

One day not long after this little affair Major Beall, being on duty as "Division officer of the Day," went into Parras with a patrol under the command of my old friend Sergeant Jack Miller. "Old Brilliant" on arriving in town drew up in the Plaza in front of a *pulque* shop, entered and informed the horrified proprietor that his entire stock of liquors was confiscated to the United States of America, which he represented!

X

A FORCED MARCH

WE remained in camp at Parras until mid-December. By this time I had pretty effectively done the place, and had made quite a collection of sketches of the prominent buildings. Some of the Churches were to me as interesting as a Museum, containing many paintings by native artists, quaint and grotesque in most cases, yet showing much boldness of design, and uncultivated talent. Then there were huge Saints, and Crucifixions, pieces of the *true* Cross, by the cord, bones of Saints by the bushel, gorgeous altars resplendent with barbaric gold.

On the 17th of December an express from General Worth, who was at Saltillo, about 110 miles to the southeast, brought word that Santa Anna, with a large Mexican force, was on his way from San Luis Potosi to attack General Worth's smaller army at Saltillo. Immediately the long roll was beat on the drums, the bugles blew "Boot and Saddle," the wagons were packed, the sick removed to the Citadel, with one company of regular Infantry left them for guard. In two hours from the receipt of the dispatches, we turned our backs on Parras and its charms, and with our faces to the South, our little division commenced one of the most extraordinary marches ever made.

The first night we halted on the bank of an arroyo that led into the "Paso el Diablo." Resuming our march at two o'clock in the morning, we marched all day over a very dusty road and made over forty miles. It was terribly severe on the footmen, though their knapsacks were hauled in wagons, and the Dragoons on the rear guard would give the weary a lift. Yet many would evade the rear guard and hide in the Chapperal, and that with the full knowledge that the Mexican *rancheros* were constantly on the watch for our stragglers. Several were lost this day and we could tell to a moment when the poor fellows met their fate by the circles of buzzards, kites, and Vultures over the place where they were being murdered.

The second night we bivouacked in the road, and slept in order of march: reveille at 2 A.M., breakfast cooked and eaten, and we were off again in half an hour. The road was dusty and without water, but we made a good fifty miles this day, and halted for the night in the chapperal, near the town of Patos. The next morning we came to a smooth level plain, where the troops could march off the dusty road, which was a great relief. At noon we reached a small stream of most excellent clear cold water; and men and animals rushed into it together. What rest and vitality it gave us to get rid of the two days' accumulation of dust that had settled on our faces, clinging to our hair and the men's long beards to such an extent that we had lost all resemblance to humanity and presented an appearance at once grotesque and horrible. We rested here for two hours and then resumed our weary route much refreshed by our halt.

Soon Staff Officers came at speed from the advance; orders were given to close up, the Dragoons and Washington's Battery were ordered to the front at a trot; all seemed to say that something was up!

General Wool, ordering our Squadron to follow as escort, galloped off to a gentle eminence well to the front. Away across the smooth plain toward Saltillo was what appeared to be an army drawn up in line of battle. Horsemen could be seen riding back and forwards. Clouds of dust rolled up, a respectable line of mounted skirmishers appeared in their front, things looked decidedly promising for a fight. Colonel Yell's regiment of Cavalry was ordered to reconnoiter their position, but they only went about a mile when they halted, yelling and brandishing their sabres at the foe five miles off!

The General and Staff sat in the saddle watching the enemy through their field glasses, when I heard Captain Benham, an Engineer Officer, exclaim, "It's a line of Spanish Bayonets (yuccas), and a drove of Mustangs!" And so it proved to be, though Lieutenant McDowell, General Wool's aide, had seen "thirty Brass guns in position."

We moved on and went into camp at Agua Nueva, a cattle ranch some 17 miles south of Saltillo, having accomplished 130 miles from Parras in under four days, an achievement unparalleled in the history of the war.

We formed a regular camp at Agua Nueva although the only advantage the place possessed was in having nine springs of excellent water. The ground was covered with a thick growth of cactus and mesquite which had to be cleared away before we could pitch our tents. The inhabitants had all fled the place, with the exception of a dozen or two old women, a few children, hundreds of dogs, fleas and lice ad infinitum. Our Quartermasters and Commissaries took possession of most of the houses, the chapel was turned into a hospital, and as the weather was growing cold, the post corral was used for fire wood. Pickets were thrown out on the San Luis and Zacatecas roads, from sixteen to twenty miles from camp. I was fortunate enough to be detailed on General Wool's guard, and thus got rid of the unpleasant duty of outposts in cold weather.

One dark disagreeable night, we were ordered to saddle up and accompany the General and staff. We moved out of camp toward the Encantada ranch, at the entrance to the pass that leads to Saltillo. It was a miserable night; a cold, drizzling rain that seem to penetrate to our bones was falling, while it was so dark that we could not see our file leader. Wrapped up in our overcoats we rode along in silence, often missing the road, and being compelled to dismount and find it again. We passed pickets who did not hail us until we almost rode over them, passed the Encantada ranch, turned to our right and continued on for some time, when the two men on the advance halted, their horses refusing to move on.

A belt of blackness, darker than the surrounding gloom, yawned beneath their horses' feet. Lieutenant McDowell told the men to spur their horses and make them move on, but the sensible animals would not budge. Lieutenant Carleton found a stone and threw it in the black streak; no splash followed, but it was heard to strike on a hard rocky bottom, far below. What a nice place to leap in! Brilliant McDowell, the most obtuse intellect in the army not excepting Dave Hunter!

We found the road and moved on, but in a few minutes came to another halt, this time bringing up against a perpendicular wall. We felt it with our Sabres, but as far as we could reach it was as straight as the side of a house; in fact we were in the famous pass of La Angostura. Getting on the road once more we moved on for some time, when the barking of dogs directed us to a ranch; here we got so mixed up in courtyards and corrals that we were compelled to rouse up a "greaser" to show us our way out. He informed us that the little insignificant place was known as Buena Vista. Beyond it the road lay over white limestone and we succeeded in keeping it better; we took a trot and in about one hour our horses' hoofs rang on stone pavement, a sleepy doughboy hailed us, and we found we were in Saltillo.

After inquiring for General Worth's Headquarters, we proceeded down a steep street, just as a town clock struck the hour of midnight. At once our ears were saluted with the most infernal noise I ever heard. The war whoop of the Comanches, the cry of a pack of Coyotes, the morning serenade of a drove of mules and Jackasses, was nothing to it! and yet it was only an honest Mexican watchman crying the hour! *"El Espiritu Santo Santissima Virgen Maria doce horas!"* ending with a shrill whistle. Our horses plunged and reared with affright, and I honestly believe that ten such watchmen would have routed our entire army.

We drew up in front of Worth's quarters in a pelting rain. The sentinel called the General's orderly to whom General Wool said, "Give my compliments to General Worth, and tell him that General Wool is here." After some ten minutes the orderly returned with this message: "General Worth's compliments to General Wool and he wishes to know what you want." "What I want!" exclaimed our little General, "what I want! Do you hear that, Mr. McDowell? Tell General Worth that I want quarters for myself. Staff and Escort." Away went the orderly and soon returned and said, "General Worth says you can stop here." The General was angry enough at this cool reception, but remained with McDowell while the rest of us found accommodations in the quarters of Company F, 1st Dragoons.

After dinner on the second day we started back for camp. General Worth and General Butler (the latter in a carriage, still suffering from a wound received at Monterey) accompanied General Wool as far as the plain back of the town. This plain is much higher than the city, so that in approaching the place from the north, it cannot be seen until you are within pistol shot of the houses, when you have a bird's eye view of the whole town. On the plain an animated Council of War was held by the three generals, as to the best way to defend the place against Santa Anna and the fifty thousand "greasers" that rumor credited him with having.

They differed in opinion. General Butler, an able volunteer officer from Kentucky, was in favor of throwing up Rifle Pits, and Redoubts on the plain covering all approaches. He remarked, "Gentlemen, I know my volunteers. If once broken they cannot be rallied, but place them behind breastworks, and we will gain a regular New Orleans victory". Worth, a splendid officer who rose by merit alone from the ranks of the 6th U.S. Infantry and believed his division invincible, got a little excited and exclaimed, "D—n the volunteers! Place me and the Regulars on this plain, and I will drive all the greasers in Mexico to hell at the point of the bayonet! Why d—n it, gentlemen, this plain was made for an infantry fought, a man must be insane to talk of breastwork when he has got such a field as this to maneuver in." General Worth's mind was fixed on the pass we encountered on our march and recommended it be examined before any decision was made.

The debate waxed warm, even our pious little General let slip an oath, but squared the account by lifting up his hand and saying, "Heaven forgive me for blasphemy." The council broke up without any decision, and we started on our way back.

We passed the ranch of Buena Vista, and reached the pass of Angostura, when we left the road, turned to our left and ascended to a high plateau, where we had a fine view of the position. The road we had left went through the pass, which was formed by a high perpendicular cliff on one side and a deep impassable *barranca* on the other. From the pass to the craggy mountains on our left was about two miles, and with the exception of the plateau, the ground was rough, full of deep ravines rendering it impassable for cavalry and artillery. General Wool was delighted with the strength of the place, and remarked to Lieutenant Carleton, "If we have to fight a superior force this is the place, this plateau commands the whole ground."

On Christmas day our mess, famous as foragers, made extensive arrangements for a capital dinner. We had secured a fat Pig, a ten pound Turkey, a dozen of eggs, and "Boss" Hastings, a veteran in war and the culinary art, had got up a plum pudding! I was tending the Pig for my share. It was spitted on a ramrod that some volunteer would find on his pay roll (we had borrowed it for the occasion). My Pig was doing splendidly before the coal fire, the skin browning to a turn, cracking open and letting the rich fatty juice ooze out and drop into a messpan, from which I ladled it over the revolving barbecue. "Boss" was superintending the Turkey and the plum pudding; the former, stuffed with bread and onions, was baking in a Dutch Oven, the latter doing in a messpan, with another turned over it. How we smacked our lips in fond anticipation of the coming feast! Benches, a table and even plates we had, all cut out of the yuccas.

Things were about ready; Hastings and myself were debating which was the right thing to do, serve Turkey or Pig first, and the remainder of the mess were seated when a Ranger dashed through camp crying out, "The enemy are on us! The enemy are on us!" and made for Headquarters. In another moment the bugler blew "Boots and Saddles"; this was taken up by the cavalry and artillery, while from the Infantry camps sounded the long roll. In five minutes "To horse" blew, and kicking out the fire we left our splendid dinner—alas! never to meet again. Just as the command was given, "By fours trot, march," a mob of volunteers passed by and made a raid on our treasure; Dutch oven and its delicious contents, Messpans and pudding. Pig and ramrod all went right before our eyes! The strength of discipline was never more forcibly shown than in the present case—regulars robbed of their dinner by volunteers! To witness this without leaving the ranks was a severe trial.

We went out on the San Luis road and as we reached the ranch found the place full of volunteers. They were committing all manner of outrages on the few women left in the ranch, fighting over their poor victims like dogs, and the place resounded with horrid oaths and the groans and shrieks of the raped. Captain Steen cried out, "Ride them down, men! Give the cowardly wretches the weight of our sabres!" and we went for them with a will.

With the memory of our dinner fresh in our minds our mess struck some hard blows, several of the miscreants getting badly cut. We drove them out of the place, placed the women, some of whom had been stripped naked, in one house, and leaving a guard, we went on.

About one mile from the ranch, we met a gang of Rackensackers, coming in great confusion at speed. They reported that while on picket in the Paso de los Pinos, they were charged on by a large body of cavalry. Steen questioned their officer, a Captain English, who described in the most minute manner their appearance, how they attacked him, and of the deadly fire his brave command poured into the ranks of the outnumbering foe! With reluctance they formed in our rear and went back with us, English riding alongside of Captain Steen. A sharp trot for one hour brought us to the scene of the desperate affair. All was quiet, for a wonder not a Buzzard was in sight, but away off on the plain, which extended as far as the eye could reach, appeared a cloud of dust. Captain English cried out, "There they go, a Brigade of cavalry at least! Hurrah Boys, we drove them after all!" and the brave Arkansas chivalry made the rocky pass echo with their wild shrill cries.

Buford, who had been watching the dust through his glass, suddenly exclaimed, "Mustangs, by God!" and as the dust lifted we could plainly see with the naked eye a drove of wild horses careering over the *llanos*. Leaving the crestfallen heroes, we returned to camp, cursing all volunteers. Our mess was completely cleaned out, others were as bad off, and we made our Christmas Dinner off of hard bread and salt pork. By some means, we had by next morning acquired a complete mess kit, and a couple of hams and a dozen smoked buffalo tongues, and there was some tall swearing by certain volunteer officers.

XI

MASSACRE OF THE CAVE

ONE day in midwinter I was on General Wool's escort, and returning from a trip to the Encantada ranch—our communications point with Saltillo—when the sound of fire arms in the mountains back of camp attracted our attention. General Wool sent his Aide, Irvin McDowell, to find out the cause of the alarm. The Lieutenant with an orderly went off at a gallop, disappearing behind a clump of chapperal bushes, when a fearful yell of anguish reached us. With our minds full of thoughts of Guerillars and ambuscades, we slung carbines, drew sabres, and even our little General drew his dress sword and charged with us.

On reaching the scene, determined to conquer or die, we found the unfortunate Aide lying on the ground face down groaning most fearfully, with a "Turk's Head" (a species of the Cactus) fast to the most prominent part of his person! In spite of discipline the escort greeted this exhibition of the "stern realities of a soldier's life in Mexico," with shouts of laughter. Poor thick headed McDowell, his horse had thrown him and he had found a landing on a cactus that had thorns an inch long! His orderly came back with his horse but "Mac" declined to ride and walked to camp. A story circulated later that a Surgeon and a pair of tweezers was required to rid the gentleman of his tormentors.

Hearing more shots away up in the mountain, General Wool ordered Sergeant Clifford to proceed with the guard to the place of firing and arrest all soldiers he found there. Taking a trot we reached the steep ascent of the mountain, where we dismounted and led our horses up. Soon we were obliged to leave our horses. Three men were left in charge and now we only numbered nine men and the Sergeant. All was quiet; overhead circled a cloud of *zapilotes*, or Vultures, that would occasionally dart down on something on the ground ahead.

On reaching the place we found a "greaser" shot and *scalped* but still breathing; the poor fellow held in his hands his Rosary and a medal of the "Virgin of Guadalupe," and only his feeble motions kept the fierce harpies from falling on him while yet alive. A Sabre thrust was given him in mercy, and on we went at a run. Soon shouts and curses, cries of women and children reached our ears, coming apparently from a cave at the end of the ravine. Climbing over rocks we reached the entrance, and as soon as we could see in the comparative darkness a horrid sight was before us. The cave was full of our volunteers yelling like fiends, while on the rocky floor lay over twenty Mexicans, dead and dying in pools of blood. Women and children were clinging to the knees of the murderers and shrieking for mercy.

Sergeant Clifford ordered the volunteers, mostly from Yell's Cavalry, to come out and give themselves up as prisoners, which order was received with shouts of derision and threats of cleaning us out if we interfered. Clifford gave the command and we dropped behind rocks and took aim on the foremost ruffians, when our Sergeant again ordered them to file out or we would fire. They became silent, not knowing our strength.

Soon a brutal looking Rackensacker advanced towards us brandishing a huge knife dripping with gore in one hand, and a bunch of reeking scalps in the other, and cried out:

"Hyer, you Regulars! I'm Bill Stamps, I'm! We don't a muss with you, we don't! I raised this 'ere har from the d——d yellow bellies that had on poor Archy's clothes. I did! Take me to 'Old Fussy' and I'll be responsible for the whole."

With this the savage cutthroat marched out with a swagger, gave a fancy Indian dance and subsided in tears. With curses and threats, more than a hundred volunteers filed out of the slaughter pen and with the muzzles of our Carbines bearing on them they sullenly marched down the mountain. We soon met our Squadron, who took charge of our prisoners while the Officer of the Day ordered us back to the cave with several surgeons. On reaching the place we could hear the low groans of the dying mingled with the sobs of women and cries of children. A fire was burning on the rocky floor, and threw a faint flickering light on the horrors around. Most of the butchered Mexicans had been scalped; only three men were found unharmed. A rough crucifix was fastened to a rock, and some irreverent wretch had crowned the image with a bloody scalp. A sickening smell filled the place. The surviving women and children sent up loud screams on seeing us, thinking that we had returned to finish the work!

No one was punished for this outrage; General Wool, in a general order, reprimanded the Arkansas Cavalry, but nothing more was done. The direct cause of the massacre was the barbarous murder of a young man belonging to the Arkansas Regiment. But this murder was undoubtedly committed in retaliation for the outrages committed on the women of the Agua Nueva ranch by the volunteers on Christmas day.

XII

VOLUNTEER CAVALRY

OUR little army was rather weakened than strengthened by the two regiments of volunteer cavalry, Colonel Yell's Arkansas and Colonel Humphrey Marshall's Kentucky. The material that these regiments were composed of was excellent—none could be better—for the men possessed fine physiques, and strength combined with activity, but they had no discipline, or confidence in their officers. Most of them were wild reckless young fellows, with the most inflated ideas of their own personal prowess and a firm belief that their own State could whip the world and Mexico in particular. This independence of character, and self-confidence was fatal to their efficiency as soldiers. Many of them were duelists and desperados of the frontier, quite famous in their own locality as fighting men, to whom the wholesome restraints of discipline seemed tyranny in its worst form. The battles of the Alamo, San Jacinto and Mier, with the exploits of their demigods Crockett, Travis, and Bowie, caused them to religiously believe that a dozen Southern gentlemen armed with the Kentucky rifle and that southern institution, the Bowie Knife, could travel all over Mexico.

Their impatience of all restraint, and egotism made them worse than useless on Picket, while in camp they were a perfect nuisance. They would visit the Ranches and, looking upon the "greasers" as belonging to the same social class as their own Negro slaves, they plundered and ill-treated them, and outraged the women, and this sometimes in the presence of the fathers and husbands, who were tied up and flogged for daring to interfere in these amusements of the chivalry. This made work for us Dragoons, for we were obliged to patrol the whole country for miles around camp to protect the wretched inhabitants and arrest these heroes.

The really fine horses that they were mustered in with, they sold to officers and the quartermaster, and were now mounted on Mules or Mustangs that they had stolen. They took no care of their arms—not one Carbine in fifty would go off—and most of their Sabres were rusted in their scabbards.

This shameful state of affairs seemed to have no remedy; the War was a southern democratic one, and ex-Governor Yell of the great and sovereign State of Arkansas, and ex-Senator Marshall, of the immaculate and still greater State of Kentucky, were men of too much importance to take advice, much less orders, from a little Yankee general like Wool.

"We come here to fight sir! not to clean old iron and groom horses sir! and doggoned if we do it sir!" was the reply to Colonel Churchill, Inspector General of the army, by Major Borland when he had been reprimanded by the Colonel for the highly culpable condition of his command. The incompetency of the volunteer cavalry kept General Wool and Staff constantly on the alert. The General seemed never to sleep; the least noise during the night would call forth the cry, "Sentinel! Sentinel! what noise is that?"

The tents of his guard were pitched directly in the rear of his quarters and his call would invariably arouse us up; many and many a time that cold winter, I had been out all day in the saddle, and had just got warm in my blankets, when the cry of "Sentinel! Sentinel! What o'clock is it?" would startle me from my hard bed to listen with anxiety to what would follow. When it was, "Call Mr. McDowell! Call the Sergeant of the guard! Dennis! Dennis!" I knew I was in for it, and with the rest turn out with muttered curses to saddle up. Dennis was the General's colored servant, and when he was called we knew it was for the purpose of saddling up the General's "bay," and then for an all-night ride in the cold, visiting the outposts, and the different encampments.

One bitter cold night we paid a visit to the camp of Arkansas Cavalry at the Encantada. We went up the dry bed of an arroyo until we gained the center of the camp without being discovered. Colonel Yell's tent was on a pillar-shaped island of sandstone, some thirty feet high, reached by a flight of steps cut in the rock. As late as the hour was (2 A.M.), the tent was lit up, and judging from the clink of silver coins and remarks such as, "I see it, and go you ten better," "I'll call you," a nice little game of Poker was being played.

General Wool dismounted and rushed up the steps, into the tent and cried out, "Surrender gentleman, your regiment is captured!"

We heard Colonel Yell's voice reply, "Welcome, General, welcome! What will you imbibe. Brandy or Whiskey Punch?"

The general staff went up and for an hour we had the satisfaction of listening to the clinking of glasses in the tent while we were shivering in the cold. The Colonel's poker party departed and one of them, Captain Albert Pike, asked our Sergeant if we had anything to drink, and on being answered in the negative went back and soon a Negro boy made his appearance with a camp kettle full of hot Whiskey Punch, with the sliced lemon floating on it. By the time the General came out, we were quite jolly, for the Colonel's merits as a punch maker were quite undeniable.

As the General mounted we heard the ring of a horse's hoofs coming at speed over the frozen plain. "There! There!" said the General. "Another of your pickets captured, only one escaped!" Sure enough, the guard on the Parras road had been surprised and taken, but one had escaped.

XIII

THE CAPTURE OF MAJOR GAINES' COMMAND

IN January, 1847, a Captain William J. Heady and nineteen men of the Kentucky Cavalry, while on picket in the Palomas Pass, were captured without a shot being fired. A detachment of a hundred and seventy-five men of the volunteer cavalry was ordered out in pursuit. Major Gaines of the Kentucky Cavalry was in command. Major Borland and Captain Cassius Clay held subordinate commands, Dan Henrie, a famous Texan Ranger, was the guide. The command left camp full of fight and mezcal.

Days passed and no tidings from the expedition, and at Headquarters considerable anxiety was felt for their safety, but the volunteer officers relying on Gaines' and Borland's merits as fighting men, said they were all right, that they had got on the trail of the missing party and would follow it to the end. But day after day passed without any word from the detachment. More volunteer cavalry gobbled up! Our officers congratulated themselves on finally getting rid of them all. Colonel Yell yelled, swore and played Poker. Marshall rubbed his fat belly, kicked his Negro boy and got drunk, but this brought no news of Gaines or Borland.

Eleven days after they left camp, General Wool and Staff left Agua Nueva for Saltillo. On the plain above the town their attention was attracted to a man on the right of the road. He was lying down and waving his hands. Two of the escort was sent to bring the man in. He was so weak and emaciated that he could not speak. Some stimulants was poured down his throat and he was carried to Saltillo. It was Dan Henrie, and under skillful treatment he recovered and related the story of

THE CAPTURE OF MAJOR GAINES' COMMAND.

After he left camp, Major Gaines marched all night and the following day, only halting long enough to feed the horses. On the second day they reached the ranch of La Encamacion situated in a vast salt plain fifty miles from camp. The only water to be had was drawn by mule power from deep wells. To water and feed the horses was a task that occupied them until dark. As soon as they had finished their supper, fatigued with the severe march, they lay down to sleep, with only one sentinel on post and that on the *azotea* (a flat roof). No pickets or patrols were thrown out; they lay down as if in camp and surrounded by a cordon of sentinels.

Dan Henrie remonstrated to Gaines against this criminal carelessness, but without effect. Major Borland remarked "that they were out for a fight, and all he asked was to have the 'greasers' come and attack him, and he would show them what mettle Southern gentlemen were made of."

Henrie was nervous and uneasy, and could not sleep. Taking his trusty rifle he walked out on the gloomy plain, and lay down and listened for any unusual noise. After some time he was about to retire when he caught the sound of a horse at a gallop. It seemed to start from near the ranch, grew fainter and finally died away in the distance toward El Salado.

Hours passed and, all remaining quiet, Henrie returned to the ranch. Finding the guard on the *azotea* was asleep, he occupied the post himself. He was soon joined by Captain Clay, who from the fleas or some other cause was also wakeful. Henrie spoke to him of his uneasiness at the insecurity of the command, and found the Captain was far from being satisfied with the condition of things.

Towards morning a dense fog settled down on the plain, shrouding everything in gloom. Once or twice they imagined that they detected the tramp of numerous horses, and a distant jingle of spurs. At daylight to their great astonishment a Brass Band struck up, within a hundred yards of the gate, the well-known air "Love Not." The sleeping heroes, aroused by this strange reveille, sprang up and thronged the *azoteas* and listened in amazement. Soon the fog lifted and disclosed a large force of Lancers drawn up around the ranch!

The band stopped playing, a Bugle sounded a parley, when an officer left the ranks and inquired for the commanding officer. Major Gaines replied that "he had that honor." The officer, who spoke in excellent English, lifted his plumed hat and introduced himself as Colonel D. Miguel Andrade, commanding a regiment of Hussars in General Vincente Miñon's Brigade of Cavalry, and with a profusion of apologies for calling on them so early, begged to know how soon it would be convenient for him to surrender, and kindly allowed him fifteen minutes to decide.

A hurried council of war was held, and an angry discussion ensued. Gaines and Borland were for surrendering and Clay and Henrie for fighting it out to the end. The Ranch was strongly built of adobe, in the form of a hollow square, and was impregnable against any arms that Lancers carried. Henrie also volunteered to break through the foe and reach camp, but no, the brave Borland, who had "come to fight," said they had no show, that it would be an act of madness to resist such an overwhelming force, and urged the surrender.

So they laid down their arms to the courteous Colonel, and surrendered unconditionally. General Miñon allowed the officers to retain their horses, but the enlisted men were compelled to march on foot, on the road towards San Luis Potosi.

During the march a Mexican officer recognized Henrie as an escaped prisoner, and the poor fellow had the satisfaction of hearing an order given for him to be shot in the morning. But he was not easily discouraged; he had been in many a tight place before, and had made many a hairbreadth escape from situations as desperate as this. Major Gaines was riding by and Henrie informed him of his prospect, and said if the Major would let him have his mare he would try to escape.

Major Gaines agreed to this, and rode up to the head of the column and asked General Minon's permission to allow one of his sick men to ride his mare. The request was granted and the Major dismounted and waited until Henrie came up. As he sprang into the saddle, Gaines, with a pressure of the hand, bid him Godspeed and added, "My pistols are yet in the holsters."

Holding the mare in until the rear guard were close on him, Henrie suddenly wheeled, and giving her the spur, dashed by the astonished "greasers," and with shouts of triumph was well away before they thought of pursuit.

All was confusion, some opened an escopette fire, others gave chase. Looking over his shoulder, Henrie saw three lancers bearing down on him at utmost speed, with lances at a charge. Suddenly he drew up and disposed of a foe at each shot from the pistols and dashing on to the third, parried the lance thrust and with the butt of the heavy pistol brought him to the ground. The reckless ranger now, instead of continuing his flight, had the intoxication of battle seize on him; he grasped a lance from the ground and with terrific yells charged down on his foes, and such terror did he inspire that these redoubtable warriors turned tail and fled back on the main body.

Henrie rode near enough to wave a farewell to his friends, and then galloped off towards Encarnacion. Hundreds of lancers now started in pursuit, but he led them easily without letting the mare out, but when near Encarnacion he was horrified at the sight of a body of the enemy drawn up at that place. He was headed off and was obliged to bear to the right towards the Cedral, and take to the mountains. Here he got lost and was without food or water. On the fourth day the gallant mare died. Henrie dined off of his late faithful companion, and this with a Gopher that he killed with a stone was all the nourishment he had until General Wool's escort found him.

Henrie recovered, and was sent as bearer of dispatches to Washington, but with his usual luck for meeting with adventures, the train that he was with was attacked near Cerralvo, and he lost an arm. I know not what subsequently became of him, but success attend the brave ranger wherever he goes.

XIV

A GHOST STORY

RIGHT after this, General Taylor came up from Monterey, escorted by Charley May's Squadron of 2nd Dragoons and Sherman's and Bragg's Batteries, and Davis' Mississippi Rifle Regiment, and made his headquarters in camp at Agua Nueva. Our Squadron was quartered at San Juan de Panama, a ranch twelve miles back on the Parras road. The place was deserted by all but Pigs and fowls, fleas and lice. The two first we soon brought to terms, the last proved rather too much for us. Our duty was to picket the Parras road some twenty miles from the ranch. This duty was extremely severe on our horses, they being obliged to go twenty-four hours without water, there being none in the pass.

Mexico was made for picket duty. The roads available for military purposes lead through passes in the Sierras many miles apart, and the air is so clear that objects on the plain ten miles off can be seen with the eye. No picket in the high regions could be surprised without gross criminal carelessness on his part. In the night time the position of the vidette was far from being an agreeable one, and two incidents happened to me that severely tried my nerve and my unbelief in the supernatural.

One dark windy night I left the reserve at midnight to relieve the outpost. It was a fearful night; the wind blew a gale, howling and shrieking through the narrow pass and the dark gorges of the mountains as if the wild Hunters of the Hartz mountains were abroad. The man I relieved remarked that "the pickets ought to be doubled, as it was enough to frighten the d— alone in such a night."

The wild night had its effect on me. I felt unusually low spirited, and a horrid undefined sense of danger and fear took possession of my mind and I suffered all the agony of a coward when danger is nigh. In the gloomy woods the trees ground and rubbed together, producing strange unearthly noises, the sighing and soughing of the wind among the pines seemed like the moaning of despairing spirits, more than once the damp cold wings of something flapped against my face while what appeared fiendish shrieks of laughter would sound behind me, then I would hear all around the human-like cry of the Coyote, ending with a dismal howl. Well wrapp'd in my horseman's cloak, with slung Carbine, I tried to reason with my fears and do my duty. My horse was greatly excited, pawing and snorting, and several times whirled and started for the rear, trembling with affright. So sure I was that some horrid thing was close to me that I cocked my Carbine and hailed several times.

I was fully alive to the great responsibility of my post. If I was surprised the reserve would be, and then the army. All depended on my watchfulness and vigilance, and I was to use the utmost discretion and not give a false alarm, which next to a surprise is highly culpable.

All superstitious fears fled at hearing the beat of horse hoofs on the hard road coming at speed. I could exclaim, "Shadows to-night have struck more terror to the soul of Richard than can the substance of ten thousand soldiers, armed in proof," and now that I could hear something that I understood I was myself again. I could plainly hear the approach of a large number of horses, but could not hear any clang of arms or ring of iron shoes. Mustangs, I thought, and I was right—a drove of wild horses dashed past.

It was now about time for me to be relieved and I was listening for the approach of the vidette when I caught again the sound of horses on the road in front. More mustangs, I thought, but the sound was different from that before. I sprang off and put my ear to the ground and was satisfied that the horses were shod, and bore riders. I mounted and backed my horse off the road and with my Carbine at full cock, and my heart beating as if it would break the ribs, awaited their approach.

On they came, and believing that they must be foes, I shouted out "*Quien viene?*" Whereupon a voice exclaimed, "Greasers by G—d!" I cried out, "Halt! Dismount, advance one and make yourself known."

One person came out of the black obscurity and said, I am Ben Tobin and Doc Irving and two others of Ben McCulloch's Rangers. Now who in the D——l are you, and have you any whiskey, for I am as dry as a powder horn!"

The relief now came up, and I showed the Rangers the way to our reserve, where though it was against orders, a huge fire was blazing under the lea of a high rock. There was a generous amount of mezcal yet left, and with songs and stories of wild adventure we passed the time until daylight. The Rangers had been out on a scout towards Zacatecas, but had seen no enemy. Ben Tobin was one of the best fellows in the world, son of an Irish gentleman, was sent to Maynooth College to be educated for the Priesthood, was expelled, came to America, and was now the wild rollicking Texan Ranger.

My other adventure in the Zacatecas pass happened in broad daylight, and was more than my philosophy could account for. I was on the outpost one afternoon, the sun a good hour high, the air clear and calm. I was in good health, with excellent digestion, had not been on a spree for a month and I had drunk but little mezcal that day. I could see for miles in my front, and the ground was so dry and parched that the jump of a Rabbit a mile off could be told by the dust. I was thinking of nothing in particular when I caught sight of an object moving on the plain about two miles off. It was moving at right angles to the road, and seem'd to be moving at a slow walk. I thought it must be some Ranger who had lost his horse while on a scout and was making his way to camp on foot.

I started down to meet it, when the fact that the advancing figure raised no dust caused me to hesitate in wonder. On it came, until I could make out a figure of a man, or what resembled a well-got-up scarecrow broke loose from some Yankee cornfield and taking a promenade out in Mexico for the fun of the thing. Its method of locomotion was peculiarly its own; it revolved like a top in a most unaccountable and mysterious manner.

My steed showed symptoms of affright, pawing and snorting, and tried to bolt with me. I slung my Carbine and waited, my predominating feeling being that of curiosity. It appeared to be a man dressed in the stereotype stage costume of an English clod-hopper, a slate-colored smock frock, knee breeches, hobnail shoes, and a slouch felt hat. Its hair was long and tow colored, and the face! No tongue can describe the awful ghastliness of the features, and the terrible despair that glared from its stony eyes. It was horrible, unearthly!

I rubbed my eyes to see if I was really awake and when the thing was within a few yards of me I hailed it, but in silence on it came, whirling and twisting around, its long hair and arms flopping, and its legs twisting around each other. It seem'd all smashed up, every limb out of joint, the head twisted over the shoulder. I could stand it no longer but gave rein to my frightened horse who dashed off for the reserve.

Shame made me rein up and look behind. The phenomenon was moving on in the same slow, silent, mysterious manner. I got desperate and driving spurs into my horse charged down to within ten yards, and after ordering it to halt, I fired on it. Though I was satisfied my shot passed through it, it produced no effect. I tried to run it down, but I could not urge my horse near it. I rode round and round it, firing on it as fast as I could load, and shouting with sheer affright. The galloping of horses on the road toward the pass drew my attention in that direction, and to my great joy Sergeant Gorman and ten men of the reserve rode up at speed.

"What in the d——l have you got there. Jack?" cried out the Sergeant.

"The old boy himself, I believe!" I replied as I gave it another shot.

Gorman exclaimed, "Hold all! It's an old friend, Tim McCarty from the old country!" and tried to ride up to it.

Holding out his hand, he said, "Tim, my boy, how are ye, how came ye out here, and what in the d——l do you mean by twisting about in that ridiculous manner for?" but Tim or whatever it was made no reply but kept on its vortical and erratic way.

Gorman caught one look from the thing's fearful eyes, turned pale, and yelled out, "A ghost! A ghost!" and went off at a run followed by all but four.

We laid several plans to bring the thing to terms. We formed about one hundred yards off and charged down on it, but our horses, that would dash on a line of bayonets, would wheel when within a few yards. We tied our lassos together and with a horseman at each end rode around it and pulled the rope tight, which passed through the figure without disturbing it in the least. We fired volleys again and again into it. The bullets would pass through, knocking up the dust on the plain beyond. Finally, getting desperate, Jack Decker (Happy Jack of Company A) and myself dismounted and dashed on it with our Sabres. Our blades passed through and through the object, while Happy Jack, who closed with the figure, was whirled off his feet and thrown to the ground.

It had now reached the foot of a high craggy mountain, which it ascended, moaning on in the same manner until a distant peak hid the horrid thing from our sight. We looked in each other's faces with fear and amazement, and our unanimous belief was that we had seen some being of another world.

We all went back to the reserve and found the Sergeant quite sick from his scare. He insisted that it was the ghost of Tim McCarty, come to warn him of his approaching death. I tried to reason him out of this absurd idea, saying that if it was a warning to anyone it must be me as it came to me first, but Gorman shook his head and replied, "Whist, Jack, what does Tim McCarty know about you?" Superstition so worked on his mind that our strange vision came near being the cause of his death for before morning he was in a critical condition.

We had no outpost that night! Two men were placed on the road, while the rest hovered over our fire and related fearful tales of the supernatural, glancing over our shoulders as if some horrid apparition stood behind us.

Next day on our return to the ranch the ghost story was told and reached the ears of our officers, and we were separately examined by them, but we all agreed on the main points. Yet Lieutenant Buford swore we were all drunk, that the ghost was the effect of too deep potations of mezcal, and Sergeant Gorman was reduced to the ranks for seeing a Ghost. The canteens of the Picket Guards were closely inspected after this, and all strong liquors confiscated, and we were troubled no more by whirling, twisting ghosts of Tim McCartys in the Zacatecas pass.

XV

RECONNAISSANCE TO HEDIONDA

ON the 20th of February, 1847, in consequence of reports that Santa Anna's advance divisions were within two days' march of Agua Nueva, General Taylor ordered a reconnaissance in force. The detachment numbered about four hundred men, and embraced the very elite of the army: three hundred Dragoons, McCulloch's Spy Company of Rangers and one section from Washington's Battery of six pounders, all under the command of the "Murat of America"—the "heroic" Charley May.

We formed line in front of General Taylor's headquarters at daylight with three days' cooked rations in our Haversacks. Generals Taylor, Wool and Joe Lane (of the Indiana Volunteers) were present and appeared anxious for our safety. Colonel May, the cowardly humbug of the war, was mounted on "Black Tom," and appeared quite indifferent to all possible dangers, but I noticed that he *chewed* his segar instead of *smoking* it.

We moved out on the San Luis road, passed a picket of Kentuckians in the Paso de los Pinos and some six miles further on took a road to our left. We continued on for three hours, and then halted and fed our horses. After an hour rest we continued our march at a trot. The advance guard discovered and run down a Mexican Lancer, who refused to give any information; he was turned over to the Rangers, who to avoid all trouble put him out of the way.

A platoon from our Squadron was now ordered to relieve the advance guard. I was in this platoon which was commanded by Sergeant Mellen, an ignorant Irishman but an excellent soldier.

On we went for hours, when reaching the top of a hill, a level plain lay open before us some miles in width; the opposite side was bounded by a long mesa or table hill at the base of which appeared the white walls of a *rancho*. I thought I could see a body of horsemen at the place, but none of the others could make them out.

Lieutenant Sam Sturgis of the 2nd Dragoons, just fresh from West Point, now joined us and took command. We started for the ranch at a gallop. To the South, away in the distance, vast clouds of dust rolled up for miles reminding me of my first sight of Taylor's army near Monterey.

As we neared the ranch men were seen to run out and disappear in a ravine that led up to the mesa. Sturgis ordered Sergeant Mellen to occupy the ranch and not to leave it; then the Lieutenant with his orderly started in pursuit of the fleeing Mexicans. We could see them ride up as far as they could, then dismount and lead their horses until they were hid behind the summit, when we heard several shots. I was in favor of half of our number going out to see what was up, but the Sergeant had positive orders to remain at the ranch.

All the *hombres* left at the place were made prisoners and confined in a house under guard. I was stationed on the top of the highest building in the place as a lookout. I could see our column winding its way over the plain from the northwest but the cloud of dust to the south fixed my attention—I was convinced that a large army marched beneath that dust.

The command soon came up and Sergeant Mellen reported the loss of the Lieutenant to Colonel May but no pursuit was ordered. Captain Steen came up where I was. I pointed out the rising dust and stated what I thought was the cause. He said it was possible, for it was known that Santa Anna's army must be near us.

Colonel May now sent out scouting parties, the Mexicans were put to work building breastworks across each entrance to the place, a six pounder was placed in position at each, the horses unsaddled, groomed, watered and fed on barley that we found in the ranch, some beeves run in and killed, fires built and supper eaten. Colonel May, Lieutenant Tom Gibbons and other officers came up to the lookout and I respectfully stated that I thought the dust clouds were caused by the march of troops. "Troops of cattle, you d—d fool," replied the captor of La Vega. At this moment I caught sight of horsemen on top of a hill not over a mile off; their figures were brought out in bold relief by the western sky, and the setting sun fairly glitter'd on their long line of lance blades. May was now convinced that the enemy was near and acted as if he had lost his head; rushing down into the court he cried, "Saddle up, G——d d——n you, who told you to unsaddle? Lieutenant, send out a detail and drive in all the horses and cattle you can find." He created great confusion and almost a panic, countermanding his orders as fast as he gave them. A large corral was filled with cattle and horses; the latter had saddle marks and regimental brands, and had evidently been turned out to graze that day. Yet Colonel May swore at the men for bringing them in, and ordered them to be turned loose again.

He cursed and swore at everybody and everything, ordered all the "greasers" to be shot, but was prevailed on to let them live.

By nine P.M. all our scouting parties (except one under Chuck Evans) had returned; they had seen no enemy troops, but had passed over ground where large bodies of cavalry had recently camped, with fires still burning. We stood to horse until ten P.M. when our temporary barricades were torn away and Colonel May gave the command "To horse!" A dozen buglers immediately blew the call, though strict orders had been given to maintain the utmost silence! All the buglers of the two Dragoon regiments hated May for claiming the capture of General La Vega at the battle of Resaca de la Palma, when it was one of their own—Winchell of Company H, 2nd Dragoons—who took the Mexican prisoner.

We went off at a trot and had scarcely cleared the place when from the hill behind the ranch a rocket whizzed up in the air, and was answered away off on the plain by the boom of a heavy gun. A faint new moon gave a weird light to the scene as we rushed on in flight. Horses fell in the prairie dog holes, men were thrown, our artillery bounced along behind the horses like playthings, prairie dogs barked, snakes rattled, owls hooted and flew up from beneath and men cursed at our headlong flight. Now and then we could see a line of horsemen racing along on a road to our left, they were trying to reach the Paso de los Pinos and hold it against us.

Our advance went off at speed, reached the pass and were fired on by our own pickets, who then ran for camp.

The column came up and instead of leaving a force to hold the place, the whole command pushed on for Agua Nueva, leaving the pass unguarded. May ordered us to gallop and we went into camp at a charge. The "long roll" was beating an alarm, the guards fired on us and ran, all appeared convinced the

Mexicans were on them. Racing up to General Taylor's tent we formed "on right into line" and found "Old Zack" standing unconcerned by a log fire with his staff.

May reported and Taylor remarked, "Doggone them, I knew it was you that was coming. But the alarm will answer for reveille."

We had made this little excursion of eighty miles in just twenty-four hours without any sleep. We were dismissed to our quarters, our horses were taken care of by our comrades, our breakfast was ready, and having eaten, we lay down to a deep slumber, only to be aroused again at nine A.M. by "Boot and Saddle" sounding. Forming line we stood to horse for two long hours until the general alarm was sounded, the tents of the entire command were struck and all our baggage sent off north in wagons to the Encantada ranch.

A line of battle was now formed on the plain, my squadron was ordered to report to General Wool as his escort, General Taylor and Staff rode up and we overheard all the news. Ben McCulloch (the famous Texan Ranger), disguised as a *ranchero*, had fallen in with and remained with Santa Anna's army all night; they were now in sight of the Paso de los Pinos, and a brigade of their cavalry under General Torrejon was closing up to that place.

General Wool was for our falling back to the strong position of La Angostura Pass, near the ranch called Buena Vista. General Taylor was for fighting where we were, not from any military advantage of the place, but because his inflated pride would not listen to anything like a retreat. "No," he said, "I'll be d——d if I run away!" The "heroic" May now had his say: "Let their Lancers come onto the plain. I will see that none of them ever go back," and he looked all he said. Charles May was over six feet in height, straight as an Indian, with long

118

black hair and a beard that swept his waist belt, and mounted on Black Tom, he appeared the beau-ideal of the dashing cavalry officer, but the truth was, it was the old fable of the "Ass in the Lion's Skin" revived. Major Mansfield and Lieutenant Benham of the Engineers supported General Wool, pointing out the advantage the enemy would have in our present position, for his artillery placed on the hills would command our entire line.

Taylor still remaining obstinate, General Wool, after a consultation with the leading officers, stated that he would take the full responsibility on himself; that he would not see the army sacrificed but would march them back to Buena Vista, and leave the result to the battle and the War Department. "Rough and Ready" raved and told General Wool to "go to h——l in his own way," and rode off for Saltillo on Old Whitey, with May's Dragoons for an escort.

It was now midday, and much valuable time had been lost. Orders were given and promptly executed for the army to fall back; Marshall's cavalry was sent out to the pass to hold it until dark; the Arkansas Cavalry was detailed to load up the Quartermaster and Commissary Stores at Agua Nueva; the sick were sent in ambulances to Saltillo, while the Infantry marched for La Angostura. Our Squadron brought up the rear; the volunteers lagged badly and we were obliged to use force in driving them up, but at Sundown they were all in camp inside the pass.

We unsaddled our weary steeds, groomed, watered and fed them, got our supper and then lay down on the frozen ground to sleep, when the unwelcome sound of "Boot and Saddle" aroused us to saddle up our shivering horses once more. Captain Chapman, the Quartermaster, had sent word that the Arkansas Cavalry refused to work in loading up the wagons, and so the Dragoons, who had had but three hours' sleep in three days, must go back twelve miles to do the work!

It was midnight when we reached Agua Nueva; huge fires of discarded supplies were burning, around them the Rackensackers were gathered, some sleeping, others playing cards, none working. Long trains of empty wagons stood ready to be loaded. All but our number fours dismounted and went to work, heartily damning all volunteers. We had loaded twenty wagons with the most useful supplies and sent them off when a shot was fired out on the San Luis road, then another, and then a regular volley.

Cries of "Run boys, run! The Mexicans are on us!" were heard and great confusion ensued. The Arkansas Cavalry became panic stricken, sprang to their saddles and fled, nearly stampeding our horses. Captain Steen gave orders to fire the place; blazing logs were thrown into the chapel and all the houses, bacon and pork thrown on, the large barley stack fired, and soon the whole place blazed up grandly. We mounted and fell back on the plain, formed line facing the ranch and with drawn Sabres awaited further developments. The fire lit up the country for miles, the occasional bursting of shells and ammunition giving a grand effect to the' scene. The hill back of the place fairly glittered with the sheen of Mexican lance points. Soon long columns of their cavalry swept around the ranch and spread over the plain. We broke into a column of fours and started for camp at a trot; at daylight we passed through La Angostura pass with the enemy close at our heels.

XVI

THE BATTLE OF BUENA VISTA

THE next morning was glorious. It was February 22nd, Washington's Birthday! The camp was alive with preparations for Battle, Staff officers and mounted orderlies were galloping to and fro, columns of Infantry and batteries of Artillery were moving out towards the pass, drums were beating, the banners were unfurled to the breeze, the volunteers were cheering, the wagons were moving on the road for Saltillo. Our Squadron moved onto the Angostura pass, since known as Buena Vista. Under the cliffs at the pass the Surgeon and his assistants were busy preparing amputating tables.

We rode up on the plateau, where we had a good view of the whole ground. On our left, some two miles distant from the pass, rose the high craggy walls of the Sierra Madre; to our front towards the Encantada was a continued series of ravines, deep barrancas and rocky cliffs. Some five miles away to our front, clouds of dust rolled up telling us the enemy were moving on our position.

Our troops came on to the ground with drums beating and columns flying; line of battle was formed with our right resting on the pass, the left extending to the foot of the mountain. At noon General Taylor arrived on the ground with May's Squadron. His arrival was announced by tremendous cheers from the volunteers, who seemed to think that "Rough and Ready" was quite a reinforcement in himself. His first act was to order two regiments, the 2nd and 3rd Kentucky Infantry, across the deep barranca to the right of the pass, where they were out of the way of all harm, and as for being of any assistance to us, they might as well have been stationed at the Brazos. General Wool addressed the different commands, reminding them that it was the anniversary of the birth of the Father of our country, and called on them to celebrate it in a way that would confer an additional honor on the day.

About 1 P.M. the advance guard of the Mexicans came in sight at the distance of two miles; it consisted of a brigade of Lancers and a battery of Horse Artillery. They advanced in fine style, winding in and out of the ravines, with a fine brass band playing, until they had approached within a mile of our line, when they deployed column, brought their guns in position and sent an eight pound shell shrieking into our left as a feeler. It produced no response but cheers. Heavy masses of Infantry and numerous batteries of guns now came in sight, marching in beautiful array, firm and steady as if on parade. On they came, until the whole country in our front was covered with their dense masses. Gayly uniformed officers left their lines and approached quite close to ours to reconnoiter, and rode back unmolested.

About 3 P.M. a large force of the enemy, estimated at about three thousand strong, moved towards our left, and began to ascend the mountain, and thus flank our position, while an officer with a flag of truce left their ranks and galloped towards us. The officer reported himself to General Taylor as Major

Liegenburg, a German Surgeon in the Mexican service and bearer of a letter from Santa Anna. The letter interpreted was as follows.

To His Excellency, General Z. Taylor, Commanding the Army of the United States of the North.

Illustrious Sir,

You are surrounded by twenty thousand men, and cannot in any human probability avoid suffering a rout, and being cut to pieces with your troops; but as you deserve consideration and particular esteem, I wish to save you from a catastrophe, and for that purpose give you this notice, in order that you may surrender at discretion, under the assurance that you will be treated with the consideration belonging to the Mexican character; to which end you will be granted an hour's time to make up your mind, to commence from the moment when my flag of truce arrives in your camp.

With this view, I assure you of my particular consideration.

ANT. LOPEZ DE SANTA ANNA

General Taylor, on getting the purport of Santa Anna, replied, "Tell Santa Anna to go to hell!" and turning to his Chief of Staff said, "Major Bliss, put that in Spanish, and send it back by this d——d Dutchman."

The reply of the wrathy old General, reduced to writing by Major Bliss read as follows:

> In reply to your note of this date, summoning me to surrender my forces at discretion, I beg leave to say that I decline acceding to your request.

This, though not so forcible as the original, reads decidedly better in history. In the meanwhile the Mexican troops continued to ascend the mountain, and General Wool dispatched Colonel Marshall with the Kentucky cavalry to meet them. Marshall rode to the foot of the mountain and then sent some two hundred dismounted men up the heights. A deep ravine separated the foes; it was some two hundred yards wide at the bottom, but joined some half a mile up the mountain. The enemy opened a heavy fire across this gulch; our skirmishers, sheltering themselves behind rocks, returned the fire with deadly effect on the solid ranks of the foe who stood square up to their work. Our Squadron dismounted and took the bits out of our horses' mouths and let them graze on the scarce dry "gammer" grass, while we seated at our ease on the ground viewed the drama being enacted in the mountain. The air was so clear that we could see every movement, could tell when a "greaser" was hit, and see them tumble down the rocky side of the ravine. Several times the Mexicans tried to force their way around the head of the ravine, but recoiled before the fire of the Kentucky cavalrymen.

General Taylor, seeing that no general engagement would take place today, returned to Saltillo with the 2nd Dragoons, and General Wool at once dispatched orders for the two regiments in position across the barranca on our right to report to him on the plateau. The skirmish did not end until some time after dark. Our loss was one slightly wounded, while theirs must have been heavy. Water and rations was sent to our skirmishers who remained in the mountain all night.

Captain George Lincoln, A.A.G. to General Wool, ordered our Squadron on picket between the two armies. How cruel! how unjust! Both our horses and men were used up by hard work and want of rest, while the Infantry were comparatively fresh. Our poor horses were groomed and fed, and then we marched out beyond the pass for half a mile. Two mounted men were stationed at the head of each ravine; the rest dismounted and tried to get some little sleep.

My messmate, "Boss" Hastings, asked me to look out for his horse, while he tried to find something to comfort us. He returned in less than a half an hour, and placed in my hand a bottle of real French Brandy. I threw myself outside of a liberal potion, and felt decidedly warmer and better. The bottle went the rounds of our mess, until it was pronounced a dead soldier. "Boss" let me into the secret of finding the welcomed stranger: He had slipped out to the Hospital beyond the pass and presented himself to Dr. Hitchcock, with the following message: "Captain Steen's compliments to Dr. Hitchcock, and wants to know if he can do anything for him this cold night in the way of stimulant." The bottle of Brandy and the good Doctor's compliments were sent at once.

At early dawn we withdrew and at sunrise were again on the plateau.

The sun rose bright and clear behind the Sierra Madre on the morning of the 23rd of February, 1847. It shone on a scene well calculated to stir one's blood to a fever heat with warlike enthusiasm and make a coward brave. I doubt if the "Sun of Austerlitz" shone on a more brilliant spectacle than the Mexican army displayed before us—twenty thousand men clad in new uniforms, belts as white as snow, brasses and arms burnished until they glittered like gold and silver.

The Battle of Buena Vista

Their Cavalry was magnificent—some six thousand cavaliers richly caparisoned in uniforms of blue faced with red, with waving plumes and glittering weapons, advanced towards us as if they would ride down our little band and finish the battle at one blow.

They formed in one long line with their massed bands in front, and then a procession of ecclesiastical dignitaries with all the gorgeous paraphernalia of the Catholic Church advanced along the lines, preceded by the bands playing a solemn anthem. The air was so clear we could see every movement: The Infantry knelt down, the Cavalry lowered their lances and uncovered, and their colors drooped as the benedictions were bestowed. This ceremony offered a striking contrast to conditions in our lines; there was not a Chaplain in our army!

The Priests retired, a smoke arose from a battery about a mile and a half off, a thirty-two-pound solid shot plumped into the road near the pass and the conflict commenced.

The skirmish in the mountain opened lively. The enemy showed great activity along their whole line, their heavy guns keeping up a continuous fire on our right but without effect. With the exception of our skirmishers in the mountain, not a shot was fired from our line. General Wool, seeing that Marshall was being pressed hard by the overwhelming force of Mexicans, sent three companies of the 2nd Illinois Volunteers under Major Trail to their assistance. During the night the foe had dragged a howitzer up the mountain and opened with this on our riflemen, but as our men were well sheltered behind rocks it did not do much harm.

While this was going on a heavy column of Infantry and Cavalry moved up the San Luis road against our right and charged the pass. Captain Washington poured into their ranks such a rapid fire of shell and canister that whole lines seemed to sink at every discharge. Led on by their officers, the survivors pressed on, only to go down before the terrible fire that actually scorched them. They recoiled, and then fled back in confusion leaving behind fearful piles of dead and wounded.

Our Squadron remained inactive on the plateau, and Captain Steen, getting impatient and seeing a Mexican officer watching us through a glass, took our best shot (Tennessee Jim) with him, and started for the gentleman. At a distance of four hundred yards he fired with a Hall's long-range Rifle and brought the officer to the ground.

Their batteries now opened in full force, causing some wavering in our volunteer regiments; men commenced to drop out of the ranks and make for the rear. Every wounded man found himself surrounded by a host of new friends, who felt the greatest solicitude for his safety. I saw one volunteer, shot through the arm, with no less than eight of these benevolent chaps assisting him off the field. One of them was even carrying his hat! General Wool sent us to drive these good Samaritans back to their duty, which we done with no gentle hand.

Our line of battle at this time, 9 A.M., was as follows: on our right, two guns of Washington in the pass, supported by two companies of the First Illinois Volunteers; then six companies of the same regiment under Colonel J.J. Hardin on the hill; then the 2nd Kentucky, Colonel McKee; next Colonel Thomas Sherman's Battery of six guns, the 2nd Illinois under Colonel Bissell; Bragg's Battery of six guns; the First Dragoons, two companies; the Indiana Brigade under General Lane; Lieutenant O'Brien's section of Washington's battery; and far to the left, the dismounted Kentucky Cavalry under Colonel Marshall.

Mexican Attack

At 10 A.M. the firing was confined mostly to the artillery and the skirmishers. Lieutenant Sitgreaves, an Engineer officer, took charge of a six-pounder and was throwing shells among the enemy light troops and Lieutenant O'Brien with his section was playing on the heavy masses of the foe at the foot of the mountain.

To rest our horses we had dismounted, and were taking a rest on the ground, when someone cried out "Look thar!" Not more than fifty yards in our front little white things were apparently crawling along the ground. All doubts of their character were cleared up by seeing a forest of glistening tubes, and the showy caps and the dark fierce faces of the Mexican Infantry rising out of a little ravine. Santa Anna had sent an entire division through the gulches without being discovered, and it came near proving fatal to us.

"And there was mounting in hot haste" as we were almost deafened by the roar of musketry; the Mexicans were firing point blank, resting their muskets on the bank of the ravine. We fell back in a hurry, re-formed and returned the fire with our Carbines; the Kentucky and the Illinois regiments threw themselves flat and fired under the smoke. The Mexicans came out of the ravine in masses and hurled themselves onto the plateau. General Joseph Lane ordered his Brigade to charge, but Colonel Bowles, commanding the 2nd Indiana, gave the strange order. "Cease firing, and retreat!" His regiment broke and fled like deer, throwing away arms; Sherman's battery beside them limbered up and went to the rear at a jump. The panic was contagious; men left the ranks in all the regiments, and soon our rear was a confused mass of fugitives, making for Buena Vista ranch and Saltillo.

It seemed as if the battle was lost, but in this moment of confusion and danger Lieutenant O'Brien advanced his guns to within fifty yards of the exultant foe, and under a fearful fire of musketry opened with canister on the multitude rushing on him. If O'Brien yielded all was lost, and destruction seemed certain if he remained. Heavy columns of Cavalry now came thundering down on the intrepid little band of artillerists who loaded their guns with double charges of canister and threw in handfuls of stones!

But though horrid lanes were cut through the hostile columns, they still advanced, and O'Brien, seeing General Wool advancing to his support with the 2nd Illinois, withdrew his guns by their prolonges, firing as he fell back. He and most of his men were wounded. His heroic resistance gave Wool time to close the gap in our lines. Captain Steen *drove* back Sherman's battery and our squadron was sent to round up the flying Indianans, and we succeeded in bringing back some two hundred of them.

A Major Dix, a paymaster, mounted on a gigantic Bay horse, seized the National Colors from the standard bearer of the regiment and waving them over his head led the men back again where they done good service. General Wool's adjutant general. Captain Lincoln, highly distinguished himself in his efforts to rally the fugitives.

The Mexican advance cut off our skirmishers in the mountain, and our Dragoon company was ordered to make a diversion in their favor. We advanced in a column of platoons at a gallop and Captain Steen had just given the command "Charge!" when the brave old man was struck in the thigh by a canister shot and disabled. Lieutenant D. H. Rucker assumed command and led us up the plateau in gallant style. The skirmishers under Marshall dashed down the mountain with clubbed rifles, and most got through safe. But the Lancers harassed their flanks and speared a few. I saw one mere boy run through while begging for mercy!

We were on the Lancers the next moment, too late to save but soon enough to revenge; they went down horse and man before our furious onslaught.

The Mexicans now advanced again on the plateau and surrounded O'Brien's battery, charging the guns with the bayonet, under a heavy fire. The conflict was brief but terrible. No troops in the world ever showed more reckless valor than did this division of Lombardini, exposed to double charges of canister from O'Brien, two guns' shells from Sherman's battery, the musketry fire of the 2nd Illinois, and our Carbines. O'Brien gave orders for the last load, a shell fuse on top of the cartridge, and then two canisters, hoping to burst his guns. The lanyards were not pulled until the foe had hold of the wheels of the carriages, and though the tough metal refused to burst the effect was frightful; the head of the column fell as if struck by lightning, but the survivors rushed on and the deserted guns were theirs. O'Brien and what was left of his men, all wounded, managed to reach us.

At this time General Taylor arrived on the field with May's Dragoons and the 1st Mississippi Rifles under Colonel Davis to close the gap in our lines. This gallant regiment passed by us with the light swinging step peculiar to Indians and hunters, their uniform a red shirt worn outside of their white duck pants, and black slouch hats, armed with Windsor Rifles, and eighteen-inch Bowie Knives. Their Colonel, Jefferson Davis, was a West Point graduate, a son-in-law to General Taylor and a brave able officer, one of the best on the field. He formed his men on the upper part of the plateau, in the shape of a letter V opening toward the foe, the flanks resting on the banks of the gulches.

General Taylor now rode up to us with his staff and watched the movements with great interest. Down the plateau advanced toward Davis' "Red Shirts" General Torrejon's splendid brigade of Mexican Cavalry; their gaily caparisoned horses seemed to fly over the ground, and it looked as if they would ride down the thin line of riflemen, who stood without bayonets disputing their passage. I heard General Taylor say, "Steady boys! Steady for the honor of Old Mississippi!" and as the sharp crack of their rifles rang out and the leading horsemen went down, the General swung his old glazed cap and cried out, "Well done Jeff! Hurrah for Mississippi!" and raised a cheer in which we all joined.

Davis' men, profiting by the confusion caused by their terrible fire, threw down their rifles, and with frightful cries dashed on the astonished horsemen, who seemed helpless now their charge had failed. Catching the horses by the bits they backed them onto their haunches and knifed the stupefied riders, who as soon as they could turned and fled with shouts of *"Diablos— Camisa colorados!"* (Devils—Red Shirts!) From this time until 1 P.M. the battle raged with great fury all along the line; the Mexicans made repeated assaults and our position became precarious. Our left was driven back more than a half a mile, the cruel foe occupying the ground and bayonetting our wounded in our sight.

General Taylor believed we were whipped and made up his mind to retreat to Monterey, ninety miles off! The order was even given for the infantry to withdraw at a given signal, while the batteries and Dragoons were to hold the rear. This would have been done if it was not for General Wool, who remonstrated with Taylor, and pointed out how fatal it would be to us to abandon the pass, and expressed his belief that we would yet whip them. Taylor, as usual, gave in to his plucky little subordinate.

I really believe that the battle of Buena Vista would have been lost to us if General Taylor had been allowed to have his own way, at any time during the day of the 23rd.

*Defeat of Mexican Lancers
by the Mississippi Rifles*

The Mexicans had a heavy battery of three guns, manned by Irish deserters from our army. These desperadoes were organized as a battalion known as the Battalia San Patricio, or Legion of Saint Patrick; the commander was the notorious Reilly, who ranked as a Colonel in the Mexican Army. A beautiful green silk banner waved over their heads; on it glittered a silver cross and a golden harp, embroidered by the hands of the fair nuns of San Luis Potosi. The deserters pitched their shells into every part of the field, some bursting in the road a good mile in our rear.

General Taylor ordered Lieutenant Rucker to take that "d——d battery." (The old gentleman was sometimes slightly profane.) Now the order was very easy to give, but rather difficult to execute, but such men as Rucker, Carleton and Buford are not apt to hesitate in the face of danger, so we tightened our saddle girths, and stripped ourselves of all encumbrances such as greatcoats, haversacks, nosebags, etc. With a firm grip on our Sabres, down a ravine we went at a trot, cheered by Sherman's battery as we passed under the muzzles of their guns, and were soon hid from the sight of both armies by the banks of the ravine. We passed many dead and wounded Mexicans in the gulches, and more than one poor wounded wretch was trampled to death beneath our horses' hoofs. We moved up another ravine and rising the bank, saw through the dense cloud of smoke and dust, the glittering cross that waved over the deserters' guns.

Re-forming our platoons, we went for them at speed. I thought we would capture the guns without much trouble, as the pieces were so elevated that the shots passed high over our heads. Just as we were on them, the Bugler sounded to the "right," in the nick of time for our wheeling flank to clear a yawning chasm full ten yards wide that opened in front of the battery. We were soon under shelter in the ravine, and we kept down this to the road, and struck for the pass. The road was literally blocked by the heaps of dead horses and men mowed down by the fire of Washington's battery in the cavalry charge that morning.

The battle was raging furiously all along the line as we regained our old position on the plateau when suddenly a heavy shower burst on us. The wind blew a gale and the thunder was fearful; peal after peal burst over us as if to mock our puny artillery. For a few minutes all was darkness from the thick clouds of dust driven along by the violent blast. The firing ceased on both sides, as if by mutual consent. The rain was as cold as ice, but was favorable to us as the wind was driving it with great force in the faces of our foes. The shower lasted some fifteen minutes, clearing off as suddenly as it came up, the sun came out, and a magnificent rainbow spanned the valley. We hailed this as a good omen, and our guns renewed their fire.

Our Squadron of the First Dragoons was now ordered to report to the "Heroic May," whose command numbered some five hundred sabres, including a Squadron of the Arkansas Cavalry under Captain Albert Pike. We hoped that something brilliant would be achieved with the "Hero of Resaca" at our head, and we did do something—finding the fire rather unpleasant on the exposed plateau, we moved down into a deep gulch where we were perfectly safe! A few stray shots occasionally dropped among us, wounding a few horses, so May sent his orderly for another horse, "Black Tom" being too valuable to be killed in battle. The new horse was brought, the saddle changed, and May, in seeing that the girths were all right, remained a long time under the lee of his steed. "Jot" McClure, a chum of mine, remarked, "Jack, it's no use for you and me to keep the saddle when the Colonel has taken cover," so we slipped off, others done the same, and soon the whole command was dismounted and engaged in examining their saddle girths. When there was a long lull in the firing. May gave orders to mount, "fours right about wheel," and we marched out of the ravine without loss!

Unfortunately for the success of this "heroic" policy, we were out too soon. On the plain above Buena Vista a brigade of Mexican Lancers who had flanked our main line was seen making for our wagon trains parked on the Saltillo road, and guarded by the Arkansas and Kentucky cavalry. General Wool, having no confidence in the volunteers, ordered May to charge at once.

We were half a mile from the wagons, the enemy much nearer and advancing at a gallop, straight for the volunteers who sat quietly on their horses. Their Colonels, Yell and "Falstaff" Marshall, were having a lively little dispute as to which was the senior in rank, and this when fifteen hundred of the fiercest horsemen in the world were coming down on them at full speed!

The gallant Colonels, not having time to settle their debate, decided to act independently, so when the enemy was within five hundred yards, Marshall gave the order to "Fire!" and Colonel Yell cried out, "Hold! Don't fire until they are nearer!" The consequence was, some fired, others did not, but all turned and fled excepting Colonel Yell and a few officers of both regiments. Colonel Yell was killed—pierced by lance thrusts in the mouth and breast—and Marshall was senior beyond all dispute! Captain Porter of Arkansas and Adjutant Vaughan of Kentucky were also slain.

Our column gave a wild Hurrah and charged the foe in the flank, taking them by surprise, and at a disadvantage. We passed through their column, dividing it in two; their advance swept by the ranch and on into the San Juan valley, and the rear retreated back to the base of the mountain.

A section of Sherman's Battery now came up, and opened with shells on the Lancers in the San Juan valley, who climbed the mesa on the further side and disappeared. We went in pursuit of the group that had made for the mountain and found them mobbed with another division of Cavalry which had been hurrying to their support; they had come together in a ravine and were jammed in confusion. Our guns threw shells into the disordered mass, and we felt confident of capturing the whole body. The enemy now showed a white flag, and General Wool ordered us to stop all firing, which was done; the Mexican cavalry immediately retreated over a narrow ridge and rejoined their main army in safety!

General Wool, who had gone forward to the enemy line on seeing the flag of truce, now returned with the satisfaction of knowing the Mexicans had outwitted him, as the battle now raged with increased fury. Santa Anna brought up his reserves and assaulted our entire line. As in the morning the plateau was the theatre of the hardest struggle. Heavy masses of Mexican Infantry rushed on in the face of our guns and gradually drove our force back; the 2nd Illinois and the 2nd Kentucky regiments were thrown in and then the 1st Illinois, and checked their progress with the bayonet. The Mexicans fell back into a ravine, where our volunteers rashly followed. In this ravine darkened by smoke and the coming night, a horrible melee took place—our men had gone too far, and the Mexicans fell on them with bayonets and musket butts, even stones were used. Curses, shouts and frightful yells arose from the dark gloomy gulch. Slowly our men were forced back to the plateau, leaving Colonels Hardin, McKee and Henry Clay Jr. dead, mangled by numerous bayonet thrusts.

Again the triumphant foe charged the plateau, but the concentrated fire of twelve guns proved too much, and after four futile attempts on the batteries they sullenly withdrew under cover of their guns. Night closed down on the field of blood, but for another hour "far flashed the red artillery"; then silence came and "Buena Vista" was lost—and won.

XVII

NIGHT AFTER BATTLE

I FULLY expected to have a chance to get some sleep that night but was cruelly disappointed. As General Taylor returned to Saltillo with May's 2nd Dragoons, our Squadron must go on picket again between the two armies. I was posted as a vidette at once, and so sleepy and tired I was that I was sound asleep in my saddle before ten minutes had passed. When I awoke I could not tell where I was, but on looking around I found I was at our old camp ground near the ranch two miles from my post. I fully realized my danger in being away from my duty and as soon as my poor used-up steed had drunk his fill I trotted back, and reached my station without being missed.

It was a cold night, with clouds scudding across the moon. The ground was strewn with ghastly corpses, most of them stripped by our foes. A picket line of Mexican Lancers, mounted on white horses, was stationed not over 200 yards in my front; as they rode back and forward I could hear them humming an air very similar to the well-known "Love Not." Their voices sounded sweet and had that mournful tone that I had noticed among the slaves of the South and the peons of Mexico—the dirge of souls in bondage, the cry of an oppressed race.

Away out toward the Encantada the horizon was lit up by the campfires of Santa Anna's shattered hosts, built, as we found next day, with the butts of their muskets. All around me there arose the groans of wounded wretches, while from the gloomy gulches came the dismal cry of the Coyote, feasting on human flesh.

These sounds made me shiver, and I felt blue enough. Lieutenant Carleton of Company A rode up and conversed with me for some time, when we noticed that the enemy pickets had withdrawn. Some movement was evidently taking place; we could see the forms of men pass in front of their bivouac fires, and the rumble of gun carriages was heard.

The noise increased and we were soon convinced that the discomfited hosts of Santa Anna were stealing away under cover of the darkness. Word was sent to General Wool, who had remained on the ground all night. At daylight all that was to be seen of our formidable opponents was their rear guard moving over a distant ridge. To us it was a sight more lovely than the fairest woman in the world!

General Wool rode out and General Taylor soon joined him; they embraced and cried for joy, while our now aroused army crowded the heights, and greeted the glad sight with many cheers.

Our ROLL OF HONOR was long. Among those slain were:

Colonel Archibald Yell, ex-Governor of Arkansas. He was killed in the attack by General Mejia on our wagon train near the Buena Vista ranch. Colonel Yell was a noble, brave and generous gentleman, but unfortunately for himself and the Service, he was no officer.

Colonel J.J. Hardin, First Illinois Volunteers. In the last terrible attack on our center, he charged against positive orders, and knowing full well that victorious or not he would be court-martialed, he seemed to seek death in the ranks of the foe. He was on foot and fought worthy of a Knight of the days of chivalry. He had cut down several of the enemy, and had just drove his sword to the hilt in the breast of the standard bearer of the Hidalgo Battalion of Zacatecas, and seized the colors, when a shot broke his thigh. Throwing the flag to his men, he cried out, "Take this to my wife as a memorial of myself and Buena Vista!" and fell pierced by a dozen bayonets. On examining his body it was discovered that the shot which broke his thigh bone was fired by his own men (there being Buckshot in it). This was considered accidental, but believed otherwise, as battles often decide private grievances, as well as those of nations.

Colonel W.R. McKee, commanding the 2nd Kentucky Volunteer Infantry. He was slain in the last terrible struggle of the day. He was a graduate of West Point, and a most accomplished officer. His regiment fought this day with the steadiness of veterans.

Lieutenant Colonel Henry Clay, Jr., of the 2nd Kentucky Volunteers. This young man was the pride of his honored father, the "Sage of Ashland," and gained by his courteous demeanor the respect and esteem of all. In the last charge of his regiment he was badly wounded in the legs. His faithful men tried to bear him off, but being hard pressed by the enemy, the gallant officer sternly ordered them to leave him to his fate, saying to one who refused to leave him, "Place me on my back, face to the foe, place my sword in my grasp, and take this pistol to my loved father, and tell him I died in honor, with my last thoughts on him and my country." The man took the pistol and fled; looking back he saw the young hero battling with his sword, as the enemy drove their bayonets into his body, letting out his life blood.

Captain George Lincoln, acting Adjutant General to General Wool. He was a captain in the 3rd U.S. Infantry, and a young officer of much promise. During the action he was mounted on a magnificent white horse, and by his gallant and dashing action and distinguished appearance drew more than his share of the enemy fire. About 1 P.M. a well-known Laundress of the 2nd Illinois Regiment, "Dutch Mary," came onto the field with two camp kettles of coffee, and Captain Lincoln cried out in a cheery voice, "Hurrah boys! Be of good cheer, for the ladies are on our side!" when a musket ball passed directly through his heart. He fell forward on his horse's neck, who bore him alongside our Squadron and then, frightened at his strange load, bolted, throwing his dead rider over the crupper to the ground. When found, he lay on his back with a proud smile on his face. His body was forwarded to his family at Worcester, Massachusetts.

Captain Jacob Zabriskie of the 1st Illinois, a Polish exile, and a gentlemen of remarkable literary and scientific attainments, lost his life, and the world a rare scholar, while Liberty lost a devoted worshiper, and Illinois a valued citizen.

Captain Porter of the Arkansas Cavalry, a rising young lawyer of Little Rock, Arkansas, was killed fighting bravely beside his commander, Colonel Yell.

Lieutenant Rodney Ferguson of the 2nd Illinois Volunteers was an intimate friend of mine. Our acquaintance commenced in Illinois and continued in the army. A few days before the battle, he called on me; he was dejected with a gloomy presentiment of a speedy death. He gave me the address of his mother and a twin sister in Springfield, Illinois. He was slain by a lance thrust in the attack on the wagon train, and I duly wrote to his mother, breaking the cruel news as gently as possible. Three months later I received an answer relating a most extraordinary occurrence. On the afternoon of the 23rd of February, Mrs. Ferguson was engaged in housework and her daughter was reading in the sitting room, when suddenly she gave a shriek and swooned. On being restored to consciousness she said, "Oh! mother, Rodney is dead," and described a vision in which she had seen him run through by a spear. She complained of a severe pain in the left breast and in thirty-six hours she too was dead!

XVIII

YANKEE GIRL IN MEXICO

AMONG the remarkable incidents of the battle which were never told in the newspapers was the part played by a Yankee mill girl in saving our army from destruction. The event took place behind our main lines, at the Palomas Pass just above Saltillo. Here rose the white walls of a Cotton Factory belonging to General Arista, and surrounded by a garden of roses and other choice flowers—far different from the ugly piles that make our New England factories. The presiding goddess of this floral retreat was Miss Caroline Porter, formerly of Lowell, Massachusetts, who had come to Mexico three years before the war to teach the señoritas how to weave cotton cloth.

At daylight on the morning of the 23rd of February three thousand Lancers led by General Miñon, the "Lion of Mexico," debouched from El Cerro by the Palomas Pass in a move to surround our main army. While they halted to close up their column, the "Lion" rode up to the factory for refreshments. On the azotea of the dwelling house stood a graceful female figure waving her handkerchief! General

Miñon recognized the lady, his old friend and sweetheart. Miss Porter, who two years before, when Miñon was commander at Saltillo, had yielded to the wooing of his "Lionship" and become his mistress!

Cruel war had separated the fond lovers; Miñon departed for the tented field, and she buried herself and sorrows in the sylvan retreat, "Arista's Mills." Meeting now after such a long separation, the Lion forgot all else in the arms of his charmer—his command, Yankee Girl in Mexico his duty, his stern military chieftain, Santa Anna, all were ignored while he surrendered to the Yankee Delilah. Hours passed, until his officers, getting impatient, went into the house and recalled him to a sense of duty. The Brigade moved on and made two feeble attacks on Saltillo, which were easily repulsed. Miñon retreated to the Mills, remained there overnight, and the next day by a roundabout route rejoined Santa Anna at Agua Nueva. He was immediately placed under close arrest and sent in disgrace to the City of Mexico.

I became acquainted with Miss Porter in Saltillo, and learned these facts from her own lips. She seemed to think she had done a most patriotic and praiseworthy act in thus cutting the Lion's claws; in fact she claimed the victory was due to her efforts in our cause. Indeed, many of our officers, as well as Santa Anna, stated that if Miñon's brigade had passed Saltillo and gained our rear, our army could not have held out one hour. The laws of compensation that put General Taylor in the White House should have placed Miss Porter there as his Lady. At least the fair heroine (she was freckled, snubbed nosed and red haired) should have received a pension from the government. But she had her reward in quite another manner—i.e., she married a Dragoon!

XIX

SCOUT TO ENCARNACIÓN

ON the 26th our Squadron, with Captain Albert Pike's Squadron of Arkansas Cavalry, went out to see if the enemy still remained at Agua Nueva. From a distance of two miles the place appeared deserted; the tents and wagons were gone, no soldiers could be seen about the place. We moved on until within a mile of the ranch, when a bugle sounded and a column of Lancers came out from behind the walls and advanced towards us. I judged they numbered about one thousand.

They came into line on the plain, and by their actions seemed to challenge us to battle. A skirmish line dashed towards us crying out, "Charge *Americanos diablos!*" Rucker would have charged them to their hearts' content if Captain Pike had not forbade him. Rucker and Buford then called for volunteers to teach the insolent foe a lesson. Satisfied there was no danger of Pike's allowing us to charge, I readily volunteered and with three others was complimented by "Black Dan" for so doing. Captain Pike ordered Rucker under arrest, when the plucky little Lieutenant threw his Dragoon Sabre into the chapperal and swore! Those who knew Dan Rucker will understand what that means.

We slowly retired, and without a fight returned to camp. The next day a portion of the army reoccupied Agua Nueva, and found some three hundred wounded wretches, without food, medical assistance or shelter. On the 28th our Squadron formed part of a detachment that was ordered to proceed to Encarnacion, scouts reporting that place full of wounded. The command was under the charge of Major Belknap, and had along several wagons loaded with provisions and medicinal supplies. We marched thirty miles on the 28th and bivouacked on the salt plain, without water or tents.

All along the way we passed terrible evidence of the complete rout and fearful sufferings of the once formidable host of Santa Anna. Bodies of man and beast, part eaten by Vultures and Coyotes, broken arms, belts and horse trappings lay scattered the whole distance. About noon on the second day our advance under Lieutenant Carleton dashed into Encarnacion as a mounted Mexican officer took off at speed. Ben McCulloch and Tobin started in pursuit and ran their game down in one mile; he proved to be a colonel left in charge of the ranch. In the chase he threw away a bag containing fifty doubloons or gold *onzas*; this was found and confiscated by the Rangers chief.

I was with the advance that entered the place. It was a den of horrors! Death was on all sides; miserable wrecks of humanity with fearful wounds lay in the square on the bare ground, and in the houses and the little Chapel nearly three hundred more wounded wretches lay without bedding or blankets on the hard cement floors, wallowing in filth, while maggots and vermin crawled in and out of their undressed wounds, and the air was so foul and pestiferous that it seemed impossible to breathe it and live. A detachment of half-starved Mexican infantry was on duty, burying the dead outside the ranch, after first stripping them of the few rags that covered them. Some four hundred women were moving around doing what they could to nurse the wounded, but there was not a Surgeon in the place!

As Carleton drew rein in front of the Chapel, a Priest came out and said in excellent English, "If you are a Christian you will assist to alleviate the misery of these poor sufferers, and not destroy them." This Priest was Eugene Sue's Gabriel in real life. He was very fair with blue eyes and pale yellow hair, which hung in wavy masses down to his shoulders. His manners were so gentle, he showed so much true Christianity in consoling the suffering and administering the last rites of the Roman Church to the dying, that the roughest Dragoons would take off their caps as he passed.

As soon as the command came up all of the Medical force went to work on the sick and wounded, and the commissary issued rations to the crowds of famished women who gathered around our wagons. Fires were built, coffee made for all, but little could be done—we were too late, over fifty dying while we were there.

There were two large Chihuahua wagons in the square, containing a little rice and sugar and several half barrels of mezcal and *aguardiente*. I was placed over this as a guard. The only water was from a well outside the gate, so brackish that our horses, though they had gone thirty-six hours without drinking, refused it. Lieutenant Rucker, officer of the guard, ordered me to let a Sergeant issue to each man a pint of the liquor to mix with the water for the horses. The cavalrymen, believing that what was good for their steeds was good for themselves, acted accordingly, and soon began to show the evil effect of drinking too much brackish water on an empty stomach. I had filled my canteen, and drank freely from my cup, until I did not care whether school kept or not.

While I was in this happy state, an artillery officer, Lieutenant Whiting, rode up to me, and in true West Point style cried out, "You G——d d——d s——n of a b——h, you have been letting the men have liquor! G—d d——n you!" and before I could reply he struck me over the back of my head with the flat of his Sabre. The blow annihilated all distinction and with the mezcal I had drunk made me insane. If my Carbine was slung I would have shot him; as it was I made for him with my Sabre, when the coward turned and run for it. I drove the spurs into my horse and started in pursuit.

Round the court we went, he making for the house where the officers was assembled. I cut at him twice; one blow cut through the brass mounted cantle of his saddle, the other gave his horse a slashing cut in the quarter. Fortunately for him and myself, some of the men dragged me off my horse and tied me up to a wagon wheel. I was soon released, at the request of Whiting himself, who found he gone too far in striking a Sentinel on post.

I went around to have a little time to myself, and among other things I found hid in an oven a costly silver mounted saddle. I did it up in a Mexican blanket also found and placed it in one of the wagons, with a good looking Señorita. The girl I never saw again, and the saddle, when I saw that again, was in possession of a wagon master, who would not give it up.

Scouts reported Santa Anna's army at El Salado, ten leagues distant, and in the afternoon we heard the boom of a heavy gun. In the meanwhile the liquor had all disappeared, night was approaching, and the command got ready to return to camp. Offers were made to the young Priest to go back with us, but he steadily refused to desert his charge. The wagons were filled with the best looking of the women, and soldiers too drunk to ride.

Our march back to Agua Nueva was that of a mob, in fact I believe the entire command was drunk! Officers, men, women, horses and mules! Officers rode through the ranks and were run down by crowds of drunken troopers, the gun carriages were loaded down with artillerymen, lashed on. How long we were in reaching Agua Nueva, I have not the faintest idea; I retained a foggy recollection of marching in a half-asleep condition for weeks as it seemed to me. We must have pushed on all night for we reached Agua Nueva next day all used up, our horses well fagged out.

XX

"OLD ZACK"

OLD ZACK was the hero of many a camp story, and the following two are reliable. The first concerns "Rough and Ready" and one of the F.F.V.'s.

When the 1st Virginia Volunteers under Colonel Hamtranck arrived they were as curious as any Yankees to see General Taylor. A certain Lieutenant who prided himself on belonging to one of the first families of the State went up to Headquarters to obtain a glimpse of the General. Seeing an old man cleaning a sword in a bower, the officer went in and with that high-toned dignity which the descendants of Pocahontas and other Virginians are so famous for, addressed the bronze-faced old gentlemen who was hard to work in his shirt sleeves, "I say, old fell, can you tell me where I can see General Taylor?"

The old "fell" without rising replied, "Wull, stranger, thar is the old boss's tent," pointing to the Headquarters.

"Lieutenant, if you please," said the F.F.V. "And so that is the humble abode of the great hero. Can I see him? And by the way, my old trump, whose sword is that you are cleaning?"

"Wull Colonel," replied the old man, "I don't see there is any harm in telling you, seeing's you are an officer. This sword belongs to the General himself."

"Ah! Then this is the victorious blade of the Immortal hero! And I suppose then, my worthy man, that you work for the General?"

The worthy man replied, "I reckon, and doggone hard, and little thanks and small pay I get too."

The Lieutenant took off his sword and said, "My good man, I would like to have you clean my sword, and I shall come tomorrow to see the General and then I will give you a dollar."

The Lieutenant was on hand the next day and seeing his old friend of the day before standing under an awning conversing with some officers, beckoned for him to come out and see him. The old gentleman came out, bringing the Lieutenant's sword. The Lieutenant was profuse in his thanks and giving the old man a poke in the ribs said, "Come, old fatty, show me General Taylor and the dollar is yours."

The "old fatty" drew himself up and said, "Lieutenant! I am General Taylor," and turning slowly round, "and I will take that dollar!" The next day the General related the incident to Colonel Hamtranck and had the Lieutenant introduced in due form.

Rough and Ready was fond of going about the camp of the newly arrived volunteers incognito and listening to their comments on "Old Zack." He was strolling one morning near the camp of Colonel Payne's 1st North Carolina Regiment that had just arrived up from the Brazos. A tall lank tow-headed Tar Riversman, taking him for a mule driver, followed him into the chapperal and inquired if he could tell him where he could get some liquor as he was "mighty" thirsty from the dusty march up from Camargo.

The General replied, "I don't think I can. Old Zack is so strict, but I reckon you *mout* find some down thar at that 'are wagon with the cover half off (a sign that the teamster sold liquor, only known to the initiated) as I have seen a number hanging round thar."

"Wull," said Tar River, "come along old hoss, and I treat, doggone if I don't."

Old Zack replied he had other matters to see to, but would see him some other time, and asked what he thought of General Taylor. The volunteer replied, "Wull stranger, he's right thar in a fight, doggone shure, but dod drot him he is a mean shoat for stopping the boys' whiskey; it's *agin nater*, and I would tell him so, if I had the chance, doggone my buttons if I *wouldn't*."

"Stranger, you talk big," replied the General, "but I will bet you a quart of old rye that you would not dare say so to his face."

"Old hoss. I'll take that bet," rejoined Tar River and departed for the wagon swinging a canteen that would hold a gallon at least.

A few days after, when the North Carolina Regiment was reviewed by General Taylor, the volunteer recognized the old gentleman mounted on a white horse as the kind old fellow that showed him where to obtain his liquor. He stared, and inquired who he was, and was frightened when informed that it was General Taylor! Rough and Ready, riding down the line, caught sight of his whiskey-hunting acquaintance, and ordered him to step to the front. The volunteer done so with much reluctance, when the General said.

"Well, my man, did you get the whiskey? And what have you to say to the mean shoat?"

Tar River replied, "You got me foul. General. I'll cave. I'll send yer the whiskey," which he actually did the next day. Taylor laughed and rode off, but the volunteer always swore that the old hero was interested in the liquor establishment in the wagon.

XXI

LADIES IN DISTRESS

DURING the spring of 1847, the Headquarters of the Army of Occupation was removed to Monterey, General Wool remaining at Saltillo with his headquarters at the Springs near the Buena Vista ranch and an advance post at Agua Nueva. Our Squadron was encamped near General Wool, our duty light and pleasant, the general and camp guard, patrolling the Alamo and San Juan Ranches, with an occasional expedition after guerillars or corn giving us just enough exercise to make us healthy.

New regiments continued to arrive at Saltillo, generally composed of the roughs of the South, without drill or discipline. The 1st Virginia Regiment, Colonel Hamtranck commanding, proved a noble exception to this; both officers and men were distinguished for their high-toned, gentlemanly bearing, while the regiment bore a most deserved character for efficiency. Men of the 2nd Mississippi Rifles, and the 1st North Carolina Volunteers under Colonel Payne, were especially unruly, committing many depredations and outrages on the inhabitants of the San Juan valley. Houses were robbed, women insulted and sometimes outraged. To keep these unruly patriots in some little subjection, a patrol was sent from our camp daily into the valley. Being looked upon as protectors by the inhabitants, our arrival was always hailed with joy, and we became great favorites with all classes.

A short distance from the Alamo ranch was the hacienda of Don Jose Maria Traveina; the place was known as Casa Blanca. Don Traveina, a Colonel in the Mexican army, was absent, leaving his charming *la esposa* (wife) and *dos hermosa hija* (two handsome daughters) under the charge of a *mayordomo* and a dozen peons. One day while on patrol in the valley, I was sent alone to the Casa Blanca to see if all was safe. My route brought me to the rear of the hacienda where an aloe hedge and an adobe wall guarded the place against intrusion. As I paused to let my horse, Lucifer, crop the short grass that grew on the bank of the irrigation canal, I heard a woman scream, and the hoarse voices of men on the other side of the wall.

I started to go round to the entrance, when a rough voice in English cried out, "Stick the d——d greaser, Bill, and pull the old hellcat off me, quick!" I had no time to spare. Galloping off for fifty yards, I wheeled and headed for the wall. The noble Kentuck rose with a tremendous bound and cleared the aloes, fence and ditch, landing me within ten paces of a scene unhappily not uncommon in Mexico. Two rough-looking volunteers, whose red shirts showed that they were members of the 2nd Mississippi Rifles, three females and an old white-haired Mexican were the actors. One of the chivalry had the old man down, one hand at his throat, while his right grasped a formidable knife. The other patriot was engaged in a desperate struggle with the three women; one, whose torn clothes and disheveled hair proclaimed the nature of the conflict, he held in his arms, the other two were paying their regards to his face and hair with their hands and nails.

166

I saw all this at a glance, and my Sabre descended across the back of the one who was engaged in the struggle with the old Mexican. With a howl of rage and pain, he sprang up and fled, while his companion succeeded in freeing himself from the women, and escaped through the shrubbery. I did not pursue, but dismounting I offered my assistance to the ladies, for such they evidently were.

The eldest was a haughty, regal-looking woman of some thirty-six years, in stature far above the common height of Mexican women; her bluish white complexion and almond-shaped eyes showed she was a *puro Castellano*. The two younger ladies were as lovely as the Peri of the Poet's dream. The old man embraced me and kissed me, his salute was followed by the ladies' and we were sworn friends for life. Francisco, the old man, was the *mayordomo* and an ex-sergeant of Lancers. The ladies introduced themselves as Dona Isadora Traveina, and the Señoritas Franceita Maria and Deloroso. They informed me that the youngest sister was walking in the garden when she was alarmed by the sudden appearance of the two soldiers who seized on her. Her cries brought her mother and sister and Francisco to her assistance, when one of the villains with a blow knocked the old man down, and but for my timely arrival, the worst of crimes would have been committed.

I passed two hours in a most agreeable manner with my new friends; then, after many pressing invitations to come the next day, I mounted and rejoined the patrol in the Alamo. Somehow I did not consider it best to report my adventure to the Sergeant.

I now sought every opportunity to go on patrol, and all my time while on passes was spent in the society of my fair friends. The mother was as kind and friendly as the sisters, and I lived in clover, as happy as possible. They would ask me a thousand questions about my country and its customs. I drew for them sketches of our ladies' costumes, our houses, furniture; all things in regard to the North seemed to attract their curiosity. My long flowing hair, especially, excited their admiration and attention. Weeks glided away, and I became as one of the family. Dona Isadora urged me to leave the army, become a *bueno cristiano*, marry one of her daughters, and fly with them to a hacienda of theirs in the State of Durango. What a temptation to a poor soldier ill paid and roughly used! Here was riches, liberty and beauty offered me, but honor and my strong proclivity for a military life made me remain firm in my loyalty to my flag, and true to my obligation.

My acquaintance with the Traveina family was not all sunshine. More than once my life was endangered and their friendship came near costing me dearly. The first danger I experienced was from the quarrelsome disposition of an Irishman of Company A. Crane was a deserter from the British Army in Canada, and being a powerful fellow, with a bulldog's temper and some science, he aspired for the position of "Bully of the Squadron."

I had no ambition to claim such an unenviable position, and was perfectly willing that he should wear the belt, and I rather avoided him. But one day, while I was on detached duty, my tin cup was stolen. None but a soldier can appreciate the importance of a tin cup to one on a campaign, when another cannot be obtained. I had etched on it a rough design of a cavalry charge, with my initials, and on my return to camp I found the missing cup in A Company's line and claimed my property. Crane soon made his appearance, claimed the cup, and cursed me for a thief. A fight was the consequence, and I was severely punished. I somehow had but a slim chance with him, and was taken to the guard house in an almost senseless state by my old friend Corporal Cory. Lieutenant Buford ordered my release at once.

Crane after this took every opportunity to abuse and insult me and several fights ensued, in which I generally got the worst of it. This was before my acquaintance with my dear friends of Casa Blanca.

One unfortunate day I was detailed to cut corn fodder in the valley. When I reached the wagon, I found that Crane was the one going from Company A. The Irishman was gay and insolent on our way, as we rode in the wagon, but I kept my temper. On arriving at the cornfield. Crane, to my joy, went with Abe Hoover up to the Alamo ranch, leaving me to cut the load. Glad to be alone I went to work with my corn cutter made from a broken Sabre, and in a half an hour I was satisfied that I had sufficient cut for a load. The field was near the Casa Blanca and the oldest sister, Deloroso, being on the *azotea*, recognized me and throwing her *rebozo* over her head came out to where I was. An hour had been passed in loving endearments when we were startled by a shout of laughter, and Crane, insane with mezcal and passion, stood before us. His language was most outrageous and insulting to the poor girl. "Oh ho my pretty one, if you wish to save your long-haired lover, come and kiss me, or I'll lick him and have my will of you before I leave this field." I whispered to Deloroso to run home, but the brave girl refused. I felt perfectly cool and confident, yet I wished to avoid a combat with the brute. However the sight of "Lolo" had excited his worst passions and he became more and more abusive.

Finally I said, "Well, if I must fight, it shall be with this," grasping my corn cutter. He drew his and rushed on me. "D——n you, I'm a better man than you are any day!"

A terrible and deadly struggle then ensued between us, with poor Lolo praying to the Virgin for my protection. I felt no fear for myself, only fear for the awful responsibility of being compelled to take a human being's life, for I felt that I should

kill him. He was crazed with liquor and vile passions, used no guard, but rushed on me with the blindness and ferocity of a wild bull, exhausting his wind and strength in furious plunges. I remained on my guard, springing aside from his onsets, and I could have easily have knifed him in the back or side as he rushed past me. Once he stumbled on a pile of the fodder and fell full length. To show my contempt I kicked him in the most prominent part of his person and allowed him to regain his feet, though Lolo cried out, *"Muerte! Muerte el ladron, el demonio."* (Kill! Kill the thief, the devil!) He was more furious than before, he labored hard for wind, but used more judgment, and I was compelled to cut his left wrist as he had caught me by the shirt. He let go and with most fearful curses threw himself on me. This time I did not dodge. Well on my guard, I turned aside his thrust and drove my blade to the hilt in his breast. He fell with a cry more like that of a wild beast than a human being, and for a moment tore up the earth in his impotent fury, then black blood gushed from his mouth. My foe was dead.

Now it was over I was as weak as a child, and would have fallen, if Lolo had not come to my assistance. I soon recovered, and prevailed on her to go home. I then covered the horrid object with fodder, and removed from my person all traces of the struggle. Going to another part of the field, I cut another load of com stalks and then went up to the ranch and found the teamster, Abe Hoover, drunk. I asked for Crane, but he only recollected of his coming to the ranch and their drinking together. We went back and loaded up. The sight of a flock of Vultures settling down on another part of the field sent cold chills all through me, for well I knew what horrid thing lay there to attract them by its blood.

On returning to camp I complained of being obliged to do all the work. Hoover told his story, and the opinion was that Crane had deserted, though some of his cronies I thought looked at me with suspicion.

Next day I obtained a pass and rode direct to the fatal spot. How my heart beat when I saw fresh marks of wagon wheels, and all the fodder gone! Nothing of the body was to be seen, and the only marks of the struggle visible was a dark place on the ground. I was thoroughly frightened at the disappearance of the body, thinking it must have been found and carried to camp. At the house, I met old Francisco, who had seen me come out of the cornfield. In a few words he informed me that he had witnessed the combat, and had seen to the body himself! What a load he lifted from my mind!

This fatal affair produced a marked change in my character and disposition. My temper became violent, I drank deeply, and was ready to take up the gauntlet on the least provocation; it seemed as if the mantle of poor Crane, for bullying, had fallen on my shoulders. My dear friends noticed the change with sorrow, and tried to win my better nature back, and supplied me with the mild wines of Parras to keep me from Mezcal and *aguardiente*. I now found that Deloroso was dearer to me than her sister, and it was understood by her mother and Franceita that Lolo was all to me, and they seemed to be glad of it, and no change in their friendship to me appeared, and our meetings were as happy as ever.

Another time my life was placed in danger through my acquaintance with the Traveina girls was owing to that spirit of coquetry that all daughters of mother Eve seem to delight in. Sergeant Jim Gorman while on patrol in the valley one day stopped at the Casa Blanca and saw for the first time the sisters, and at once fell in love with one or both of them. They for the sport and to kill time encouraged the Irishman, and invited him to renew his visit. Soon after this our squad rode out on patrol in charge of Gorman. Leaving the other men with the Corporal, he said, "Come with me, Peloncillo Jack, and I will show you the two prettiest girls in the country."

We rode up to the white house, the Sergeant telling me on the way how fond the dear creatures were of him, and I congratulated him on his conquest. When we rode into the court of the Traveinas' casa, two glorious brunettes ran from the house, leaped up on each side of my horse and throwing their bare arms around my neck gave me *muchos besos*. Whew! There sat Gorman, his countenance showing much amazement. The coquettes, seeing his woeful phiz, laughed and teased the poor fellow as only woman can. Francisco came and took Lucifer; I, with an arm around the waist of each of the roguish doncellas, turned to Gorman, and inquired if the "dear girls did not look remarkably well" considering they were dying for him?

With an oath he ordered me to leave the place and report to the Corporal at the ranch, and never dare show my face there again!

I only laughed at the poor fool, and started for the house, when the jealous Sergeant sprang off his horse, drew his Sabre and advanced on me swearing that he would cut me down if I did not obey him. My reply was to draw and come to a guard, when our steels crossed. A cold chill run through me, as a vision of a similar conflict in the cornfield passed before me. By a violent effort I threw off the weight of horror that almost benumbed me and paralyzed my nerves, and met the fierce onset of the passion-crazed Irishman with coolness. He rushed on me, wasting his wind and strength in terrific windmill-like blows, which I parried with the utmost ease. His blind fury, and want of judgment, reminded me forcibly of poor Crane and I resolved to spare him, for I really liked the fellow, and the girls were somewhat to blame.

These darlings, instead of running away or fainting, wrapped their *rebozos* around their left arms, and drawing small dirks (which they earned since their adventure with the Mississippians) placed themselves one on each side of me. This incensed Gorman still more and he took a vicious cut at Franceita. For this savage act he received the point of my Sabre through the fleshy part of his right forearm. He sprang back with a fearful curse; at the same instant I heard the whiz of a lazo and saw the rawhide noose encircle his neck, bringing him to the ground. Then old Francisco sprang by me, with a long thin Spanish knife in his hand, and if I had not interfered he would have given the Sergeant his quietus as he lay as quiet as a choked kitten. To the great astonishment of my friends, I relieved Gorman of his uncomfortable cravat, and made him take off his jacket and after bathing his wounded arm in mezcal I had Francisco beat up the pulp of a maguey leaf to bind around the wound.

The Señora Traveina now made her appearance, accompanied by a sleek fat *padre*. An explanation was made to them, and the Sergeant, arm done up, mounted and left us without a word of thanks. Frisco repaired to the azotea to report when the patrol left for camp, while my dear friends and myself had a wild frolic in the garden. In a short half hour a warning exclamation caused me to take a hasty leave. Mounting Lucifer, I dashed out of the *puerta* (gateway) and soon overtook the patrol. I rode up to Gorman and reported, "All quiet at Casa Blanca," and then inquired what he intended to do with me when we reached camp. The crestfallen non-com answered sullenly "that I would find out," but I convinced him that he had better let the affair drop as his wound was a mere flesh one and soon healed.

Sergeant Gorman now appeared friendly, but he studied revenge, and got it. Some ten days after, I was at the Traveinas', without a pass. We were at lunch in the garden when Gorman, with half a dozen men of Company A, rushed in and demanded my pass! Not being able to show the article, I was taken in charge, when the Señora Isadora invited the patrol to dismount and partake of the lunch. The invitation was accepted, and soon the whole party was engaged in devouring the rich cakes and preserves.

Gorman I judged had been drinking freely, and I whispered to the padre to keep the girls and Francisco out of the way, for I was satisfied that he meant mischief, and his men were the most dissolute fellows of his company. Old Frisco retired, but the ladies with women's obstinacy would remain, and not knowing what I was arrested for, commenced weeping. Then Gorman caught Deloroso in his arms and in spite of her resistance fastened his polluted lips to hers. I sprang forward and struck him to the earth, and just in time to save his worthless life, for as he fell an escopette ball cut through the space occupied by his body a moment before, and Francisco who had fired the shot came running towards us with a drawn machete in hand. I received a crushing Carbine blow from behind, and I fell like a slain bullock on top of Gorman.

When I recovered I looked upon a sad sickening sight; the grounds were filled with the alarmed peons of the place, the two sisters were held by their mother and a number of women, the padre was kneeling and supporting the head of poor old Francisco, whose life blood was spurting out in black jets from a cruel Sabre thrust in the breast. Sick and faint from my scalp wound, I staggered to the dying man and grasped his hand while the Priest gave him the last absolution.

If some of the men who thought they had gone far enough had not held Gorman, he would have run me through, as he tried to do. He ordered the men to tie my hands behind my back and drag me to Camp behind a horse.

The *padre*, finding that Francisco was dead, asked permission to dress my injury, and only the fear that Gorman had of exciting a Priet's anger made him grant the privilege. The Señoritas, being now quieted, assisted. My head was bathed, the hair cut away around the wound, and a poultice of cobwebs and pulp of the maguey bound on with a delicate cambric handkerchief, and I started for Camp on foot.

The day was exceedingly hot, and I knew I could not make it, but I would ask no favors of the Sergeant. Near the arroyo I swooned and fell. I was brought to and placed on a horse, and my hands untied, for the men felt ashamed to go into Camp dragging a wounded boy with his hands tied behind him, and one of their own Squadron too. And I doubt if the force of discipline was sufficient to have prevented my own friends in my own company from interfering in my behalf. Gorman abused me and would have struck me if the men had not restrained him, and this for only giving him a look, but he snatched the handkerchief from my head, causing the wound to bleed afresh. I then spoke for the first time since I left the casa.

Looking the brute in his uneasy eyes, I said very quietly, "Jim Gorman, I will kill you for that."

He tried to laugh it off, but I knew he feared me.

I was brought before Rucker, who seemed to believe all the lies told by the Sergeant. I was then taken to the Hospital, my wound stitched up and dressed, and then to the guard house and handcuffed. I shall remember that night to my last hour! How fearfully I suffered! Agonizing sharp pains in my head, a terrible thirst with no water, loathsome vermin that my irons prevented me from interfering with, anxiety for my friends at

Casa Blanca, and my own fate, all combined to give me a foretaste of Hell.

Captain Rucker came down to the guard house at guard mount the next morning and ordered my irons to be taken off. He said he had approved the charges preferred by Sergeant Gorman, and if they was proven I would be shot to a moral certainty! He also said that three ladies had been to see him and he had given them permission to see me. I knew they must be the Traveinas, and they soon made their appearance.

Our meeting was one of sorrow mingled with joy. They brought me some shirts, a fine blanket and some cakes and jellies. Before they left I gave them a solemn promise that in case the worst should come, I would escape and fly with them to their hacienda in Durango, and marry one of the girls. But which one? My heart answered Franceita, for the fatal secret known now only to Deloroso and myself seemed to open a broad gulf between us. Dona Isadora pressed on me a liberal supply of money and with her daughters departed for home.

My dear friends done all they could to assist me. They called on General Wool and related the full particulars of the affair and the story of our acquaintance, and presented the General with a beautiful black pony, which became his favorite riding nag. By invitation the General and staff visited Casa Blanca and dined with the Traveinas, and the good old gentlemen assured the dos hermanas that no harm should come to me.

INTERLUDE:

SUPPLEMENTARY ILLUSTRATIONS BY CHAMBERLAIN

Lolo Dancing

Sam saving Mexican Girls from Americans

Santa Anna and his Generals

Sam Riding with Carmelita

184

Parras

Two Views of Mexican Guerillars

General Wool's Army Marching into Mexico toward Monclova

Rancho San Juan Bautista

188

March from Parras to Saltillo

San Antonio

On Guard at Parras

Sam on Picket Duty at Paso de los Pinos

"Colonel May, Your Squadron is Thar"

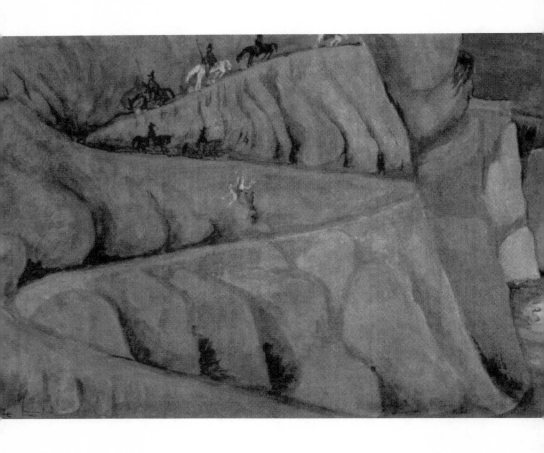

The Barranca

XXII

A RIDE FOR LIFE

MY wound healed rapidly and gave me but little or no trouble. On the sixth day of my confinement Lieutenant Abe Buford came to the guard house, and said in his usual courteous manner, "Jack you d——d s——n of a b——h, you can have one more chance for your life," and proceeded to explain that General Wool had authorized him to offer me the chance to ride the express to Monterey, when the charges would be withdrawn. Though the danger was great I accepted the offer with thanks. To be free once more was worth all the risks.

Romeo Falcon, with his bloodthirsty gang of Salteadores, was between Saltillo and Monterey, stopping all communication except a large force. Three express riders had started for Monterey during the last ten days. The last returned badly wounded and reported seeing the dead bodies of the two others before he reached the Rinconada Pass, where he was wounded and only escaped by the fleetness of his horse.

I was released and was received by my "mess" with much joy. I took Lucifer down to the blacksmith shop to have his shoes overhauled. The men of the company not on duty gathered around me, for all knew that I was to ride for my life. I found the rough old soldiers had quite an affection for me. Even

Corporal Cory offered his hand and best wishes. Jim Sherrod, our company farrier, made a new set of shoes for my horse, which were fastened on with the utmost care, for an ill-fitting shoe or an ill drove nail might cost me my life.

I was to report to McDowell at three o'clock in the morning, and getting permission to be absent from the roll calls, I was soon with my dear friends, I informed them of my desperate chance, and while they rejoiced to see me free, yet they looked upon me as good as dead, the dangers were so great. The *padre*, Antonio, gave me his blessing, Franceita placed around my neck a relic of much sanctitude, a protection from all dangers and from evil spirits, and then with their prayers for my safety, I bid *buenas noches* and was soon in camp.

I visited Lucifer, and found him in charge of three of my friends, who had volunteered to watch him for fear that Gorman or some of his crowd might tamper with him. I was soon fast asleep and but my mind was so active that I rested but little.

I was aroused from my uneasy slumber at two in the morning, ate a hearty breakfast, shook hands with my comrades, and mounted Lucifer, who had been well groomed and fed by the stable guard. Lieutenant Buford came out of his tent and placed in my hand a long-range Hall rifle to carry instead of my Carbine, and said, "Take care of yourself, Jack," and then added as if ashamed of the momentary exhibition of feeling, "D——n you, Jack, if you lose that rifle, I will flog you to death."

I reached Headquarters and reported to McDowell at 3 o'clock, received the dispatches, and with a "Success to you, Jack," from McDowell, I was off. The morning was delightful, the air was cool and bracing and I felt in the best of spirits and hopeful of success. Passing the guard, I entered Saltillo, and stopped and got my canteen filled with "old Rye." I soon left the sleepy town behind, and passed through the maguey plantation that extended for six miles beyond Saltillo. Lucifer felt the exhilarating effect of the morning air and was impatient to be let out, though he was now going at a sharp trot, a good twelve miles the hour.

At the last ranch six miles from town was stationed an Infantry Picket. The officer in command seemed to doubt the propriety of allowing me to pass out, though my dispatches had endorsed on them an order to all guards to pass me. He said I would not get two miles before I was killed, that the guerillars were constantly in sight.

Telling him to look out for his own safety, and report the time I passed out, I went on at an increased pace, and when old Sol showed his fiery face over the Sierra Madre, I was at the stone wall twenty-six miles from camp. I halted at a spring and found my good steed apparently as fresh and as lively as when we set out. I raised up his head and gave him a drink of the whiskey (he was a regular old soldier), took some myself, let him drink at the spring, in which I bathed my head, and then tightening the saddle girth I was off again.

I rode with slung rifle, and kept a sharp lookout on all sides. The stone wall ran along on my left for some five miles; at the end was the ruins of two ranches. I had seen for miles a flock of Vultures circling around in the air above this place, and was somewhat prepared for the horrid sight that greeted me at the end of the stone wall. The body of an American lay in the road, surrounded by a yelping pack of coyotes; the air was full of Vultures, Turkey buzzards and eagles, while on the body was seated an enormous bird like a buzzard, in fact, a condor, who kept all the rest at a distance while it finished its disgusting repast. As these birds will not attack a man when alive, the poor fellow must have been alive the night before, because in a few hours the bones would be as cleanly picked as if done by a Surgeon.

This part of the route had been the favorite haunt of the *ladrones al caballo* (highwaymen) for years and the numerous little wooden crosses erected on each side of the road told of the many fearful tragedies enacted here. I passed two more remains, mere skeletons, the red ants finishing the work begun by the Vultures, and soon reached the three unfinished earth works on the summit of the Rinconada Pass thrown up by General Ampudia on his retreat from Monterey. This pass, from the numerous murders committed in it, was known as "El Paso del muerte," or Pass of Death. It is a wild dreary place, the road winding down the hill for nearly a mile, and quite steep. Dismounting and with rifle in hand I commenced the descent. The associations connected with the place, the numerous crosses on each side, the strange stillness that prevailed, depressed my spirits.

When nearly down, I caught sight of a leather-clad "greaser" watching me from the top of a small hill on the opposite side of the little stream that wound around the foot of the pass. He shook his lance at me, and with a fierce *"carajo! burro Tejano"* disappeared. I mounted and made for the Rinconada Ranch as fast as the ground would permit, the road being the bed of the arroyo, and full of small boulders.

With my rifle cocked I rode into the ruined ranch, through the *plazuela* where a number of ill-looking rascals were lounging wrapped up in their gay serapes. They saluted me with *"buenos dias, Americano, como esta, Señor?"* Without replying I passed on to an open place outside, near a row of alamo trees. I rapidly formed my plan, and coolly dismounted, calling for one of the "greasers" to approach. They all came forward, when I warned them back, and told one to bring my horse some corn and water. This was done, and holding

Lucifer by the lariat I had him fed and watered, with a liberal mixture of whiskey. I stood with rifle in hand and pistol in belt, expecting to be attacked at any moment, for there was at least twenty *hombres* in the miserable place, most beyond doubt guerillars.

I asked how much corn they could sell me, saying I wanted enough for two hundred horses that would be on hand in one hour! This had the desired effect; the cutthroats gathered together gesticulating in a furious manner, then horsemen rode out toward the pass, no doubt to report if the two hundred horses was coming. I engaged "veinte fanegas de maiz, tres pesos la fanega" (twenty bushels of corn at three dollars a bushel) to be paid for when the column arrived. Seeing the girths and surcingle were tight, I mounted and with a "Adios Señores" I rode off at a walk. I had to ride a few hundred yards to clear the open space, with the unpleasant idea that I might receive an escopette ball in my back, but I reached the shade of the chapperal in safety.

I was now halfway on my journey and my horse showed no signs of fatigue; the road was nearly level to Monterey, all seemed hopeful and cheering. I had left the Rinconada some five miles behind, and could see the little adobe *fonda*, known as the "halfway house" (it standing halfway between the ranch and Monterey), when a cloud of dust rising on the road, about a half mile ahead, attracted my notice. I withdrew some fifty yards from the road and concealed myself and horse behind a clump of yuccas.

A party of wild-looking horsemen soon made their appearance on the road and halted not two hundred yards from my place of concealment. They seemed to be looking for the cause of the dust that I had raised, and which still hung over the road. One who from his air of superiority and distinguished appearance I judged to be the leader was mounted on a fiery white Mustang, who snuffed the air and gave a loud whinny. To prevent Lucifer from answering I jerked him in with the curb, causing him to plunge, when a ferocious yell from the guerillars told me that I was seen. I threw up my rifle, drew a bead on the leader and fired, but unfortunately missed him, yet tumbled one of the gang out of the saddle.

Another yell arose in my rear. The cutthroats of Rinconada had found out my corn ruse, and were in pursuit. I struck off in the chapperal to my right, receiving a volley of escopette balls without damage. The chapperal grew in clumps, which at the speed I was going I found impossible to avoid. My horse cleared some at a flying leap, but most of them he dashed through. The sharp thorns tore my flesh and drove my steed wild with their cruel thrusts. After a short run I was satisfied I was leaving my enemies behind, so I drew up into a trot, inclining my course to my left to regain the road; after a long ride 1 reached it within two miles of the "halfway house."

Here I halted, and surveyed my situation. Ahead all appeared clear. I could just discern the White walls of the Arista cotton mill on the edge of Monterey, seventeen miles away, while that singular peak, *Cerro la Silla,* or Saddle Mountain, showed its unmistakable outlines beyond, I felt safe, for if pressed I could reach the Mill in one hour, and I was informed I would find a picket of the Second Dragoons stationed there. In my rear, little clouds of dust puffed up above the chapperal, and the glint of Lance blades showed that my foes were still in pursuit.

I dismounted, loaded my rifle, and after fixing my saddle, I went to work to pull out the thorns from my own and horse's legs. This being done, I went on a-foot to rest us both. I had walked for half a mile, when the guerillars came in sight. Their Mustangs seemed to fly, but they lacked stride to get over the ground. Mounting, I kept on at an easy gait, my spirits rising with the prospect of a race and my apparent safety. The "greasers" came on with triumphant yells, thinking no doubt that my horse was used up and that they were sure of me. When they came too near for comfort I gave a shout and let my glorious Kentucky thoroughbred out.

The way I left them, they seemed to have halted! I turned in my saddle, and gave them shouts of derision and defiance. But I was premature; I was not out of the woods yet, for as I neared the little adobe hut, a crowd of leather-clad rascals, the counterpart of those in my rear, formed across the road with Lances at a charge.

I was decidedly in a trap, a band of Salteadores in front, another coming up in my rear, on my left high, craggy mountains that a goat could not climb, on my right the infernal chapperal. The very idea of taking to it again made me shiver. I held up and like a woman who hesitates was lost— almost, for bullets hummed over my head. Several of my foes were gliding into the bush to head me off in that direction.

With feelings akin to taking a plunge into ice water, I once more turned my poor steed into the chapperal and again we was tearing and dashing through clumps of mesquite and cactus. Savage cries and the tooting of horns rose on all sides. I felt dizzy, and was in danger of losing my coolness, and if I did I was lost. After giving some distance, I came suddenly on three guerillars, coming in an angular direction. I passed them like a shot, they following me in pursuit. I soon struck on a mule trail, and being free from my thorny tormentors I increased my horse's speed and went on at his best for several miles, until the noise of pursuit died away.

I now brought Lucifer down to a trot, when to my great alarm, I discovered that he had cast one of his fore shoes! A cold chill went over me at this sight. I felt doomed. But I kept my poor horse well to his work, when suddenly a deep chasm opened right in front of me, the trail disappearing into it. It was one of those barrancas peculiar to this country, cut out by the heavy rains of ages. I dismounted and found that the trail went down in a zigzag manner, and not three foot wide. Seeing this was my only chance I tried to lead Lucifer down but he refused and pulled back snorting with affright.

The yells of my remorseless pursuers again rose from the dark chapperal and I became nervous and frightened. I took a deep drink from my canteen and gave some to my trembling steed, when a sudden thought flew into my mind—the blinders used by the Mexicans on stubborn mules! My handkerchief was tied over Lucifer's eyes and worked to a charm! the intelligent animal feeling his way slowly but surely after me. It was a position of great peril! Coming after me was a cruel, barbarous foe, while I was crawling down the almost perpendicular walls of a precipice, the cliff on one side rubbing my horse, while the other was a sheer descent of unknown depth. A false step would hurl us to eternity! Confident in the intelligence of my noble companion, I removed his blind. He looked around, and seemed to comprehend the situation in a glance, and when we came to a turning point in the zig-zag trail, the judgement he showed in gathering himself up in the least possible space, and placing all four feet close together, was something human.

As I neared the bottom my nervousness left me and I felt calm and collected. I was now in a deep gulch or barranca, the walls rising hundreds of feet on each hand. The sky looked dark blue, so deep was the cut. A small stream of clear water ran down the barranca. I was watering Lucifer when a shout from the bank above, a shot, and then another, informed me that my pursuers had arrived.

I judged it would take them as long to descend as it did me, but to my surprise their light, active ponies came down without difficulty. I drew up and fired at the head horse, and had the satisfaction of seeing horse and rider plunge down the frightful abyss. Then as a parting salute, I gave the Dragoon shout, and went down the ravine at a round trot. The trail went up on the opposite bank in the same zigzag manner, but I had no desire to climb the precipice, in the face of my active foes. I was satisfied I was going in the right direction; in fact the little stream was the head water of the Rio San Juan that flows past Monterey. The course of the ravine was very crooked, making many horseshoe bends, so I could not see any great distance either way. The cries of the guerillars came echoing down the barranca and served me well in letting me know their distance, and I felt confident in getting through safe.

According to instructions I had placed my dispatches rolled up tight in the barrel of my holster pistol, in order that when all hope was gone the discharge of my pistol would effectually destroy them. Twice I had thought the time had most come to shoot a "greaser" with a government dispatch, once at the Rinconada, and again when headed off at the halfway house, but I judged now all danger was over. But on coming to a longer stretch than usual, I was startled to catch a glimpse of glazed hats bounding along above the left hand bank! A part of the gang undoubtedly had kept to the chapperal plain to head me off when I came out of the ravine.

The high walls grew lower and lower as I flew along, for now I urged Lucifer on under the spur. On we went for miles when I came to a broad road crossing the gulch. I sprang off and led my reeking steed up the right hand bank, when but for the sight of the glazed hats I should have gone up the left, as on that side lay Monterey.

I soon reached the top of the bank and took a look at the condition of things. Nothing was to be seen of the guerillars but little clouds of dust rising over the chapperal on the other side, a mile back. The serrated chain of mountains that run on the left of the road from the Rinconada to Arista Mills seemed as close at hand as when I left the road, though the little adobe *casa* was barely discernible miles away. Towards Monterey, I was rejoiced at the apparent nearness of well-known objects around the city. The little village of San Catarina was close at hand, the hills of Federacion and Soledad rising behind, while the Obispado rose grand and gloomy as if to bar all approach from the north.

But more important matters than these claimed my attention. My saddle blanket had worked loose, and another shoe was off, and the hoof badly worn. I unsaddled and carefully adjusted the blanket, resaddled, and drew the girths and surcingle as tight as possible, seeing from the dust that the human bloodhounds were still in pursuit. Raising Lucifer's head, I gave him about all the whiskey that was left, drank the remainder, mounted and was off, just as the "greasers" came pouring out of the ravine.

Lucifer now labored hard. The halt had stiffened his joints, and the guerillars gained on me and came so close that some of them were swinging their *lazos* for a throw. Was I to go up after all? In pure desperation, I pulled out a small dirk, and gave my suffering steed a cut in the neck, drew my pistol for my last shot as the blood spurted out. My gallant darling increased his speed, his limbs regained their vigor, and as we dashed through San Catarina, I was a good four hundred yards ahead. They followed on to a short distance beyond, and finding it in vain, gave me a parting salute of Escopette balls, and shaking their Lances in impotent rage and baffled hate, they went back and I was SAFE!

I crossed the ravine on a road leading to the Mill, dropped from the saddle, embraced the neck of my panting horse and cried like a child. Now the excitement was over I was weak and faint, and I must own a little drunk, yet I did not forget to thank the Almighty for his protection during my perilous ride. A clatter of horses at a gallop on the Monterey road made me start, but oh joy! I recognized the orange bands of the 2nd Dragoons, and was soon surrounded by a squad of Cavalry from the picket stationed at Molino del Arista, and mounting one of their horses I reached the reserve.

I reported to the officer in charge of the picket, who was my old acquaintance, long Tom Gibbons. I was received very kindly and furnished with a horse to ride to Walnut Springs, the Headquarters of General Taylor. Lieutenant Gibbons promised to send Lucifer to camp by the road that led around the town by the San Jeronimo Ranch, to avoid the paved streets. I mounted and galloped off, passing into town by the Calle de Monterey and on for the Grand Plaza, the inhabitants and the soldiers of the garrison looking at my forlorn appearance in wonder. Keeping on at a gallop, and not stopping to answer questions, I passed over the Queen's Bridge by the Black Fort and drew up under the shade of the magnificent woods of San Domingo, known as Walnut Springs.

Showing my dispatches to the sentinel, I was passed into the presence of General Taylor, who was seated in his shirt sleeves at a table conversing with his Chief of Staff, Major Bliss. I delivered the papers to the General himself. As he reached out his hand for them, he noticed the hour that I left General Wool's Headquarters marked on the envelope, and on referring to his watch he found that I had been just *nine and a half hours* in getting through. It was eighty miles, and I must have made many a mile more by being drove into the chapperal and the barranca. My noble Lucifer, how proud I felt of your gallant achievement!

Officers now gathered around and made many inquiries about my ride. In a few words I stated the principal facts, when General Taylor ordered me to give my name, age and company to Major Bliss, adding, "I will remember you." I was then taken in charge by an orderly and conducted to the quarters of my old friends, H Company, 2nd Dragoons.

The rumor had spread that one of the 1st Dragoons was in camp, having rode through from Saltillo alone, and my reception was a perfect ovation. After a hearty drink of *aguardiente* I was taken to the creek, bathed, clothed in new garments, mine being torn to rags, and then sat down to a splendid dinner (what excellent foragers those 2nd Dragoons must have been!) and related my adventures over again. I then slept until night, when I was sent for by Major Bliss, who was a Massachusetts man. He said that if my officers would recommend me I would be commissioned, but I made a clean breast of it, and told him all my troubles, and he saw that my record would prevent my promotion. He gave me a pass until cancelled, and much good advice.

Next day I went into town with some of the "Seconds" and had a glorious time. At the end of a week I returned to Saltillo with troops guarding a large Quartermaster's tram. I reported to General Wool and was turned to duty, and the charges withdrawn.

XXIII

VIRGINIA HOSPITALITY

COLONEL Hamtranck and the officers of the First Virginia Volunteers gave a dinner to General Wool and staff on Monday, July 5th, 1847. This was shortly after my return from Monterey while I was on extra duty as standing orderly to Lieutenant Sitgreaves, Topographical Engineer. The banquet was held in the old ranch halfway between camp and Saltillo.

When the General arrived there was a large number of officers waiting who rushed forward to receive us with true Virginia hospitality. A Lieutenant who had had considerable to drink if not more so, grasped my hand and dubbed me "Major," but looked very stupid when Sitgreaves ordered the "Major" to "lead the horses into the shade and not to leave them."

Dinner call sounded; the officers marched into the casa, leaving a dozen or so poor devils of orderlies to see to the horses and kill flies, while we listened to the music of knives and forks within and regaled ourselves with the savory odors of the highly seasoned dishes of good things inside. This state of affairs did not suit me. I persuaded an Artillery orderly to look out for my charge as well as his own, and I would go a-foraging. I made a flank movement on the dining room, and gained a good position commanding the kitchen.

An aged darkey with snow white whiskers who looked strangely familiar was in charge of this important place, and I judged his suspicions was aroused from the way he eyed me. Believing that a bold attack was the best, I opened the skirmish with, "Hello, Uncle, ain't you from Boston?" and to my delight I found he was. He came out to Mexico in Colonel Caleb Cushing's Regiment of Massachusetts Volunteers as cook for one of the officers, had left them at Monterey and come to Saltillo, where he opened a restaurant, and had been engaged to cater for this occasion. I spoke to him of the Boston Common on Independence Day, the shows, the fireworks, above all I dwelled on the refreshment booths that crowded the Mall, and the delicious Fried Eels served there.

The delighted colored gentleman gave a shout. "God bless you honey, dis chile kept one of dose places hisself."

Of course I had purchased Fried Eels of him, and they was the best ever sold on Boston Common; and I hinted that something of the kind would not go amiss now. He opened a bottle of Brandy and we drank to the success of the good old city of Boston, to the American Independence and our own good health. I mentioned my comrades, and departed taking what was left of the Brandy with me; before this was drunk, he came bringing a part of a Turkey, a pudding and a pitcher of wine.

We made an excellent dinner but I was not yet satisfied, and started this time for the dining room. Approaching the door, I examined the position of things. Toasts were the rule, and from the loud talk and the number of empty bottles lying around, I was convinced things was getting lively. One

Kentucky Dragoon officer, Lieutenant Thompson, was already "hors de combat," being under the table. I never let a good chance slip, so I took his chair at the festive board between a fat Major of a North Carolina Regiment and the Lieutenant who had greeted me so warmly on our arrival. The Lieutenant did not recognize me, but put one of his arms around my neck and hiccoughed out that his name was Cooke, Philip St. George Cooke, one of the F.F.V.'s, and the fact that he was in love! Also in confidence he informed me that but for a mistake he would have been the colonel of the regiment; as it was he was only a lieutenant and Provost Marshal of the Division, and then he subsided in tears.

The mirth waxed loud and furious, the fat Major tried a song, I assisting in the chorus, and then the toast master gave the third regular toast—"*Our Army in Mexico*, they are provided for better than any other in the World. Their military *Taylor* is of great *Worth*, furnished with the best of *Wool* for making breeches; a faithful *Butler* attends to their inward man, with a full *Pierce*, while they repose on *Pillows* and *Cushings*, and are protected from the dews of night and the *Summer* heat by *Shields* of *Twiggs*. While our army is thus furnished, without *Bragging*, the enemy cannot expect to get off *Scott* free." This was responded to by Colonel Churchill, Inspector General; then came the fourth regular toast—"*Our distinguished Guest*—the Hero of Queenstown Heights, Lundy Lane and Buena Vista. General John E. Wool."

Our little General arose and replied, and had gone on very happily as far as "This is the proudest moment of my life—" when his sharp eyes singled me out, and the irascible old hero cried out, "Orderly, you rascal, what are you doing here? Leave, you rascal, leave!"

As I arose to go my worthy friend of the F.F.V.'s, the Provost Marshal, struck at me with a Champagne bottle. I dodged the blow which took effect on the nose of the fat Tar River Officer, bringing the claret. The Major returned the compliment, just as I landed one, laying him on top of "Little Boots," Lieutenant Thompson. Officers rushed up and a free fight was about to be inaugurated, but Colonel Hamtranck and the more sober ones restored order, I having in the meanwhile gained a corner of the room. There, seated on the floor, with a barricade of dishes and the debris of the feast around me, and a bottle of Brandy for a companion, I felt master of the situation.

General Wool and his staff soon took their departure, and I was feeling quite glorious when I heard Sitgreaves calling "Orderly!" I managed to gain my feet and amid the clatter of falling dishes succeeded in reaching the door by holding on the wall.

"Orderly," said Sitgreaves, "have you had anything to drink?"

"Not a drop, Lieutenant," I said, whereupon he ordered a bottle of Champagne with which I drank his health in a bumper.

Thanks to my colored friend our horses were ready and at the door, and we started off at a gallop to overtake the General. Lucifer (who had fully recovered from his run to Monterey), probably thinking it a challenge for a trial of speed, let himself out, Sitgreaves followed suit, and away we went. We overtook and dashed by the General and his Staff who, not noticing that one of the party was only a buck private, cheered on the race. Leaping the ravine back of Headquarters I received a sharp blow across the waist, and found myself performing a somersault in the air bringing up against the General's Negro servant Dennis, sending him backward into his cook tent among his pots and kettles, with myself on top. The festive Lieutenant of Engineers cleared the obstacle (a picket rope) in the same happy manner and landed in Captain Chapman's tent, much to the indignation of the Captain's worthy lady, who was in dishabille taking an afternoon siesta.

The General arrived and the Sergeant of the Guard, Mellen, took me before him and reported me for drunkenness. General Wool, leaning against the Flag Staff, listened to the Sergeant's complaint with much gravity, and did not choose to recognize the "orderly."

"Dragoon" he said, "you are drunk! I am ashamed of you! You rascal, where have you been?"

I steadied myself, saluted and replied, "Drinking with the General and Colonel Hamtranck, Sir!"

"Sergeant, confine him, by my orders!" was the answer.

Lieutenant Benham, one of his engineers, told General Wool that I was the Dragoon that rode the express to Monterey; but I was marched off to the guard house.

I awoke in the morning cold, thirsty, and with a splitting headache, sans jacket, pants, boots and spurs. I had been cleaned out in my sleep by the other prisoners. At Guard Mount I was released by order of General Wool, ordered to report to Rucker, who gave me a blessing, swore that I was more trouble than all the rest of the company, and ended by issuing me a Colt's Revolver, one of twelve sent to him for trial. He tried to conceal this partiality by swearing he knew I would shoot myself, and he would in this way get rid of his greatest trouble.

XXIV

TRAGEDY OF PATOS

ONE day's march from Saltillo on the Parras road, hid from the great world without by high hills that formed a natural amphitheater, lay the Hacienda del Patos belonging to the great Sanchez family whose property extended for a hundred leagues. The Sanchez being on good terms with General Wool and the U.S Government, the inhabitants of Patos as well as those of Abuja remained peacefully in their homes, raising flocks of sheep and goats, and cultivating large fields of corn.

Our Squadron often visited the place for forage, the corn being paid for by our Quartermaster, and we was always treated with the greatest hospitality and kindness by the people, whose unsophisticated manner reminded me of what I had read of the primitive ages. We always bivouacked in front of their pretty little church in the *plazuela*, and roguish-eyed *poblanas* would bring us *frijoles*, oranges, eggs, grapes and sweetmeats. When night came they always gave a fandango, and what frolicking and love making the bold Dragoons had with the *doncellas*, and many a dark eyed Señorita of the place gave her whole heart to the sworn enemy of her country.

On one fatal occasion, our Squadron being absent on a scout, a detachment of Texan Rangers, under the command of Captain Bayley, reached Patos with twenty wagons late in the afternoon, passed through and went into camp half a mile beyond. One man remained behind and entering a *pulqueria* drank freely of mezcal. Frenzied by the fiery liquor he entered the church and tore down a large wooden figure of our Saviour, and making fast his lariat around its neck, he mounted his horse, and galloped up and down the *plazuela* dragging the image behind him. The venerable white-haired Priest, in attempting to rescue it, was thrown down and trampled under the feet of the Ranger's horse.

The people assembled in the square at first were so astonished at the sacrilege that they offered no opposition, but when they saw their beloved *cura* lying all bloody in the dust, their horror was changed to madness. With fierce cries of "*Que meuren los Tejanos diablos*," they lassoed the wretch, tied him to a large wooden cross in the square and flayed him. His horse escaping found his way to Bayley's bivouac, who, thinking something was wrong, mounted up his men and went back to the Hacienda at speed.

As they charged into the square they saw their miserable comrade hanging to the cross, his skin hanging in strips, surrounded by crowds of Mexicans. With yells of horror, the Rangers charged on the mass with Bowie Knife and revolver, sparing neither age or sex in their terrible fury. The miserable cause of all this was yet alive and in his awful agony cursed all and everything and begged his comrades to shoot him and end his sufferings. He was cut down and finding him beyond hope the Rangers' Captain put a bullet through the brains of the wretch.

The inhabitants that survived had fled to the chapperal and hid, and the Texans, glutted with blood, returned to camp.

Don Jacobo Sanchez laid the facts of the tragedy before General Wool, Bayley made his statement, and for the credit of the army, the matter was hushed up, and kept secret from the world.

XXV

MASSACRE OF THE WAGON TRAIN

ON the 24th of February, 1847, a large government train of wagons and pack mules loaded with Quartermaster and commissary stores, on its way up from Camargo, was attacked by the united bands of the guerillars of Tamaulipas and Nuevo Leon. The train, consisting of some two hundred wagons and as many pack mules, with an escort of two infantry companies, had reached a ruined ranch known as Ramos, nine miles from Marin, when the guerillars charged on both flanks, front and rear. The guard offered no resistance, but threw down their arms and became prisoners. A scene of wildest confusion and horror ensued; some of the teamsters defended themselves, and all whipped up their mules and tried to park the wagons but were lanced or lassoed by the guerillars who surrounded the wagons, cutting off all retreat.

I am indebted to a wagon master, one Captain Mick Box, for a description of the massacre. He was riding along near the center of the train, which was well closed up, and about one mile in length. They had reached the Ramos ranch when columns of smoke was observed rising in different directions, and a Lancer appeared on a hill behind the ranch, waving his lance. Then leather-clad "greasers," with terrific yells, dashed out of the chapperal, and the work of death commenced. Captain Box made for the hills when he was charged on by two of the band, one with a lance, the other swinging the more fatal *lazo*. The Captain with his holster pistols sent them to grass, ran down a third who tried to bar his way, and gained the shelter of dense thicket. From there he witnessed the most fiendish acts of wanton cruelty committed by the guerillars. Teamsters were lassoed, stripped naked, and then dragged through clumps of cactus, and horribly mutilated; a boy of sixteen who drove a forge was lashed in front of the bellows, a charcoal fire kindled and a fire hole blown into him, until he expired in the most fearful agony. Another had an incision made in his abdomen, cartridges inserted and the victim blown up!

The Salteadores, after plundering the train of the things they wanted, loaded the mules with the goods, and then set fire to the train. Three wagons loaded with ammunition blew up, killing a number of the yelling devils. The guard, commanded by a Captain Brown, offered no resistance but cowardly stood and saw their countrymen butchered under circumstances of unheard of cruelty. One hundred and thirty wagons was destroyed, and one hundred and ten teamsters killed.

A young Miss of sixteen, the daughter of a Sutler, was with the train. She was taken to Montemorelos, and after being compelled to sit in a nude state on the table at a banquet given by the guerillar chiefs, she was released without any further outrage being perpetrated, and reached Monterey, on foot.

The loss to government amounted to over one million dollars, which was assessed on the inhabitants of Nuevo Leon and Tamaulipas.

General Taylor not only collected the money assessed by force of arms, but he let loose on the country packs of human bloodhounds called Texan Rangers. Between the Rangers and the guerillars the unfortunate inhabitants of the states of Nuevo Leon and Tamaulipas had a hard time of it during the summer of 1847, plundered by both sides, their lives often taken, and their wives and daughters outraged and carried off. The names of "Old Reid," Captain Bayley, Harry Love, Ben McCulloch and, more terrible than all, "Mustang" Gray will always remain fresh in the memory of the Mexicans, as the fearful atrocities committed by them now form part of the Nursery Legends of the country.

Mustang Gray with his command on one occasion started out from camp at midnight and after a two hours' ride reached the San Francisco ranch on the Camargo road near Agua Fria. The place was surrounded, the doors forced in, and all the males capable of bearing arms were dragged out, tied to a post and shot! Most of them was shot by an old mountain man known as "Greasy Rube" who had been castrated by Mexicans in Chihuahua. The victims were tied to a post on which was placed a light, the grim old Ranger would coolly fire his rifle from the distance of one hundred yards and send the ball crashing through the poor devil's brain, keeping tally by cutting a notch on the stock of his fatal Rifle. Thirty-six Mexicans were shot at this place, a half hour given for the horrified survivors, women and children, to remove their little household goods, then the torch was applied to the houses, and by the light of the conflagration the ferocious Tejanos rode off to fresh scenes of blood.

For weeks this work of carnage and devastation continued until the entire country from Monterey to Camargo, a distance of one hundred and eighty miles, with the exceptions of the towns Marin, Cerralvo and Mier, was depopulated.

The guerillars, if possible, were guilty of worse acts than the Rangers, and the conflict was no longer war but murder, and a disgrace to any nation calling itself Christian. Our officers became disgusted with the many revolting acts committed by volunteers and Rangers, and no reports were ever made of these cruel raids.

In extenuation of Captain Gray's ferocity, he had had the terrible experience when a boy of witnessing his parents butchered, his only sister subjected to the most hellish outrages and then murdered, by a gang of Canales' men in Texas, in 1840. Gray, at the time of his raid on the San Francisco ranch, was not yet twenty years of age, but had acquired a reputation under the names of "Bravo" and "Mustang" for daring courage, not second to Jack Hays himself. He died at Camargo at the close of the war.

XXVI

SCOUT TO ZACATECAS

GENERAL CALEB CUSHING came out to Mexico as colonel of the 1st Massachusetts Volunteers, the only command sent by the Old Bay State. This "Yankee" regiment was essentially an Irish one, the best material in the world to make infantry of, but requiring great efficiency on the part of the officers to enforce discipline. Unfortunately, Colonel Cushing was only efficient in military knowledge in being inefficient, and the credit of Massachusetts suffered some by the conduct of his command, the regiment gaining for itself a most unenviable reputation for outrages on the inhabitants and insubordination.

One day the General came up to Saltillo from Monterey to visit General Wool and the battleground of Buena Vista. In his honor a grand review was ordered, Colonel Hamtranck commanding the brigade. The day was all that could be desired, the troops looked their best, and our Squadron outdone itself. The gallant General was delighted. He said that "the National Lancers could have done no better." What a compliment! What rare military discernment!

When the General returned to Monterey, I was detailed on his escort. I went to visit the Traveinas the night before and passed a very pleasant evening, but with two drawbacks: one the presence of a young Swede, Walberg, a bugler in E Company, and the other a tall stern military-looking *gauchpin* who seemed very much at home—in fact Colonel Traveina himself.

He was very cool and polite, I thought too much so. Dona Isadora was, with her daughters, as kind and gracious as ever, she informed me that her husband had come home to remove them to their Hacienda in Durango, that Walberg was going to desert and go with them and marry Deloroso, and urged me to fly with them and take Franceita for my wife. I could not consent, but agreed to remain with them when the war was over and I received my discharge.

I took an affectionate leave of my affianced and returned to camp with Walberg, and early the next day set out with General Cushing for Monterey. On our return to Saltillo I found that the Traveinas had gone, and Walberg had deserted, and I never saw or heard from them again!

Ten days after our return, our Squadron, a section of Sherman's Battery, and one hundred Texan Rangers, all under the command of Lieutenant Abe Buford, the red headed giant, left on a reconnaissance toward the city of Zacatecas. Leaving camp at daylight, we moved up the valley and ascended to the gloomy Paso de los Pinos that leads through the Sierra Madre, halting at the tank of water at the southern terminus. From here to the next water was sixty miles.

This place was our old picketing ground during the winter of 1846, and we could see our route across the salt plains for miles; the only vegetation at this time of year was mesquite and yuccas, the dry bayonet-like leaves of the latter looking like rusty old iron. We travelled all day in blinding dust that covered us with a mantle of greenish hue, and did not halt until ten at night; we slept without unsaddling in the line of march, With our mouths so parched by the villainous salt and coppery dust that it was impossible to eat, we passed a miserable night. On the road again at daylight we reached a tableland about noon, and to our great joy discovered a mud ranch a few miles ahead. It was a *ganada* or cattle farm, with an abundance of clear water. We remained here the rest of the day and night and feasted rightly on fat beef belonging to the place.

Our horses were picketed near the corral under a strong guard. As usual I was detailed on this duty (owing to my name being near the head of the Roster). My tour was from ten to twelve. I went on post and I never felt so lonely and so uncomfortable before. Yet the command lay sleeping in plain sight, I could see the dark forms of other sentinels on each side of me, all seemed quiet and peaceful.

If cowards suffer as much from their fears as I did those long two hours, I pity and sympathize with them. I walked back and forward with a quick step, wheeling suddenly and casting sharp glances into the surrounding darkness. A thick clump of chapperal some twenty feet from my post attracted most of my watchfulness, and once I would have sworn that I saw a pair of fiery eyes glaring at me from its gloomy recesses. To cock my Carbine, take aim between the glowing orbs, was the action of a moment, but they were gone and I withheld my fire and believed it was the effect of my excited imagination. After the longest two hours I ever spent, I was relieved, and the fear of ridicule kept me from telling of my scare.

When I laid down I could not sleep, the same unaccountable feeling of dread remained, and I was glad when the bugles sounded Reveille, but I was confounded and horror struck on

223

learning that the man who relieved me had been assassinated! He was found dead with a long Spanish knife sticking in his spine, and a valuable horse gone. I felt condemned for not warning the poor fellow, but I don't think he would have heeded it and the result would have been the same. That the strange presentiment of danger saved my own life I have no doubt. The murdered Dragoon was buried in the road and the command marched over the grave, obliterating all signs; this was done to prevent the body being robbed by the "greasers."

Continuing our march, we passed through a wild country, with high craggy hills, lofty blue mountains in the background, with the ruins of Haciendas and smelting furnaces standing here and there in the barren solitude. The fell Comanches had penetrated even here, and all was desolation. Some of the scenes reminded me of those described by Scott, and G.P.R. James, the mined white walls of a Hacienda at a distance having a striking resemblance to the Feudal Castle of some bold Baron, and when about noon on rising the crest of a hill "a solitary horseman" was seen on the road coming towards us, I would not have been in the least surprised to have seen him draw up and challenge one of our number to break a lance in honor of "fayre Ladye" and chivalry. But he proved a recreant Knight, for as soon as he espied us, he turned and fled.

Two of the Rangers on the advance dashed off in pursuit and run their man down, and he was brought in badly frightened. He was a regular Lancer of Miñon's Division, now commanded by General Garcia Conde whose Headquarters was at Mazapil, a small town ten miles ahead. The Division numbering some three thousand had been ordered there to guard a valuable silver train, the property of the British government, down to Tampico. The Lancer was pressed into service as a guide, with the promise of being released if he acted honestly, or death if he proved false.

We pushed on and soon came in sight of the town and forming line of battle advanced across the plain until quite close, with no signs of the redoubtable Lancers. Our two guns were placed in position, and then we charged into the place, drew rein and formed in the plaza. Strong pickets were thrown out on all approaches to the town, while the guns formed in battery in the square to rake the two principal streets leading from it.

In the plaza, piled up in pyramids, was a vast treasure of silver in pigs awaiting transportation. Visions of prize money flitted through our brains when a dignified little yellow-faced man, dressed in a suit of Nankeen, cut English fashion, came from the *cuartel* and stuck a pole surmounted by the Union Jack of England in one of the piles and, in the most pompous manner, informed our officers the silver was the property of Her Majesty Queen Victoria, and that the United States Government would be held to a strict accountability if it was molested!

How potent is the power of Great Britain! Here thousands of miles away from all apparent power of that nation a miserable little cockney, with only the insignia of his country's greatness, defies and threatens three hundred of Uncle Sam's roughest riders. I believe that one of the Silver Pigs was sequestered by a graceless artillery officer, who not having the fear of Her Majesty's displeasure, hid one in one of his guns, and thus it was brought to camp.

We remained here two hours, watered and fed our horses, and then passed through the place on our way towards Zacatecas. We were now in the midst of the richest mining district of Mexico; the hills were destitute of vegetation and of a dull iron rust-red in color, and honey-combed by mining shafts. A wild-looking shepherd boy, a few lean goats, or a melancholy-looking donkey, was the only objects of life we met with. The water had a coppery taste, the dust that covered us was of an olive green hue, even the sky appeared of a brassy tint, and the sun glowed down on us like a huge ball of fire. For four hours we toiled through this copper region, when reaching the summit of a small rise we found ourselves in a different country, a tableland well watered and stocked with cattle farms.

At a ranch on the road we found an abundant supply of corn and cattle and here the command halted to pass the night. Pickets were thrown out and Lieutenant Carleton proceeded with a small party to make a reconnaissance in our front. I was with this detachment, and we reached a high mesa, an island hill rising from the plain. Carleton dismounted and climbed the almost perpendicular face of the hill. He soon came to the crown and said, "Jack, bring up your sketch book, you will find a grand view from here."

I went up and certainly the scene was magnificent! The plain that we looked down on extended ahead for some six miles, beyond this through an opening in a range of hills appeared a beautiful valley of bright green, thickly studded with the white walls of Haciendas, ranches, churches and convents, while away in the distance rose the towers and domes of a great city, the city of Zacatecas, the third in size and the second in wealth in Mexico. I seated myself and sketched a rough outline of the view, when the Lieutenant, who was using his field glass, turned it towards Mazapil, and said, "Jack, look there," and gave me his glass. By its use I could plainly see a long column of dust on the road we came on, not ten miles off, with the glitter of steel points flashing in the setting sun.

We galloped back to the ranch, where a strange scene met us. A little fat old Mexican, stripped to his waist, was tied up to the wheel of our travelling forge, while Jim Sherrod, our company Farrier, stood by brandishing a formidable mule whip, awaiting Buford's order. Some of the farrier's tools had been stolen, and as this is a serious matter where so much depends on having the horses well shod, Buford, after having searched the place in vain, had ordered the *alcalde* to be tied up and flogged, and it was that dignitary we saw embracing the wheel.

"Give the old rascal a taste of the black snake, Sherrod," said the Lieutenant, when the whip descended with a sickening thud on the poor devil's bare shoulders, leaving a dark red welt. The *alcalde* groaned in agony, but another blow and a third followed, tearing bits of flesh, when the missing tools were thrown over the heads of the crowd, the thieves knowing well that the *alcalde* would find them out, and then his vengeance would be terrible.

While this was transpiring, Carleton informed Buford of his discovery and the Rangers with one gun was sent to hold the road where it ascended from the plain, our pickets were recalled, the command got in readiness to start, the horseshoeing going on to the last moment. At dark we took the back track, and rejoined the detachment on the bluff, who reported the enemy massed on the plain below. To all inquiries the Lancer's only reply was the universal "*Quien sabe?*" (who knows?) until a pistol placed to his head so refreshed his memory that he recollected that there was a road to our right that passed around Mazapil leading to an old silver mine, and coming back into the Saltillo road on the salt plain at the ranch where the sentinel was assassinated.

Under his guidance we started on this route and travelled all night, the next day and next night. The heat and dust was fearful, our horses and ourselves suffered from thirst and the salt dust that pained our eyes. On our rear hung another cloud of dust, that of the enemy in pursuit, while still another, well on our left flank, showed us that a party was detached to reach the pass before us. But by daylight the following morning we were back in the Pass, except for three Dragoons, and found it in possession of a large detachment sent from camp. The enemy halted two miles off, and then retired the way they came. They must have suffered fearfully on their return over the salt plain for sixty miles without water. We remained at the tank of water until late in the afternoon, and then returned to camp, having released our guide with two days' rations.

Query: Did the flogging of one *alcalde* pay for the expedition and the loss of four Dragoons? Was the Lancers in the service of Her Majesty also?

XXVII

A NIGHT AT VICTORINES' CASA

IN the fall of 1847, General Wool removed his Headquarters to Monterey. Our Squadron and Sherman's Battery accompanied him and went into camp in the woods of San Domingo or Walnut Springs. Here live oak and pecan trees, festooned with silver streamers of Spanish moss, made a most agreeable shade, and streams of cold, crystal water gushed out of the ground. Our camp was well supplied with all kinds of tropical fruits, while the villages of San Fernando, San Domingo and San Nicolas, with their bewitching Señoritas and poblanas, their Fandangos, *combate giour* and their national game of "Monte" afforded abundant pastimes for us when off duty, which was nine days out of ten. Walnut Springs was a true Soldiers' Paradise. What glorious times we had in our eight months' experience in camp at this place! What reckless adventures with guerillars, and scrapes with the intriguing *margaritas* of the surrounding ranches.

Soldiers of the army may be divided into three classes: FIRST, the DEAD BEATS, men who never can be trusted; they are dirty or on the sick report most of their time. This class is hated by their comrades, and despised by the officers. SECOND, the OLD SOLDIERS, men who do their duty in a quiet mechanical sort of way, always on hand in camp, never in the guard house, never known to get drunk or spend their money, often made corporals but rarely sergeants. They are disliked by the men, who suspect them of being tale bearers to the officers. THIRD, the "DARE DEVILS." These men are first in a fight, frolic or to volunteer for duty, with uniforms fitting like a glove and faultlessly clean, arms, horses and accoutrements always in inspection condition, faithful in the discharge of every duty, but when off no camp can hold them. They often turn up in the guard house, but never in the hospital; they are the "orderlies" of the regiment, the pride of the officers and the admiration of their companions. I was considered a fair representative of the third order.

And as Mexico is a country of romance, I had my share of adventures. Officers often spoke to me in regard to my irregular life, and pointed out how I was injuring my chances for promotion by my dissipation; but what did I care? One night at a Fandango in Victorines' Casa had more charms for me than the chevrons of the Sergeant Major.

The San Nicolas ranch lay on the road that led to the Obispado, one mile and a half from camp. A *Casa el Valer* at this place was kept by two sisters, Ramonda and Pasquale Victorine. The house of these charming but mercenary girls was the favorite resort of *all*; officers and men, Dragoons, Artillerists, Rangers and volunteers all were welcome as long as they were provided with *mucha plata* (much money). But this state of affairs did not suit our officers, who forbid all Dragoons leaving camp at night, and ordered out patrols to bring in all soldiers found in the place, while they would get up parties, visit the dance hall and pass night after night in the society of the graceful Señoritas of San Nicolas.

Now this did not suit us Dragoons any more than the former state of affairs did our officers, so we took council together. The result was that no officer could visit the Victorines after dark without being fired on and attempts made to lasso the frightened monopolizers. This put an effectual stop to all *Fandangos de los oficiales* and by wise management we soon had the ranch all to ourselves and our friends. One regular frequenter at Victorines' was Martie Martiznes, a Priest and guerillar. He sought no concealment, but seemed to court observation; dressed in the picturesque costume of the *ranchero rico* (rich rancher) he would come into the room, treat the soldiers to *vino, pulque* and mezcal, dance and flirt with the *poblanas*, "buck" at Monte, in fact make himself the most popular man in the house. Between this typical Mexican *padre*, and myself a strong feeling of friendship sprang up which proved of great service to me, more than once.

One night with a party of chosen comrades I visited the Victorines, and after some hours of indulgence in the festivities of the place, feeling tired and sleepy, I slipped out of the dance hall into a side room and was soon fast asleep on the banqueta (bench) which ran around two sides of the room. How long I slept I know not, but awoke to find Ramonda in the room disrobing by the dim light of a candle. A blanket hanging from a line hid me by its shadow but when she stood with only her *camisa* (chemise) on, I said with a laugh, "*Su humilde servidor, mi bonita camadre*" (Your humble servant, my pretty gossip).

Ramonda seemed frightened, but not for herself; she begged me to go out the back way and run for camp. Being overwise and obstinate, from the effects of mezcal, I refused, thinking there was a lover in the matter, and I resolved to remain out of pure mischief. Hearing voices in the dance hall, in spite of the girl's remonstrance, I forced myself into the room.

One look was enough! I was completely sobered, cold chills shot all over me, succeeded by a deathly faintness. How I wished I had taken Ramonda's advice and was now flying for camp. Around the room smoking and drinking was seated at least twenty as villainous-looking cutthroats as ever drank *pulque*, threw a *lazo*, or as Salvator Rosa painted. My hurried entrance caused them to spring up, draw murderous-looking knives and with fierce *carrajos* crowd around me.

I thought my time had come, but resolved not to be rubb'd out without a struggle. With a bound I sprang behind a large table used for a bar, drew the chamber of my Hall's Carbine (that I always carried in my pocket), said a short prayer and stood cool and collected, at bay before those human Tigers, guerillars.

There was one grizzly old fellow who seemed more ferocious than the others; he had but one eye that glared on me with the fierceness of a wild beast. He rushed for the table as if he would spring over, when the sight of the little iron tube pointing straight for his solitary optic caused him to pause. A few tallow dips cast a feeble light on the savage faces in my front; cries of "*Muerte! muerte! el ladron Americano, que meure el yanqui burro*" came from all parts of the room, but none offered to strike. For the moment twenty brigands were held at bay by the strange weapon which they seemed to know was sure death to one of them, then there was a rush to the corner where their Escopettes were piled and the scene was about to close. Yet I thought I perceived one slight chance for escape— the door by which I entered, leading to Ramonda's room, was not yet closed; gain this, dash through a rear door, and once outside in the darkness and the dense chapperal, I would be safe.

Gathering all my energies, I struck out with my left and landed a terrific blow on the single glaring eye of my grizzly foe, and as he went down I grasped his knife, kicked over the table, and with a wild yell rushed for the door. I had gained Ramonda's room when I was seized in a powerful grasp. I struck wildly with the knife but in vain, was thrown down, disarmed by Padre Martiznes himself. The Salteadores gathered around me like wild animals, thirsting for my blood, but the guerillar Priest waved them back and cried out, "*Compañeros! Esta mi amigo!*" But "old grizzly" got up, his face covered with blood, and swore by the Virgin of Guadalupe that he would have my heart's blood before he left the house!

Martiznes made quite a speech to the rascals which was listened to in silence and at its conclusion was hailed with shouts of laughter and cries of "*Bueno! Bueno! el combata! el Tuerto y el Yanqui burro!*" (Good! good! a fight! One-eyed with the Yankee jackass!)

Martiznes now spoke to me in broken English and said he had made a proposition to his men that "El Tuerto" be allowed the privilege to kill me himself in a fair fight with knives, with the restriction of no throwing allowed, and that the idea took immensely with the facetious cutthroats who said it would be better sport than a *corrida de toros* (bull fight). He said he had witnessed the whole affair, Ramonda having warned him of my danger, and asked me if I was willing to fight the duel; he said if I did not wish to take the risk he would protect me until I was safe in camp. Although I wished myself in camp and well out of the scrape, I assumed an air of bravado, and replied that I met his proposal with pleasure.

The Brigands prepared the room for the conflict, the heavy tables were pushed back against the wall, and to my great surprise half a dozen smiling Señoritas in scant night dresses appeared and grouped themselves on the tables. We were to peel to our buff and soon stood with nothing on but our pants. The "greasers" were highly elated, and bet freely on the result, and to my great surprise I seemed to be the favorite. I felt cool, and now my foe was stripped I was satisfied that I should come out all right, for he appeared weak and emaciated, and his only eye was nearly closed from the effect of my blow.

The holy relic, the gift of Franceita, that I wore around my neck attracted attention, and was examined with much interest, and when for effect I kissed it there were cries of, "*El soldado no heretico, mucho bueno Cristiano!*" while the *ladies* all took sides with me and chattered away like magpies.

Martiznes placed us in position and cried out *vaya!* when the old fellow threw himself on me with the agility of a cat. I parried his thrust with my knife, and on the impulse of the moment launched out with my left Duke, which took effect on his vulture-like beak with such force as to flatten that appendage and send him with a dull thud to the floor. The fight was over. Though disappointed that no one was killed, the guerillars gathered around me and each dirty scoundrel insisted on embracing me and kissing the "Holy relic." My unlucky opponent was carried out senseless, and the guerillar chief Martiznes assured me I was perfectly safe, that with the exception of El Tuerto each one of his band would defend me with their lives. As gratifying as this information was I felt still more safe when he restored to me the chamber of my Carbine and gave me El Tuerto's knife.

XXVIII

REWARD OF
MERIT

THE next evening at Dress Parade an order was read by the Adjutant signed by Major D. H. Rucker, appointing me to the high and important position of a corporal! Shades of Napoleon, rewarded at last!

How particular I was to the cut and fit of my Chevrons as stitched on by Mrs. Charley McGerry, and what pride I took in their pristine glory on their background of red, my "battle stripes." How prompt I thought the poor privates were to obey all my orders—not a ghost of a chance to exercise my authority by putting some disobedient common soldier into the guard house.

But I done better; I got a pass for all my mess and gave them a grand dinner at the Victorines at San Nicolas. Each bold Dragoon had his *moza* seated by his side, while my *amigo*, Martiznes, honored me by his presence. Ramonda with the rest congratulated me on my *well-deserved promotion!* We had a jolly time, and I was careful to keep sober and to see that all were back in time, at Stable call.

But really the appointment made me a better man and a soldier. It gave me more respect for myself, and I resolved that Rucker's confidence in me should not be misplaced, and that in future I would try to deserve the honor. But Dame Fortune, one short week later, kicked down all my airy castles of glory! But I anticipate.

Major Thomas W. Sherman with his Battery of Horse Artillery was encamped on the other side of the creek known as Walnut Springs. His company with Braggs' Battery formed an Artillery camp, quite independent from ours, the Dragoon camp. Sherman was an eccentric, weak, tyrannical officer, allowing his men no privileges, and resorting to the most severe punishment for the most trivial offenses. One dark day, the most unfortunate day in my history, I was on duty as corporal of the guard, Major Rucker was absent in Monterey, Lieutenant Sam Sturgis was Officer of the Day, and, as usual in these days of easy duty, Executive Officer of the camp.

About one P.M. I saw Major Sherman cross the creek and approach our Guard House. As he came up no one presented arms, and the Major in an angry tone demanded "why the Sentinel did not order the guard to turn out?" I advanced, saluted and in a respectful manner replied that the Sentinel had no instructions to do so, as I was not aware that he was entitled to that honor.

"G——d d——n you!" he said. "Who is commander of this camp?"

I said that I considered Major Rucker was. "But when Major Rucker is absent who then commands, you d——d hound?"

I replied, "Lieutenant Whittlesey, as senior officer, Major," when Sherman, with many oaths, gave me to understand that he commanded both camps in the absence of Rucker, and ordered me to send a file of men to the Lower Springs, and arrest a man there engaged in selling liquor to the soldiers, to destroy his stock, turn loose his ox team, and bring him to the guard house, and then report to him.

He went back to his quarters, I sent the men, and then went to find Lieutenant Sturgis, but that festive officer had left camp with his orderly, and the only officer I found in camp was a Lieutenant Wilson, who had recently joined us from New Mexico. He appeared alarmed and said "if I knew what was good for me I would obey Major Sherman's orders."

I returned to the guard house, and on the arrival of the prisoner, instructed No. 1 and crossed the creek and reported that fact to the courteous Major, and then went back to my guard. The prisoner was a poor little Irishman, one John Dougherty, who had been discharged from the First Regiment of Illinois Volunteers for disability arising from wounds received at Buena Vista. With his discharge money he had purchased an ox team and a supply of liquor, and followed up the army to retail his stock to the men. This day some utterly depraved scoundrel reported him to the meanest officer in the service, "Battery Sherman," and his arrest followed.

Sherman soon appeared, the guard was promptly turned out, the customary salute given and returned, and then the Major proceeded to interrogate the trembling culprit to make him confess to the fearful nature of his crime. Grand Inquisitor Sherman, not satisfied with the answers received, ordered the accused tied up to a tree, and the "question" applied by *fifty lashes!* laid on with a mule whip, and said to me, "Corporal, detail the strongest man of your guard to flog the villain."

I most respectfully declined to do this, when he broke out in a most furious rage, and with curses tried to tear off my chevrons, but thanks to the faithful sewing of Mrs. Charley McGerry did not succeed. He then ordered my belts to be taken off, and for me to be "bucked and gagged." I ventured to remonstrate, when the maniac cried out, "You talk back to me, you d——d s——n of a b——h! I'll flog you within an inch of your life! Strip, G——d d——m you, strip, you d——d hound!"

I was standing in front of our piled Carbines, with my left hand resting on one of them. Again that singular feeling came over me that I had often experienced before when in situations of extreme danger—cold freezing chills, succeeded by a deathly faintness, as if the Angel of Death was near. The beautiful world seemed to recede far away from me, and it never appeared more dear than it did in that brief moment. But I had formed this decision: that if Sherman insisted on my being flogged, I would send a bullet through his brain, mount my horse and ride for Martiznes' haunts, and even if captured I preferred death by shooting to have my back torn to pieces by a mule whip.

Looking the Major full in the eye I quietly remarked, "Major Sherman, you won't flog me," and without being aware of the act brought the Carbine forward.

Sherman started back and replied, "Well! well! I will have you Court Martialed, d——n you! Seize him, men, and buck him!"

I submitted quietly to be bucked but the villain, when he had me helpless, had me gagged with a large tent pin, causing me intense pain. He now ordered one of the guard to flog Dougherty; the man refused, and was bucked alongside of me. Another was ordered with the same result, and another, until six of the guard was bucked with me on one tent pole! The seventh man on being ordered replied, "I suppose I must obey the Major," took off his belts and jacket and in spite of the curses of my trussed companions commenced his inhuman task.

Swinging his fearful weapon, an instrument of torture far more terrible than the Russian Knout, he brought it down with a heavy sickening thud on the poor fellow's back, who screamed in agony and begged of his tormentor to shoot him and finish his misery at once. It was terrible! I could feel every blow myself! I forgot my own misery in the terrible torture of the poor fellow, who now was imploring the Holy Virgin to protect him. The executioner, Davis, seemed insane with fright. He showered down his blows at random; some overreaching lapped around and cut the skin in strips from Dougherty's abdomen.

I was mad with myself for not shooting the monster Sherman when I had the chance, and if I could have broke my bonds, there would have been a sudden promotion in the 3rd U.S. Artillery. Fifty lashes were laid on before the fiend cried "Hold!" and then the limp senseless body was cut down by Davis, and Sherman ordered the guard to carry it out of camp and leave it, regardless whether the fellow lived or died. But the rough Dragoons sent him on a litter to the San Nicolas Ranch, and left him in the care of the good *cura* Gonsalvo. Our Squadron raised quite a sum for him and I believe he reached Illinois, a miserable wreck.

Major Sherman, after sending for a new guard, ordered us to remain bucked for two hours. I was suffering greatly; the gag spread my mouth to its extent, causing a violent pain in my jaws, while I was afflicted with a throbbing headache. I felt I could not endure it much longer, that I would soon go mad with my horrid sufferings. Even my old enemy Gorman, who was Sergeant of the new guard, seemed to pity me but was too craven to take the gag out, though requested to do so by all of the guard.

Sturgis rode into camp just as Rucker returned from town, and they rode down to the guard house together, and our release was ordered. When the huge gag was taken out of my mouth my jaws snapped together, giving me such a severe twinge of anguish that I fainted, but was brought to by the free application of stimulants.

Major Sherman now made his appearance and a lively altercation between the two Majors took place. Sherman ordered Rucker under arrest, but Rucker refused to recognize his authority and rode back to town, and reported the whole affair to General Wool. Sherman was sent for, a reconciliation effected between the two Majors, who returned to camp the best of friends.

All of the guard was released but me. Sherman preferred charges and specifications against me which, if proven, would shoot me a dozen times over. A court martial was soon convened, of which Major John M. Washington, 3rd Artillery, was President, and a Lieutenant Whiting, an officer I had been in trouble with before, Judge Advocate. What chance had I, when the President had been heard to say that he "would give more weight to the 'I think' of an officer, than to the direct sworn testimony of a dozen enlisted men?"

To all of the long list of charges read by Whiting, with a sarcastic grin, I pled "Not guilty" though I knew the court was a farce, that the sentence was understood before the court met, and that sentence was DEATH! Sherman gave in his evidence, the men on guard at the time bore witness, the case for the government closed, and I was asked if I wished to call any witnesses for the defense.

"Yes," I replied, "one."

"His name," asked Major Washington.

"John Dougherty," I answered, "the man that was flogged."

But my only witness was never summoned.

Major Washington asked what I intended to do with the Carbine I took hold of. The old spirit of recklessness came over me, to act the Bravo outwardly when all was faint and terrified within, and I answered, "to shoot the Major if he insisted on having me flogged, for I had rather be shot than flayed."

"I think in all probability you will have your wish" was the consoling reply and I was returned to my snug quarters in Company Q.

What my original sentence was I never knew, but it must have been death. In a week's time I was brought in irons to the company parade ground, and the findings of the Court Martial, with the exception of the sentence, were read; the statement continued, "the findings approved, the sentence not approved, but commuted to hard labor for twelve months with a 12-pound ball attached by a ten-foot chain to the left leg, a stoppage of all pay with the exception of fifty cents per month for the Laundress during that time. By order of General John E. Wool, Irvin McDowell, Lieutenant and Adjutant."

I was taken to the Blacksmith Shop, and received my decoration with becoming modesty, Jim Sherrod riveting on the shackle, and I found on my return to the guard house that the bolt could be withdrawn by my fingers. Thanks, Sherrod, thanks!

What a humbug the execution of the sentence of a Court Martial is when one is confined to the company quarters! My "hard labor" consisted in occasionally sweeping the parade ground, with others, and playing Poker with the guard! More than once by the connivance of a friend in charge of the guard,

I slipped my shackle and with my revolver in my belt, visited San Nicolas, and appeared the gayest of the gay. I kept myself neat and clean, even my "order of merit" I sandpapered and polished, until the Ball and each link shone like silver; in the traditions of the First Dragoons that polished Ball and chain will be long remembered.

I had been exposed to this rigorous confinement two weeks, and was getting quite *fat*, when General Wool paid the camp a visit. The guard had to be inspected, of course, and the prisoners paraded on the left. Now I knew of this visit the day before, through the kindness of the General's colored man Dennis, and I got myself up for the occasion regardless of expense. There I stood, six feet two, dressed in a new uniform fitted like a mould, every button polished, while the massive links of my chain hanging in graceful festoons from my neck actually outshone the carbines of the guard. When this gorgeous spectacle met the General's vision, he appeared dazzled, and well he might be. He recognized me and said, "It was you they wanted to shoot, was it? You are a sad rogue I fear, a sad rogue," and next day I was pardoned! Free once more, but a private again in the ranks.

The first use I made of my liberty was to pommel the huge brute Davis to almost a jelly, which sent him to the Hospital, and I back to my old quarters the guard house, but for one night only. Davis on being returned to duty was "tabooed" by all, and led a miserable dog's life until at his own request he was transferred into the 16th Infantry.

A 19th century ball and chain from the National Prisoner of War Museum —
though certainly less polished than Chamberlain's

XXIX

THE PICTURE
THAT COST A LIFE

FATE was decidedly against me. Do what I would I was constantly in trouble; striving to do my duty and make friends, I found new enemies confronted me, some of whom I was unable to contend with, being officers, who after my late escape I was disposed to give a wide berth.

One day after coming off guard, I obtained a pass for myself and horse until "stable call," signed by Major Rucker. I started for Monterey and when about halfway I met Lieutenant Wilson, with a party coming from town. I gave them a respectful salute, when Wilson said, "Jack, you go to the American House, get a bundle marked with my name and bring it to camp immediately."

I replied, "Lieutenant, I am on a pass until Stable call, and I will bring it out at that time."

"You bring it out at once, or you will suffer for it!" he said as he rode off.

My spirits fell, all the enjoyment I anticipated in town was crushed by this unlucky encounter. The simple fact that he had no right to give me such an order, or interfere with me while on a pass, did not help the matter, for what officer ever respected a private soldier's rights! But I made up my mind to stay my time out and keep sober!

I rode into Monterey, filled my canteen with *vino nuevo* and my pouches with *frutas* and *confites*, and remembering that Major Rucker had asked me to give him a view of Monterey as seen from the Bishop's Palace, I thought I could not do better than to sketch it now. I rode up to the Obispado, and hitching Lucifer to the Flag Staff in the old Half Moon Battery, I seated myself in the shade and commenced to outline a sketch of the beautiful view before me.

Monterey lay directly beneath me, and so complete was the "bird's eye" view from my position that I could see every street and house in town. The whitewashed walls and the flat-roofed houses, half hid by the dark green foliage of the palm, the orange and the cactus, with the picturesque towers and Moorish domes of the Cathedral, the Chapel and convents, gave it more the appearance of an Oriental city than one of the New World. To the east of the town all of the massive details and the ground plan of the Black Fort appeared as plain as an Engineer's design, while beyond rose the grand shade of the woods of San Domingo or Walnut Springs. To the South, on the opposite side of the town, rose the Comanche Saddle, one of the most singular formations in the country. It is a detached mountain rising from the plain some three leagues from town, to an elevation of over five thousand feet. To my right the serrated peaks of the Sierra Madre filled the background while within gunshot lay the green slopes of the hills of Federacion and Soledad, crowned with now deserted batteries, with the white walls of the pretty little village of San Catarina peeping out of the orange groves just beyond, at the very base of the

Sierra Madre. All seemed peaceful, yet my experience of the manner in which the *leperos* of the country would dispose of an *heretico* for the clothes he wore made me have my revolver lying under my sketch book, and while I rapidly sketched the scene I watched every covert that would hide a "greaser."

I had been there about one hour when I noticed two dirty-looking vagabonds come around a buttress of the Palace and saunter in my direction. They came on slowly with their everlasting smirking grin and "*Buenos dies, amigo*" to which I with equal politeness (but with my revolver cocked) replied, "*Muy bueno para servile, sientese ustedes un rato, Señores.*" (Very well to serve you, be pleased to sit down, sirs.)

One of them replied, "*Gracias, cavallero, usted fuma?*" and reached out a corn husk *cigaritto* with his left hand, while his *compadre* walked up to Lucifer, and cried out, "*Pronto! Pronto! Punga vuestros cuchillo!*" (Quick! Quick! Stick with your knife!) My kind friend with the *cigaritto* threw up his dirty *serape* and with a long gleaming knife grasped in his right hand sprang for me. But he turned fairly green as he confronted a pistol bearing on his *cabeza* (head)! I fired but must have missed the rascal, for he bounded through an embrasure and disappeared down the hill.

His comrade cut the lariat of Lucifer, sprang on and dashed down the winding road at speed. I leaped on the breastwork just as the *ladrone* came around below me, riding like a Comanche, hanging down on the other side of the horse. I fired, aiming for his shoulder, and at first thought I had missed again, but soon had the satisfaction of seeing him fall while Lucifer kept on for town. I ran down the hill in pursuit of my horse, passing the robber, who was groaning in agony, with a bullet clear through his neck. Lucifer was halted by two Dragoons, who turned him back to me. I rode back up the hill to find the poor *ladron* nearly gone; he held his Rosary in his hand, and was muttering a prayer to the Virgin. As he rolled up his large oxlike eyes to me, they seemed eloquent with rebuke for his death. For the moment I felt sorry and a little guilty, but what matter? If "greasers" will steal horses they must take the consequences.

I rode on down to the American House, kept by Sarah Borginis, the so-called "Heroine of Fort Brown," and generally known in our army as the "Great Western." Here I remained several hours and then with Lieutenant Wilson's bundle I returned to camp, one hour before my pass was up. I reported to Major Rucker and then carried the bundle to the Lieutenant's tent. He asked me why I did not bring it out sooner, as ordered to, and when I showed my pass, he replied, "D—— your pass! I'll teach you to obey me when I give you an order!" I answered somewhat insolently "that I was not the Lieutenant's servant" and was ordered to report at the Guard House, confined again.

The "Great Western", Sarah Borginis

XXX

WRONGS REVENGED

I WROTE to Major Rucker, asking permission to make a statement of my troubles to him. This was granted, and I was sent to the Major's tent without a guard. I made a clean breast of it—the shooting of the "greaser" as well as the rest—and gave him a tinted pencil sketch of Monterey as seen from the Bishop's Palace, the sketch that cost the *ladron* his life. The Major appeared interested but the only reply I received was, "You give me more trouble than all the rest of the Squadron, and I shall be d——d glad when the Mexicans kill you."

He tried to have Lieutenant Wilson withdraw the charges against me but without success. I was again tried by a Court Martial, and to my great astonishment acquitted on every charge, and Lieutenant Wilson was cautioned to be careful in the future.

Lieutenant Wilson was a very poor horseman, an unpardonable fault in a Dragoon, and one day while on drill his horse ran away with him and under a picket rope, throwing the gentleman some distance and injuring him quite severely.

I must draw a caricature of him and drop it accidentally near the officers' tents. It made some fun, but did not advance me any in the good graces of the luckless Lieutenant.

One day during Stable hours, our mutual dislike reached a crisis, and I being the weaker party suffered. The care of my best friend, my horse Lucifer, was with me a labor of love. To see to his food, and that he was well bedded, was a pleasant duty, and I groomed him by the hour until his coat was as glossy as silk. I was often complimented by the officers on the excellent condition of my horse, but Wilson could never see anything satisfactory in what I done, and this day as he inspected the horses, he said to the Sergeant on duty, "Peloncillo's horse is not half groomed; make him work on him half an hour longer."

This when Lucifer shone like a polished boot! So absurd did his petty malignancy appear to me that I gave an involuntary smile, when this courteous West Pointer turned on me with, "G—d d—n you, who are you grinning at? None of your impudence you d——d of a b——h!"

I came to attention and, touching my cap, replied, "The Lieutenant takes advantage of his rank to insult a man who he dare not offend if on equal ground."

Wilson ordered the Sergeant to tie me up and again called me a dog, when desperate and indifferent to the future, I answered, "My mother was a lady, but judging from the son, yours must have been a bitch."

I had had my say and was ready to take the consequence. I was lifted up, and fastened to a limb of a tree by a cord tied around my thumbs, so that I could only touch my toes to the ground! The pain was dreadful for nearly my whole weight bore on my thumbs.

I gasped out to the Sergeant, "For God's sake, something to drink!" He brought me a canteen of mezcal, and held it to my mouth, until I drank a full pint.

The fiery liquor maddened me. I shouted, swore and sang, swung by my thumbs until the blood spurted out from under the nails. Charles Hardy, Orderly Sergeant of my company, seeing the Doctor crossing the parade ground, went and told him that my life was in danger, and the Doctor hastened to my assistance and I was cut down at once, when I swooned.

The next ten days I occupied a bunk in the Hospital. I became moody and reserved, haunted day and night by the thoughts of my fearful punishment, and would awake with wild cries from a sound sleep, having dreamed of being again tied up. I studied revenge and swore that the Lieutenant should pay dearly for his brutal abuse of power. At the end of ten days I was sent to duty still weak but anxious for excitement and something to drive away the horrid thoughts that clouded my mind.

My revenge soon came, but in a different manner from what I anticipated. With a detachment of twenty Dragoons under the command of Lieutenant Wilson, I was sent to the little town of Pesqueria Grande with four wagons for corn. The inhabitants of this sequestered place were kind and hospitable and sold their corn at a fair price. On our way back, passing through a maguey plantation, the Lieutenant's attention was attracted to the door of a rude hut by a dark skinned and roguish eyed *poblana* who was seated therein. The susceptible Lieutenant ordered Sergeant Bennet to move on with the wagons for half a mile, and halt until he came up; then with his arm around the slim waist of the smiling Señorita, he entered the hut. When we had gone a short distance I asked permission of the Sergeant to return to get something for supper. He granted my request, but sent Hastings with me.

As we entered the place I was struck with the change that a few minutes had made at the ranch. When the Lieutenant stopped, the place had been alive with women and children, the doors open and many *hombres* standing around. But now all was quiet, the doors closed, and blankets and dried bull hides placed up to the *reja*. A few "greasers" peered at us from behind them. I felt sure that some deviltry was afoot, and my own project, whatever it was, went from my mind, for a sense of danger filled me with anxiety and dread.

The house into which the Lieutenant had gone was still closed, and nothing was to be seen of his orderly. Giving Lucifer to Hastings to hold, I searched the back enclosure and found the horses tied up in a corral, and after a while found the orderly stowed away with an old *bruza*. Both were quite alarmed at my appearance, and I was compelled to kick the half drunken fool out of the hole before he would listen to reason. Ordering him to bring the horses into the street, I mounted and rode out to where crossroads came in from the east and west. A faint, distant noise was borne over the chapperal; it came from the direction of Salinas, a town some ten leagues to the eastward.

Satisfied it was made by a body of Cavalry, coming at no mean speed, I dashed back and sent Hastings flying down the road to the detachment to tell the Sergeant that guerillars were about, then I rode up to the door and thundered away on it with my revolver.

Wilson came to the door; he was quite startled at my looks, and asked what was the matter and grasped his Sabre; but when I informed him of the danger, he showed himself a man, and a brave, cool one at that. As he started for his horse, I saw the rascally orderly turn to run with both horses; at the same moment a confused noise of jingling spurs and clattering hoofs came from a cloud of dust rolling in at the end of the street not a half a mile off. A few bounds placed me alongside of the coward, when seizing the reins of Wilson's horse I rode back and met Wilson coming at a run. He tried to vault into the saddle but the horse, frightened at the noise, plunged so violently that he failed. I dropped my reins, and while Lucifer stood like a rock, I raised my Carbine and fired at the oncoming horse, with the good fortune to knock one out of the saddle. They held up and opened an escopette fire, the rough balls shrieking over our heads.

Lieutenant Wilson was now mounted, and we went off at a jump, the guerillars coming on yelling like fiends and keeping up their escopette fire. We took the affair coolly, until Wilson's horse showed signs of weakness and looking down I saw that it had been hit in the shoulder and was bleeding freely. Wilson, pale as death, said, "Chamberlain, you must leave me, and I can only say that I regret what I have done to you, and if you can, forgive me." I replied I did not discharge my duty in that cowardly manner and must venture to disobey him again and risk another court martial.

Advising him to push on, I said I would try and check our pursuers for a moment. I reloaded and held up until the guerillars were within one hundred yards and then fired. But a yell of derision showed my shot was thrown away. When they were so close that they commenced to swing their lassos I gave them the contents of three of the chambers of my revolver, bringing down one horse and throwing them into momentary confusion, during which the Lieutenant got well away. I now let Lucifer out, and soon overtook Wilson, and we reached the command all right. The leather-clad Gentry followed us close in, fired a volley and then fell back out of range of our Carbines.

It was now quite late and Lieutenant Wilson concluded to remain where we were all night first hitching up and crossing over the ravine. About midnight we were all aroused by the loud hail of the Sentinel on the other side of the arroyo and his call for the Sergeant of the guard. The non-com went over and soon returned with a Mexican woman who proved to be Lieutenant Wilson's late *dulcinea*, the frail *poblana*, but in what a state! She was covered with blood from having both ears cut off close to her head!

Her story was as follows: The guerillars were Canales' band and were bound on some mysterious expedition towards Saltillo; the ranch had been notified to have rations ready for four hundred men. On their arrival some of the men of the place accused her of warning the American officer of his danger, and assisting him to escape. The guerillars then lashed her down to a bed, where for hours she was subjected to the most hellish outrages, and then her ears were cut off. On being released, she had made her way to our bivouac. Her wounds were washed and dressed as well as the circumstances would permit, and she soon forgot her sufferings in sleep.

At daylight we got ready and started for camp, the wounded Señorita riding on top of the corn in one of the wagons. We expected an attack on the march, but we were not molested, and after leaving our earless prize with Ramonda Victorine at San Nicolas we reached camp without seeing our foes again.

Lieutenant Wilson requested Rucker to reinstate me as Corporal, and always showed much kindness to me. Such was my wrongs and such was my revenge. The little *poblana* resided at San Nicolas, and with her loss artfully concealed by her raven tresses, proved not the least attraction of the place.

XXXI

CARMELEITA VIEGHO

SHORTLY after this affair, I went out with several Dragoons to San Nicolas, and gave them a dinner in the *Salon de baile* (dance hall) of the celebrated Victorines to honor my re-appointment. The three Graces were present, in the persons of the two Victorine sisters and our earless prize.

All went as "merrily as a marriage bell," but when matters commenced to get lively I went out to get some fresh air, my head swimming from the potency of *vino* and *aguardiente*. I wandered away among the orange and *granada* trees until I was a good mile from the party. I came to an old *jacal* or hut surrounded by a picket fence of yucca plants, and should have passed it without a second look if a cracked voice, cursing in Spanish, had not attracted my attention. I found an opening in the fence and looked through.

What a sigh greeted me! A young and lovely female, in a nude state, a girl as fair as any Anglo Saxon lady, stood in front of the ruined hut. With crimson cheeks, eyes flashing with scorn and indignation and her blue-black hair hanging below her waist, in grace and beauty she surpassed all of womankind. In front of this vision stood a "greaser" who I recognized as an old acquaintance, El Tuerto, my partner in the combat with knives in San Nicolas some weeks before. The cutthroat was brandishing a strip of rawhide, with which he threatened the alabaster shoulders of this strayed Peri from Paradise while he gave utterance to the vilest curses in the Mexican tongue.

I gleaned from what he said that this glorious divinity was the wife of the old monster, and that he was about to exercise his conjugal authority on her for running away on the day of their marriage. I resolved that she should be a widow before he left the corral. Drawing my revolver I aimed for his head but a foolish dislike to shoot the cuss behind his back made me say "*Buenos tardes mi viejo tuerto*," when he turned and found the barrel of my revolver bearing direct for his eye.

He gave a yell of affright and with a cry of "*El demono Americano!*" sprang through the opening and disappeared. I let him go; chickenhearted fool that I was, I could not kill the old fellow in cold blood, leaving me afterwards like another Richard III exclaiming, "I'll have her—what! I that killed her husband."

I now turned to the strange beauty, the forlorn damsel in distress, who had sunk to the ground with face hid in her hands. I gently raised her and carried her into the hut telling her as well as I could not to fear, that I would be her friend and protect her from all harm. She put back her hair from her face and gave me a look full of wonder, interest and confidence, and then as if satisfied she said in the sweetest voice in the world, "*Mi amigo, lo envio el Bueno Dios para ayudar pobro de mio?*" (My friend, did the good God send you to save poor little me?)

She retired behind a screen formed by a blanket, and soon appeared dressed in a less Edenlike costume and seated herself beside me. My mind was busy thinking what I should do with this charming little waif. I asked her if she had a home—"Ay de mi!" she said. "*No tengo padre, no tengo madre, no tengo amigo, ninguno!*" (No father, no mother, no friend, not one.) I was already far gone in love; wild schemes flittered through my brain to adopt her as a sister, but alas!—man proposes and God disposes—platonic attachment between a wild Dragoon not yet out of his teens, and a young, passionate daughter of Mexico was an impossibility.

I told her I loved her, that she was as dear to me as my own soul, that nothing should part us, and that I would take her to camp. With a wild cry of joy she threw her arms around my neck and sobbed like a child. We bundled up her little clothing and started for camp hand in hand, she with perfect confidence trusting her fate to a stranger, and that stranger a half-drunken soldier, an enemy to her country. As we walked along she told me her little history. She was the daughter of an Irishman and a full blooded Spanish woman, her name was Carmeleita Moro, or Moore, but her father died in debt, and she and her mother were sold as peons to an old *mestizo* named Veigho, the one-eyed gentleman of the hovel. By threats and cruel treatment her mother had compelled her to marry the old wretch, and the marriage took place the day before. She ran away and hid in the little hut, but El Tuerto found her and was about to chastise her into compliance at the very moment I made my appearance.

And she not yet fourteen! But this was in Mexico, where mothers at twelve are not uncommon. This child woman was as voluptuous and graceful in shape as the Venus de Medici, full of rich blood and with a pure heart that had never yet throbbed with the ecstatic bliss of love. I led her to the Lower Springs near our camp, hid her in a dense grove, and quieting her fears with a promise to hasten back, I tore myself away from her embrace, and went into camp.

I confided in Orderly Sergeant Charles Hardy, who was pleased to help me, having just received an order to detail an "intelligent Corporal" to Headquarters in Monterey for permanent duty. Right soon I had all of my worldly possessions strapped on the back of Lucifer, and was on my way back to the Springs. I found my birdie safe, and taking her on the saddle in front of me I rode to Monterey. As I was not to report until 10 A.M. the next day I rode to the casa of a friend of mine, a Forage Master, who like all the Americans quartered in town, kept house with a good-looking Señorita. He gladly accommodated me with a room and

She loved, and was beloved—she adored,

And she was worshiped; after nature's fashion,

Their intense souls into each other pourd,

If souls could die, had perished in that passion—

But by degrees their senses were restored.

Again to be o'ercome, again to dash on;

And beating against my bosom, Leita's heart

Felt as if never more to beat apart.

In the morning without being weighed down with that terrible sense of guilt which I suppose would be the correct thing for the awful crime of making two souls perfectly happy, I reported to Headquarters and went on duty as orderly to Colonel Sylvester Churchill, Inspector General U.S. Army, a kind, benevolent old gentleman who reminded me very strongly of the statue of Washington by Chantry. To my request to be absent from the quarters he replied with a smile, "What! a Señorita already? What a sad rogue, well! well! But if you get sick I'll send you back to camp!"

I found a room with a widow and "no questions asked," and settled down to all the joys of double blessedness. Fortune smiled on me on all sides; one night at a Fandango where we went together for the first time I won one hundred and ten gold *onzas* ($1,760). We lived on the best that the Monterey market could afford; my darling dressed in the richest silks, her *rebozo* was replaced by a mantilla, and she wore stockings for the first time. She was truly happy and sang from morning to night. No thoughts of the future troubled her, no sorrow for her present position, and one day when I said I thought we had better get regularly married, she was frightened and begged of me to never mention it again. Love was all to her— Heaven, home, friends and all was made up by love; and I did absolutely worship her. She grew more handsome if possible every day, new charms developed as she grew in wisdom and more womanlike in character. Once I took her to the Theatre, where she was taken for an American and created quite a sensation among the officers. I felt just pride in being the lord paramount of the most beautiful woman in Monterey.

Fortune still befriended me. I was very lucky and also *skillful* at cards, and one day in a Poker game with Jack McNab, a 2nd Dragoon sport, won over a thousand dollars and a handsome black Pony which I presented to my esposa, for I really considered Carmeleita my wife. I bought her a Side Saddle, American style, and we had many a nice ride in the vicinity of the town. The other soldiers' wives made her a fine riding costume, the jacket of red velvet trimmed Dragoon style with gold lace, and a saucy little jockey cap with white plumes.

Six weeks passed, six sweet loving weeks, when Colonel Churchill was relieved and I was ordered back to my company. I saw Major Rucker and told him the whole story and asked to have my wife mustered in as a laundress. He informed me that old Veigho had been in camp with a written order from General Wool for all officers to give her up if she was found inside our lines!

I told him what I knew about El Tuerto being a guerillar, and one of the cutthroats of Martiznes' gang and finally he gave me permission to bring her to camp. That night I brought my treasure to Walnut Springs, leaving her in the care of Mrs. Charley McGerry while I reported to the Major. He went down to the tent with me, and to my delight he took off his hat and treated her with as much courteousness as if she was a General's wife. In fact, Carmeleita possessed so much innate dignity of character that, combined with her extreme beauty, no one could stand in her presence without paying her the respect that a true woman should always command. In her pretty broken English, she asked permission to remain in camp with me, and said she would die if we were parted. The Major was obliged to yield, a wall tent was issued to me and he later told me, "Jack, you have got the handsomest woman I ever saw, and if you don't treat her well you'll deserve to be shot! I hope now, you rascal, you will stay in your quarters nights."

All was joy once more. I really was a reformed man and drank nothing stronger than native wine. My duty was light, Mrs. McGerry done our cooking and washing, and I had more money than any other man in camp, without it was the quartermaster. At this time I had over two thousand dollars, deposited with Major David Hunter, the paymaster, quite a sum to save from my $7-a-month pay! *Viva el monte!*

We had lived in this elysium for three months, our happiness growing more perfect every day, when the Provost Marshal appeared in camp with El Puerto and an order to take my wife! I was on duty and knew nothing of it until I saw her come running toward the Guard House with two of the Provost Guards in pursuit. I caught her in my arms and learned the horrid truth. My assurance that I would protect her calmed her at once, for she believed in me as she did in her God. I did not believe it possible that any officer would authorize her being taken from me and seeing Lieutenants Sturgis and Wilson, I called on them for assistance. They advised me to *give her up* quietly and said that the *alcalde* of San Nicolas had vouched for the character of old Veigho, who had promised to treat her kindly and forgive the past.

It was no use for me to state what I knew of Veigho, and my poor Carmeleita, seeing no protection from my officers, begged me to kill her before she was given back to El Puerto. Seeing Veigho standing in the crowd with a satanic grin on his vulture-like features, I sprang for him with my revolver cocked, but was secured and disarmed by the guard. Carmeleita flew to me, and for a moment we were encircled in each other's arms, our last embrace! Then she was torn away. She cried out, "*Adiós mi marido, adios el Rey mi alma! Vamos! Vamos! Pronta de mi el cielo,*" (Farewell my husband, farewell King of my soul! Come, come quickly to me my darling!) and then, happily, swooned.

I was taken to my tent under guard and confined there one hour, after which I applied for a twelve hour pass, but was refused. Sergeant Hardy secretly offered to excuse me from roll call until reveille, my comrades slipped out my horse, and soon I was tearing over the road to San Nicolas. I searched the country for miles, questioned all, but not the least trace of my lost love could I find. I sought out Padre Martiznes who informed me that El Puerto had left him and joined Canales' band of guerillars.

For days and nights I continued my search, when the guerillar Priest met me one night at Victorines' and related a tale of horror. El Tuerto had carried Carmeleita to a lone ranch where she was outraged by Canales' whole gang of demons and then cut to pieces!

She died, but not alone, she held within

A second principle of life, which might

Have dawn'd a fair and sinless child of sin,

But closed its little being without light.

And went down to the grave unborn, wherein

Blossom and bough lie wither'd with one blight.

In vain the dews of Heaven descend above

The bleeding flower and blasted fruit of love.

XXXII

GUERILLAR HUNTING

I WAS again reduced to the ranks for being absent without leave, and found on my return to camp that I had been reported as a deserter, for I had been absent five days—five days of desperate riding and hunting, with despair driving me almost to madness. My distress of mind was so great that the officers neither sent me to the guard house nor put me on duty. They all must have felt guilty in delivering her up to such a fearful death. I tried to drown my agony by drinking deeply, but I could not drive her dear image from my mind. I dwelled constantly on my great loss; in my sleep, I would see her struggling with the fiends and hear her calling to me to save her. Bitterly I cursed myself for not shooting Veigho in the first place. But regrets were useless—and El Tuerto still lived!

A chance came at last for revenge. Canales—*El Zorro*, the Fox—became too troublesome to our line of communication; his depredations must be stopped. Hordes of Texan Rangers were let loose on the country and though hundreds of his men were slain, *El Zorro* always succeeded in getting clear. This man-hunting though exciting was a very disagreeable duty, and gained no honor. No quarter was given by either side, and in many a fierce conflict with the Salteadores the total casualties were greater than in many battles fought during the war—yet no report of them was ever printed.

A detachment of Dragoons under Lieutenant Abe Buford was ordered to join this grand hunting expedition, and I was among the first to volunteer my services. With four days' rations and one hundred rounds of Carbine ammunition, we left our camp at Walnut Springs before daylight one morning in the month of October, 1847.

Moving out on the Camargo road, sunrise found us at the ruined ranch of San Fernando, where we encountered the *Alcalde* of San Nicolas, completely disguised in a serape. I had not seen this *alcalde*, Don Pedro Galvez, since he vouched for the respectability of El Tuerto, and the sight of him aroused all my bad passions. I knew he was leagued with the guerillars and wishing to have a few words with him privately, I remained behind while the rest of the column rode on. I made a few inquiries about the health of his dear *amigo* El Tuerto and then I rejoined the column, while carrion birds circled over the spot where we parted, and the cries of coyotes came clear as they drew together to breakfast on the remains of a miserable, treacherous *Alcalde*.

At daylight on the third day we came in sight of a large house standing on the bank of a small stream. Manuel, our guide, said it was a *casa el Diablo* (Devil's house). Deploying as skirmishers, we surrounded the place at a gallop. It was a quaintly built and ruinous structure of small slate stones, rising in four stories like steps, the upper one being the smallest. Scrub oak, mesquite and a variety of the cactus family grew out of its weather-beaten sides, so that at a distance it might readily be taken for one of the mesas common to the country.

I suppose it was one of those strange buildings of a strange race called "Houses of Aztec."

Lieutenant Buford with a party explored the ruin, climbing up by means of the trees and creepers that clung to the walls. The only entrance was through the roof of the highest story. It was full of small rooms, opening into each other, and I should judge that the architect took his plan from a bee hive. There was no signs of life about the place, and it was strange that the guerillars did not occupy it for a stronghold, for nothing but heavy guns would breach its hill-like walls, but I suppose that some superstition kept them away.

The following afternoon we came to a mesa from the top of which a ranch could be seen, with horsemen around it, not three miles off. Guerillars at last! We charged on the place raising our Dragoon shout. My mount was good, though not equal to Lucifer, but I kept him well up to his work, taking the dirt from only Buford and three others. We overtook a lone "greaser" who made frantic efforts to escape but was hurled from his Mustang, both rolling over and over, and no doubt breaking their necks. As we came close, we could see guerillars driving cattle and horses from the corral through an archway into the ranch; glazed hats appeared on the *azotea* and we were fired on with muskets. The ranch was in the usual Mexican style, a square of buildings around a court, but in front the central building sat back so that the corners projected like the bastions of a fort. There was only two windows on the front side, and these were placed in the walls at right angles with the front face, and defended with the *reja* or iron grating. Built all of stone and cemented outside it was a hard nut to crack without artillery.

I noticed that the large doors of the gate opened inward and I spoke of this to Buford who caught at the idea. The men were dismounted, the horses sent to the rear under a guard, and a skirmish line thrown around the place to fire on the "greasers" on the roof, while four men picked up a heavy plough that lay on the ground and dashed at the gate, using this novel projectile as a battering ram. In spite of our covering fire the Salteadores shot down two of the four. The other two dropped the ram and sought shelter under the walls.

The Mexicans screamed triumphantly in their shrill treble voices and kept up a fire on our two wounded who were trying to crawl out of danger. On seeing this cruel action we all made a rush for the stronghold, picking up the plough and driving it with such force against the gate that it soon gave away. As it flew open a carbine fire was poured in and then a rush, shouts, cries of anguish, a fierce melee for five minutes, and the place was won.

I had a narrow escape. I was looking for El Tuerto, I had no interest in any other, I wanted him all to myself. I passed a party of Mexicans desperately defending themselves in the patio against our men, and seeing that Veigho was not one of them I dashed up the *escalera* (stairs) to the roof, where I found myself attacked by a crowd of *bravos*. I was glancing among their faces for El Tuerto; rather carelessly I held my revolver in my left hand and my Sabre in my right, and not finding my man, tried to pass when one brutal looking "greaser" cried out, "Americano soney-bitchey" and fired on me point-blank with a huge flintlock pistol. Fortunately he missed, but then lunged out with a machete while his companions closed on me. A shot from my "Colt's" brought one down, and then there was a shout and a dozen Dragoons came pouring onto the roof and I and my complimentary cuss were left to settle our own difficulty. I thought his black face was familiar and soon recognized. Antonio, the guide to General Wool, and the hero of the bedroom in our little affair at Parras!

I was agoing to shoot, but the fool seemed to think he could pink me with his sword. So after a little play I parried a thrust and gave a clean stroke to his bare neck; the steel cut through bone and gristle to the center, and the renegade guide fell with a curse on his lips, dead.

The place was ours with a loss of two killed and five wounded; of the robbers, nine were dead and the rest, seventeen, prisoners, many of them wounded.

It was now after sundown, our horses were brought in, the wounded seen to, the gates closed and strongly fastened, and we went to work to make ourselves comfortable for the night. After supper the prisoners were brought up and questioned by Buford as to the whereabouts of Canales, and myself as to El Tuerto. But to all inquiries the sullen rascals only replied, "Quien sabe?" Manuel, the guide who had deserted our column just before the fight, was with them, and while Buford was cursing him, an accommodating Ranger proffered his services to assist the rascal in "shuffling off this mortal coil." So much kindness touched the Lieutenant's heart, and he gently replied, "Yes take the d——d s–n of a b——h out and hang him."

When the Ranger, in the most delicate manner possible, went to place the noose around Manuel's neck that ungrateful renegade made a snap and caught the left hand of the friendly Texan in his teeth, biting it to the bone. The Ranger tried to choke him off but in vain, and fearing that he might lose his temper if the pain continued, he drew his Bowie Knife and drove it to the hilt in Manuel's heart. Then a most horrible scene ensued, all of the prisoners threw themselves on us with frightful yells, many brandished knives they had concealed, and inflicted some serious wounds before our men could rally. But it was soon over; when the brief but savage struggle ended, there was not one "greaser" left alive. In all of this I took no part; I had been holding a torch to light up the hanging, and acted as a candlestick until the tragedy was over. My principal emotion was disappointment and rage at not finding El Tuerto.

That night finding rest impossible, I got up and walked out into the courtyard. A full moon lit up the pile of ghastly corpses and turned their staring, stony eyes to a horrid green. Our horses lay quietly resting but the Mustang and cattle, secured by lines of lassos at the farther end of the patio, were restless and uneasy from the smell of blood. By one of the fires a group of Dragoons were playing Poker with money obtained from the slain Salteadores. I watched the game awhile, and then visited our wounded; they appeared quite comfortable lying on piles of blankets with two men to attend to their wants. The kind-hearted Ranger was sitting up and engaged in a game of Eukre with three companions, with the same benign look that he wore when he volunteered to put a rope around the neck of Manuel.

I went up to the *azotea* and joined the Sentinel on post. The night was lovely, the moon shone bright and clear, quiet reigned, the only noise came from the cattle, and the dismal howls of coyotes who came close up to the walls scenting blood. When a corporal came up with a relief I volunteered to stand until daylight. I don't know what kind of a watch I kept, but I know that my heart became as soft as a child's and many tears were shed and many a prayer was offered up from that lonely roof that night, and through all there ran a hope that I might die and join my lost love.

XXXIII

MILITARY EXECUTIONS

1. The Death of Victor Galbraith

VICTOR GALBRAITH was a Prussian emigrant, of a superior musical education, who settled in Illinois and taught music for a living. On the call for volunteers by Governor Ford he enlisted in Colonel Hardin's 1st Illinois Regiment. When his time expired (12 months) he re-enlisted in a cavalry company organized from disbanded volunteers, called the Buena Vista Guards, Captain Meers commanding. Galbraith was appointed Bugler of the Company, which encamped near the Buena Vista Ranch.

Bugler Galbraith, like many soldiers, had a señorita living with him in camp. Returning unexpectedly one night from picket he found some other man under his blankets. There was a row of course and Galbraith threatened to shoot the intruder, who proved to be his commander, the gallant Captain Meers! Poor Victor was dragged off to spend the night on the bare ground of the guard tent to reflect on the enormity of the crime of interfering with the pleasure of a commissioned officer.

Captain Meers preferred charges against the unfortunate Prussian, he was tried, found guilty and sentenced to be shot to death "for threatening the life of his superior officer." The sentence was approved by General Taylor, and Dec. 28th, 1847, was the day fixed for the execution. Repeated efforts had been made to obtain a pardon, but in vain. The frail Señorita travelled to Monterey, had an interview with General Wool, and begged for the life of her doomed lover. But the volunteers had been unruly of late and an example had to be made; Galbraith must die.

I had gone to Saltillo on an escort at the time, and with a companion rode out to Buena Vista on the morning of the execution. The troops were formed on the old wheat field, presenting three sides of a Hollow Square. On the open side, a grave was dug, with a plain pine coffin beside it. Perfect silence prevailed in the ranks, all seemed deeply affected at the fate of the talented stranger who was to die a dishonorable death in a strange land. The sound of muffled drums sent cold chills through everyone, and when the sinister procession came in sight, a perceptible tremor ran through the ranks. My old acquaintance, Lieutenant Philip St. George Cooke, as Provost Marshal, commanded the escort and firing party.

Victor Galbraith walked with a firm step; dressed in his best, he looked soldierly and handsome. As he passed in front of the lines his eyes seemed to seek out sympathy but appeared resigned. He was stationed beside the coffin and the sentence of the Court Martial, the order for execution, was read to him by Lieutenant Cooke. The poor fellow looked around for the last time. The sun was rising over the mountain peaks east of Saltillo, flooding the valley with a soft golden light, and the sky was one grand mass of crimson and gold. Victor gave one look on all; then, closing his eyes, and in a voice of the sweetest melody, he sang in German one of Luther's grand hymns, and then said, "Good-by all, I am ready." His eyes were bandaged, twelve men moved up, the word of command was given, twelve muskets belched forth their contents. As the condemned fell back a woman's scream was heard and the Señorita who was the cause of all rushed to him and raised his head into her lap. To the surprise of all he was still alive and cried out, "Water! for God's sake water!"

Lieutenant Cooke gave him some from a canteen, and then loaded up two of the muskets himself. After the guard tore away the shrieking *poblana*, the muskets were discharged close to the poor fellow's head, blowing it to atoms. Thus the military butchery of Bugler Victor Galbraith was completed.

2. *The Hanging of the Legion of San Patricio*

The "Legion of Saint Patrick" was organized from the Irish deserters from our army. At one time they numbered over seven hundred men, regular desperados, who fought with a rope around their necks. Their commander was the notorious Riley, a former Sergeant in the 4th Infantry now holding the commission of a Colonel in the Mexican Army. They fought like Devils against us at Buena Vista, and at Contreras the Battallion held the Convent and fortified walls of a Hacienda *two hours* after the Mexicans had run away. Nearly one hundred of the Patricios were captured. They were tried by a Court Martial, fifty sentenced to be hanged, the rest to dig the graves of their executed comrades, and "to receive two hundred lashes on the bare back, the letter D to be branded on the cheek with a red hot iron, to wear an iron yoke weighing eight pounds with three prongs, each one foot in length, around the neck, to be confined to hard labor, in charge of the guard during the time the army should remain in Mexico, and then to have their heads shaved and be drummed out of camp."

Riley having deserted previous to actual hostilities, received the last sentence, served out his sentence, and married a wealthy Mexican lady, and lived respected—by the "greasers." Of those doomed to the halter *sixteen* were hanged on the 9th of September, 1847, at the village of San Angel; on the following day *four* were hanged at Mixcoac, and on the 13th *thirty* more were strung up at the same place, fifty in all!

The execution of the last number was attended with unusual and unwarranted acts of cruelty. The day selected was the one on which the Fortress of Chapultepec was to be stormed, and the gallows was erected on a rising piece of ground just outside of the charming little village of Mixcoac, in full view of the attack on the Castle. Colonel Harney, on account of the proficiency he had acquired as an executioner in hanging Seminoles in Florida, was selected to carry out the sentence. The man who "had ravished young Indian girls at night, and then strung them up to the limb of a live oak in the morning" was certainly well fitted to carry out the barbarous order: "To have the men placed under gallows with ropes around their necks, to remain until the American flag was displayed from the walls of Chapultepec, and then swing them off." A long beam supported by four uprights formed the gallows, from which dangled thirty lariats. As General Pillow's division moved forward to the assault, the Patricios were brought out with their arms and legs tied, seated on boards laid across wagons, and faced to the rear. When twenty-nine had been brought the Surgeon informed Harney that the other one was dying, having lost both legs at Contreras.

Harney replied, "Bring the d——d s——n of a b——h out! My order is to hang thirty and by G——d I'll do it!"

So the dying man was brought out and laid in a wagon and hauled to the gallows. When the order of execution was read to them, these reckless and desperate men, many of them wounded, made it the subject of mirth. One said, "If we won't be hung until yer dirty ould rag, flies from the Castle, we will live to eat the goose that will fatten on the grass that grows on yer own grave, Colonel."

Others cheered for "Old Bravo," the Mexican commander in the fortress. While the fight raged in the dense grove at the foot of Chapultepec and the result seemed doubtful, they became more reserved, but when our troops appeared beyond the copse driving the Mexicans up the hill their levity returned. One said, "Colonel! Oh colonel dear! Will ye grant a favor to a dying man, one of the old Second, a Florida man. Colonel?" When Harney asked what he wanted, the Irishman replied, "Thanks, thanks. Colonel, I knew ye had a kind heart. Please take my dudeen out of me pocket, and light it by yer eligant hair, that's all, Colonel!"

The red headed Colonel struck the jester a dastard blow on the mouth with his Sabre hilt, knocking some of his teeth out. As the poor wretch spit out blood he cried out, "Bad luck to ye! Ye have spoilt my smoking intirely! I shan't be able to hold a pipe in my mouth as long as I live."

The battle raged for hours, with varying fortune, before Chapultepec was won. When Harney saw our flag flung to the breeze from the highest tower of the Castle, he gave the order for the wagons to start up, and thirty bodies hung whirling, swinging, kicking and rubbing against each other in a fearful Dance of Death. Just as their legless comrade died, one of the desperados cried out, "Oh, ye old brick top, is it kind ye are to make Murphy dance on nothing, now that he has lost his legs!"

Such was the miserable end of the infamous Legion of San Patricio.

XXXIV

THE HORSE FORT

RUMORS of peace continued to reach us during the spring of 1848; the victories of General Scott's army seemed to confirm them, and we all expected to see the United States before long. We remained encamped at Walnut Springs, with light duty and few drills. I had but partially recovered from the gloom of mind caused by the terrible fate of Carmeleita, and still kept a keen lookout for El Tuerto.

In May, 1848, I was detailed on a detachment that was ordered to go to Cerralvo to bring to Monterey one Miller, a former clerk to the English Counsel in Monterey. He was wanted at Headquarters as a witness in an important smuggling case of contraband goods across the Rio Grande at Mier. The detachment consisted of twenty privates, one Sergeant, two Corporals, commanded by Lieutenant Campbell of the 2nd Dragoons.

We reached Cerralvo without incident, received our man, and started back. On the second day of our return march, June 4th, we passed through the little town of Marin at noon and were nearing the Agua Frio river when the two men on the advance fired on some horsemen in the road ahead and came back at a run. Lieutenant Campbell gave the order to "draw sabre and charge!"

We run on to a considerable column of guerillars, cut right and left as we rode through and over them, then drew rein and rallied at some three hundred yards. We had received no material damage. The road was full of dust that completely hid the ground but the tooting of horns from the chapperal showed that they were in force.

Campbell with much gallantry but poor judgement gave the order to charge back. Off we went at speed, passed a confused mass of struggling men and horses and had cleared the cloud of dust when fierce yells arose on all sides, and a scorching fire from Escopettes was poured into our column with fatal effect. Down we went, man and horse. Lucifer gave a mighty leap and fell headlong, dead. I sprang off in time to save myself from being crushed, and throwing myself on the ground behind my poor dead companion, I lay low to avoid the fire.

At first I thought I was alone, as the dust and smoke hid everything from sight, but as the cloud lifted I saw that the road was full of my comrades. Lieutenant Campbell was on the ground a short distance behind me holding his mare by the lariat; he sang out for us to get our horses together and take our Carbines from the gun boots and secure our extra ammunition from the saddle pouches, form around him, and keep low. Some twelve of us had done so when the firing ceased, and the blowing of horns announced a charge. Campbell told us to keep cool, and only half of us to fire at a time and that at the word of command.

As we lay on the ground behind our live and dead horses, we could hear the orders given by the guerillars, the clash of weapons and the jingle of spurs as they formed up the road, then came a fierce shout, a rushing sound, and fifty yards in our front the bright lance points and the swarthy faces of the "greasers" shot out of the dust, coming down on us at speed. At the command six Carbines poured in their fire, and then as they still came on, the other six and two Colts revolvers, told on them with such fatal precision that instead of riding us down as they easily could have done, they turned tail and went back faster than they came.

We now went to work to strengthen our position. Men crawled out and collected all of the arms—Carbines, pistols, Escopettes, Lances and ammunition; our wounded were collected, and lariats fastened to the dead horses which were hauled into position by the live ones. Our loss was appalling; five lay quite dead, twice that number wounded, and no less than fifteen of our horses were killed or wounded.

One of the wounded men, a German by the name of Nockin, volunteered to make an attempt to reach camp if the Lieutenant would let him have his mare to ride. Campbell accepted the offer with joy, when the mare was found to be wounded in the neck. Nockin said he would risk her, and the wound being staunched, the brave fellow mounted and rode off just as the Mexicans re-opened fire. As both ways the road was occupied by the guerillars, Nockin took to the chapperal on our left, to try and flank them. We listened in anxiety for any sound announcing his discovery by the foe. A minute passed, and then a distant yell, a shot, then another and another, told that our messenger was seen and fired on! Was he or the gallant steed hit? Soon a clear ringing war whoop, the Dragoon charging shout, rose high and clear above all the coyote-like cries of the "greasers." It was Nockin's voice giving us the joyful news that he was past their lines, that he was safe! for no mustang in Mexico could overtake the Lieutenant's mare, a fast Kentucky thoroughbred. We answered with three genuine American hurrahs to let him know his signal was heard.

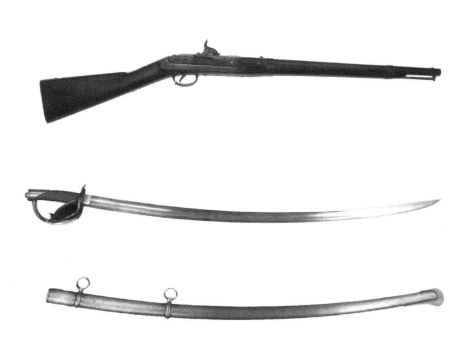

Photos of weapons issued to Dragoons:
Model 1843 Hall's Carbine & Model 1840 Saber

We now felt in good spirits, for if we could hold out for two or three hours we was safe. Everything that could be thought of was done to make our position stronger; the dead horses were arranged in a circle, a trench dug with our Sabres on the inside and the dirt and cactus plants piled against the dead bodies. On the outside a circle of lassos and lariats were made fast to bushes some three feet from the ground, the Lances planted over the breastwork forming quite a formidable abatis, and all the fire arms were loaded and placed ready at hand. Our wounded were seen to as far as possible; all but four could help in case of attack, and for a while we felt quite elated.

In the meanwhile the dust had settled and we obtained a view of the situation. We lay in a good position in the road, a clump of cactus and yuccas on each flank; beyond was a clear space some sixty yards wide, and beyond this the chapperal was open and scattered, so that we could see for some distance. About four hundred yards in front of us on the road towards Marin was a group of horsemen; behind us the road ran straight to the river, the banks of which we could see, with the blackened walls of the ruined ranch of San Francisco on the opposite side. On this road was posted another body of guerillars, and horsemen could be seen riding through the chapperal on each side. We were surrounded. Puffs of dark smoke flew up from all points. The dull reports and the screech of the rough-cast copper bullets as they flew over and around us, showed that the Salteadores were trying the range.

But now another enemy threatened us—thirst! The fierce rays of a tropical sun beat down on us, our blood was heated to a fever point, our throats parched from the dust and powder, and this when we were so near the Agua Frio that we could hear the gurgle of its cool waters over its stony bed. We had in fact just emptied the warm water from our canteens when the fight commenced, in order to fill them at the river. The sufferings of our wounded was heartrending, their cries for water unceasing.

The guerillars had got our range, and their balls struck into our horse breastwork with an ominous thud that told us to lay low. A young and generous Irishman, named Grady, volunteered to go for water. Campbell remonstrated, but he would go. Armed with a Sabre, and taking a dozen canteens, he secured a Mexican sombrero and *serape*, crawled through the chapperal to the open space, and without any judgement started on a run. He was soon shot down, and a horseman dashed out, lassoed him and dragged him into the chapperal to be butchered at their leisure. If it was not for our wounded, we would have charged down the road, gamed the river or died in the attempt, but no one thought of leaving our disabled comrades.

The increased cries of the brigands, and much galloping to and fro, made our hearts beat with renewed hopes of succor. A cloud of dust on the Salinas road showed that something was approaching! Friends or foes was the question. Oh! that it might prove to be "Mustang" Gray, Old Reid, Bayley or some other Ranger and his command. But how our hearts fell when we were convinced that it was a reinforcement to our enemies. A band of at least fifty horsemen came in sight, and formed line in the open space, showing considerable drill and discipline. They held council with our foes, and there was much gesticulating and pointing towards our position. A couple of Burros were brought to the front, with something lashed on their packsaddles; we wondered what new devilment was about to take place. We had not long to wait to solve the mystery. The Burros were wheeled round, bringing their rear towards us, with lassos hauled taut from each leg; a dashing looking guerillar dismounted and aimed the "something" towards us, a port fire was applied and a pound ball plumped into the road and ricocheted over our heads. The other was fired and overshot! Jackass Artillery! We had heard of them, but had never seen the article. While they had no effect on us, the result with them was quite serious: the recoil kicked over both of the gun carriages as the Burros were thrown down; one was disabled by having a leg broke.

A gallant *caballero* now rode towards us whom I recognized as my quondam acquaintance. Padre Martie Martiznes, the guerillar chief. Without orders four of the men fired on him and Martie fell to the ground, his faithful well trained Mustang remaining with him. The wounded chief reached up and took the lasso from the pommel of the saddle and fastened it under his arms, when the intelligent animal dragged him slowly from the field.

The enemy now opened a furious fire with Escopettes, and the "Jackass Guns" gave out their sullen roar. At a bugle call the firing ceased, and from three sides came the rush of charging Squadrons! We expected death, but resolved to die like wolves, to rend and kill to the last. We poured in a volley with the captured *escopetas*, then with Carbines, and as we had four or five loaded fire arms each, our fire was incessant; even our worst wounded loaded for us. Lances gleamed through the dust and smoke, fierce cries of "*Matar! Matar los americanos ladrones*" sounded on all sides, their horses ran against the ropes and fell; while our fire told fearfully on the struggling mass. The brigands again retreated in confusion into the chapperal, leaving more than twenty dead "greasers" on the ground. Wounded horses stood by their dead riders, and many lay by the ropes.

That proved our salvation. We collected more arms, and oh joy, found three of the double-headed gourds that the Mexicans carry, full of water! This was sparingly dealt out to all, and gave us much benefit. All arms were carefully loaded. Mustangs added to our breastwork, the Mexican *serapes* brought in, and though again under a heavy fire, we felt we could hold all day.

One of the wounded suddenly said, "Hark! I hear our Squadron coming!" Lying flat on the ground we could hear a faint but distinct rumbling noise, away across the Agua Frio, and soon could make out the roar of iron shod horses coming on the road from Monterey at speed. Saved! We fired as fast as we could to drown the noise of their approach from the guerillars, but the splash of water at the river crossing gave the alarm, and all that was living disappeared in the chapperal. The Dragoons came up the road with such fearful speed that we were in danger of being run over.

We sprang onto our breastwork and tried to cheer, as the head of the column divided and two hundred bold Dragoons dashed by on the right and left of us. One company remained by us, and Surgeons, hospital stewards and ambulances came up. All were put into the ambulances—dead, wounded and unhurt— and carried to the Agua Frio. Our appearance was distressing, our clothes were saturated with blood and sweat, and covered with dust, faces begrimed with powder. The ambulances stopped in the shade of some alamo trees on the river bank and all were stripped and washed; the dead, wrapped in blankets, were tenderly loaded in a wagon, the wounded received treatment. Those of us who were unhurt took a bath in the river, ate a hearty supper, and then being supplied with some hospital Brandy, got jolly drunk, and went in the ambulances to camp in that condition.

Our loss was seven (7) killed, twelve (12) wounded, and seventeen (17) horses killed and all of the rest so badly wounded as to be unserviceable; these were shot. Of the Mexicans, twenty-nine (29) lay dead as they fell, and two wagon loads of saddles and arms were collected and brought to camp.

The Dragoons returned next day with twenty-two prisoners, some of them wounded. They were examined before General Wool, and a crowd of *alcaldes*, *Padres* and *Curas* came forward and testified that they were all honest *rancheros* on their peaceful way to a festival at Salinas when attacked by us, and that they only defended themselves! They stated also that peace had been made three weeks before! The prisoners made the same statement, and said that the good Father, Martie Martiznes, lost his life as he went to tell us that we might go in safety to camp!

The innocent chapperal rangers were released and suffered to go in safety. But as it happened there was many Dragoons and Rangers out on all the roads and trails through the chapperal a-hunting that day. And as game was scarce, and not wishing to return with empty game bags, it unfortunately happened that the released innocents met the hunters and were bagged, and this not five hundred yards from camp. Every one of them was shot, with the new *alcalde* of San Nicolas. This was the last guerillar fight of the War.

Mexican equipment, sketched by Chamberlain

XXXV

FIENDS AND FIREWORKS

IT was not until the middle of June that we received the official notice that the treaty of peace between the United States and Mexico had been signed at Guadalupe, May 30th, 1848. Cheer after cheer went up from the volunteer camps. Hurrah for New Orleans! for the United States and home! All of them were in high glee.

But for the Regulars, the real Uncle Sam's Boys, peace made but little difference; they had to serve their time out, peace or war. I myself was enlisted only for the war but on the advice of Major Rucker decided to stay with my Squadron guarding the enormous quantities of Ordnance and Quartermaster stores in Monterey until they could be collected and shipped out of the country.

I was satisfied, for I liked Mexico, and had a serious notion to remain in the country, turn Salteadore, hunt down El Tuerto and avenge Carmeleita, and then marry some *señorita rica* (rich lady) and return to Boston as Don Juan Peloncillo, and rejoin the Church.

But fate, fortune or Providence ordained otherwise. As the last wagon started from our camp at Walnut Springs we bid *adios* to the weeping Señoritas of San Nicolas, and started down on the Camargo road, accompanied by hundreds of our fair friends. Some were mounted on Mustangs, some on Burros, but most on foot, all striving to get out of the country, to escape the most horrible outrages by the "greasers," who seemed resolved to kill all the "Yankedos," as the women were called who had lived with the Americans.

The next morning we had just reached the grand plaza of Marin when a courier came up at a jump and handed Major Rucker a letter. It was an order for the Dragoons to report back to Monterey to refit for a journey to California—to us, then, a *terra incognita*. Some of the Dragoons deserted before we reached our old camping ground, and most were dissatisfied. But I was rejoiced, it promised adventures, and new scenes, and I resolved to go if I had to re-enlist. We went into our old camp, much to the joy of the "Yankedos" of San Nicolas.

During the war many of the females of the country had proved firm friends of "Los Gringos," and we were often indebted to them for valuable information regarding the movements of the enemy, their own countrymen. Our fair female friends showed the utmost contempt for the weak dissolute "greasers," and were public in their outspoken admiration of the stalwart frames, fair skins, blue eyes, and the kind and courteous demeanor of *Los Barbarianos del Norte*. This feeling was not confined to the lower classes; the *señoritas ricas* and the "*doñas puros Castillanas*" of the towns shared it with the poblanas and margaritas of the villages.

As might be supposed, this did not increase the love of the *hombres* for us, or render the position of the "Yankedos" now that their protectors were leaving the country, a pleasant one.

They suffered fearful outrages from the returned Mexican soldiery and the ladrones of the country—they were violated, ears cut off, branded with the letters "U.S." and in some cases impaled by the cowardly "greasers," who thus wreaked their vengeance on defenseless women.

At Saltillo there were a number of women who had lived with the Americans, and were models of their class. When our troops evacuated the town these unfortunates were compelled to remain behind, some of them ladies of unusual beauty. After General Lombardini's Mexican division re-occupied the place, the authorities got up a grand celebration to commemorate the treaty of peace. At midnight the Grand Plaza was all ablaze with fireworks, and full of drunken soldiers, *pollos* and *ladrones*, when a fat Dominican Monk, one Padre Olitze, got up on the fountain in the center of the square, and in the most fiery language denounced these poor "Yankedos" to the mob. With yells of fiends, they searched out the miserable creatures, dragged them from their beds in their night clothes to the plaza, where for hours they were subjected to nameless horrors; an unheard of atrocity was perpetrated on them by the agency of the less brutal Burros, and then in their dying agonies they had their ears cut off and the finishing stroke (a merciful one) given by cutting their throats. Twenty-three women were tortured to death at this time, and no notice was taken of it by General Lombardini, or any one else among the Mexican authorities.

XXXVI

EXPEDITION TO CALIFORNIA

THE expedition intended for New Mexico and California was fitted out at Walnut Springs in the most complete manner. It consisted of D and E Companies, Second Dragoons, and Troop H of the Second Dragoons; three troops of the First Dragoons, and Bragg's battery of light artillery, now under the command of Lieutenant Kilburn. The cavalry was under the command of Major Laurence P. Graham, while Brevet Lieutenant Colonel John Washington commanded the whole detachment. Our camp was alive with preparations, wagons were overhauled, tires re-set, new horses and mules purchased at Camargo, all drills discontinued and everything done by the officers to make the men satisfied with the change.

All of us who were enlisted for the war were now mustered out of the Army and paid off. I felt sorry to part with my comrades, who seemed to be my only friends, and I also had a strong desire to see California. I called on my friend Mrs. W.W. Chapman, whose husband was going along as Quartermaster. Through her influence I obtained the position of wagon master, at sixty-five dollars per month and two rations—a much better arrangement than the $7 a month I had been receiving as a Dragoon.

On the 18th of July, 1848, we bid farewell to Walnut Springs for the last time. The morning was delightful, birds of the gayest plumage filled the grove, the air was redolent with fragrance from the orange and pomegranate trees, all nature wore a holiday look as if rejoicing at the departure of the last of the invaders from Mexico. The bugles sounded loud and clear "To horse!" and the finest appearing column of United States Troops that was ever seen debouched from the woods and wound its way past the "Black Fort" toward Monterey.

The entire command was dressed in bright red flannel shirts and black broad brim felt hats; this, with their white belts, burnished arms, gay banners, and dashing horsewomen galloping up and down our flanks made an effect seldom witnessed in the dull routine of Uncle Sam's service.

We went into camp at Arista Mills and I got my charge of 50 wagons parked, my tent pitched, and was about to dine, when a woman rode up with one of the Quartermaster clerks, who pointing me out said, "This is the man you want," and rode off. I asked the lady's pleasure, and she handed me a note addressed to "Peloncillo Jack, B.M.D. (Boss Mule Driver)". The note as near as I can remember was as follows: "Dear Jack: The bearer of this, Miss Ellen Ramsey, is desirous of going to California, and I have recommended you to her as a suitable party for her to contract a 'Scotch marriage' with, to enable her to do so. She will explain all. Yours, &c, Hugh Elmsdale." This extraordinary epistle was written by a friend of mine, a clerk in the commissary Dept.

I gave a look at the "bearer," and certainly my eyes never rested on a finer specimen of womankind (physically) than this same Ellen Ramsey. She was full *six feet* in height, splendidly proportioned, complexion clear pink and white, eyes a deep blue, with bright golden hair that fell down her back in heavy ringlets, and dressed in a riding habit of blue velveteen with a cavalier's black hat, from which floated a white plume. And this apparition wanted to go to California with me—Whew!

She told me her story—she had landed in Texas in 1847, with other emigrants from Scotland; the Small Pox and Measles carried off many of them, amongst others Ellen's parents. Reaching San Antonio, she obtained a situation with a lady whose husband was a commissary in the volunteers. With them she came to Monterey, and now they were returning to Texas. She was desirous of going to California, but an order prohibited all except married females from going with our troops.

With blushes I tried to decline her offer but she laughed at my bashfulness and said, "After we have lived together for a year we will know one another better and then if we wish we can marry. If we don't agree we'll separate in peace." What could I do? There sat this six feet of female perfection, with a winsome smile on her lips, and the innocent look of a child shining from her blue eyes. Do? I done as any sinner would have done, threw down the sponge, surrendered at discretion, and consented, saying, "There's my tent and kit, make yourself at home."

She done so. Her horse was unsaddled and hitched to the same picket rope as mine, a Burro drove up with her baggage, and in fifteen minutes I scarce knew my own tent. There was a rug on the ground, a looking glass fixed to the pole, a comfortable looking bed with snow white sheets and pillow cases! Miss Ellen, with her riding habit changed to a short dress and sleeves rolled up showing a plump white muscular arm, was hard to work setting the dinner in better shape. "Scotch Ellen," as she was called, made herself mistress in more sense than one. And as she was an excellent cook, owned her own horse, and a good supply of clothing, the arrangement was not so bad after all.

I reported my new partnership to Captain Chapman, and he kindly approved.

Her example seemed contagious, for just as we were ready to start the next morning a train of three large Chihuahua wagons came in sight around the bend of the road by the Obispado, preceded by a horsewoman who was recognized by all as Sarah Borginnis, the celebrated "Great Western." She rode up to Colonel Washington and asked permission to accompany the expedition; the Colonel referred her to Major Rucker, who informed her that if she would marry one of the Dragoons, and be mustered in as a laundress she could go. Her ladyship gave the military salute and replied, "All right. Major, I'll marry the whole Squadron and you thrown in but what I go along." Riding along the front of the line she cried out, "Who wants a wife with fifteen thousand dollars, and the biggest leg in Mexico! Come, my beauties, don't all speak at once—who is the lucky man?"

Whether the thought that the Great Western had one husband in the 7th Infantry and another in Harney's Dragoons made the men hesitate, I know not, but at first no one seemed disposed to accept the offer. Finally Davis of Company E (the same that flogged Dougherty) said, "I have no objections to making you my wife, if there is a clergyman here to tie the knot." With a laugh the heroine replied, "Bring your blanket to my tent tonight and I will learn you to tie a knot that will satisfy you, I reckon!"

Such was the morals of the army in Mexico. Mrs. Davis *nee* Borginnis went down on E Company books as "Laundress" and drew rations as such.

Besides the Great Western and my Scotch Lassie, there was with the command Mrs. Chapman, Sergeant De Lancey's wife, Mrs. Charley McCerry, and a young girl servant to Mrs. Chapman.

About noon we resumed our march, Miss Ellen riding by my side, while I gave her a description of my dangerous ride when pursued by guerillars down this same road. I found my partner more practical than sentimental; when I related how my pants and flesh were torn by the thorny chapperal, without any inquiries about my own sufferings she coolly said, "Pity you threw them away. I could have mended them for you." No romance about that. More than a week later we finally reached the hacienda of Don Manuel de Sanchez near Parras, having with much hard work got the teams safely through Paso el Diablo. Colonel Washington remained here two days to rest the animals. The horses of the Dragoons showed much distress after the long march but my long-eared charges seemed as fresh as when we left Monterey.

After I had my wagons overhauled, and some tires set, I went with the fair Ellen into Parras, to do a little shopping. In a store we met with Mrs. Chapman and Mrs. De Lancey. At first I held back, but to my surprise the ladies called me and said I must introduce my lady to them. I did so, when all conventions of society were thrown aside and the *ladies* chatted and tried to cheapen the goods together as if on the same footing. After numerous purchases, we stopped at a *pasteleria* and partook of the sweets and fruits, with some excellent Parras *vino*. A merry happy hour was spent, and then with the bundles strapped on behind we returned to camp, when social restraints were again enforced.

After two days' rest, we moved on, and at night we reached the large Hacienda El Poza (deep well). It was built like an ancient castle, with towers and castellated roof. There was quite a garrison of armed peons, for this estate belonged to the Sanchez family and was very rich in cattle and sheep, but suffered from the annual visitation of the Comanches. It was at this place that a party of Doniphan's command the year before defeated a large party of Comanches, killing fifteen, and rescuing twenty-three Mexican girls from captivity. Next day we reached the small town of Alamo de Parras, where Colonel Washington and Major Graham found the hospitality of the *Alcalde* so great, his wine so good, the Señoritas so extremely pretty and accommodating, that they ordered Captain Chapman to have all of his wagons repaired, regardless whether they required it or not. This took four days, during which we were treated to *la corrida de toros* (bullfight), in which a female matador appeared and showed considerable *muscle* and little skill in dispatching some poor old oxen that they tried to persuade us were bulls.

Ellen attended all places of amusement with me and I began to really like and respect the poor girl, who was yet only eighteen, and until the arrangement with me, virtuous, and her living with me she did not regard as being the least wrong, as it was one of the customs of her country. She was perfectly faithful to me and was in truth a model mistress. I lived better than any officer, dressed well, and my clothes were always in the best of order. She made excellent pies which she sold (as well as whiskey), sewed for Mrs. Chapman, was always busy and good-natured and I am sorry to say had no better sense than to give her affections to that roving vagabond Peloncillo Jack B.M.D. Well, with all his faults, he treated her kindly and lovingly, and protected her from all insults, and once bled a Forage Master by putting a leaden pill into his shoulder for making an improper overture to her. After that no one even by look would insult the Scotch Lassie.

Our next stop was at the Noria de Pozo Calvo, a cattle farm on the great road to Chihuahua. Our red shirted Dragoons attracted much attention from the inhabitants of this part of the country, for the only American troops they had seen before were the half civilized command of Colonel Doniphan that plundered the country from Santa Fe to the Brazos.

What an earthly paradise the country from Parras to this place was! The white walls of Haciendas, ranches and hamlets, were to be seen as far as the eye could reach, rising from fields of corn, sugar cane and barley, while Figs, grapes, pears and watermelons grew in great abundance, and the delicious Parras wine was as free as water. Thereafter the country became more rugged and barren, with few signs of cultivation, but excellent grass. In about a week we reached the lively little silver mining town of Mapimi, at the foot of the Bolson de Mapimi (purse of Mapimi, so called from the extraordinary richness of the silver mines in the mountain). We remained here two days and from there on we followed Doniphan's route to Chihuahua. It led over a high table land, with scattered cattle Haciendas and little cultivated land. There were but few objects on the route worthy of notice. Most of the towns consisted of a few miserable adobe houses, with a ruined church on one side of the plaza and the Casa de Cabildo (town hall) on the other, a *patio el gallo* (cock fighting court) and a *salon de baile* (dance hall) without which no Mexican could live. At Santa Cruz de Rosales, about 60 miles from Chihuahua, I sketched a monument built to commemorate a victory over the Comanches, who terrorize the country. This quaint affair, the only one in northern Mexico, was designed by the Cura of the place. It was built of adobe, rough plastered with cement, and could certainly claim the merit of being original. At the top was a coarse colored print of the ubiquitous Virgin of Guadalupe, underneath this was a soldier looking badly frightened. Innocent, practical Ellen who visited with me, artlessly inquired "if it was built to frighten the coyotes away?" Santa Cruz de Rosales is famous as the place where the last battle was fought between the Americans and Mexicans in

Chihuahua, March 17th, 1848. Our troops, commanded by Colonel Sterling Price of Missouri, stormed the place and captured General Trias, and the entire garrison.

At Bachimba, only 15 miles from Chihuahua, we laid over one day to enable the command to clean up for the grand entry into the capitol of the North. The belts of the Dragoons were newly pipe-clayed, the arms burnished, and next day, August 26, we entered Chihuahua, making a fine appearance. There was a large garrison in the city commanded by Colonel Justiniani; Don Angel Trias was Governor. We passed through the city and went into camp near a large building known as Casa Blanca on the bank of a small stream.

Chihuahua is the great depot of the States and Santa Fe Trade and the inhabitants have become well acquainted with Americans through their intercourse with the traders, but they don't seem to have acquired much love for the gringos by this contact. The population of the city is stated to be fifteen thousand, but I should judge this was too high a figure. In honor of the Governor, a grand review was given by Colonel Washington, which concluded with a sham fight in which His Excellency was shown the way we whipped his *paisanos* (countrymen), this no doubt proved quite satisfactory, for he expressed himself as highly delighted.

While we remained at this place my ill fortune led me into an adventure in which I came near losing my life. One evening Sergeant Moore and Jack Jones of my old company took supper with me and Ellen. After it was over the Sergeant proposed a ramble in town. The fearful events of that evening deserve a separate chapter.

XXXVII

A NIGHT'S ADVENTURE IN CHIHUAHUA

WE reached town and strolled around for some time, drinking freely at different *fondas* until we brought up at the *salon de baile*, where a fandango was in full blast. The room was full of ugly looking cutthroats who greeted our entrance with fierce *carajos* and ribald jests. Common prudence should have caused us to retire, but that wasn't our style, so we swaggered up to the bar and called for the drinks. Then selecting for partners three of the best looking señoritas in the room, we took places on the floor and called for a dance, when Moore cried out, "I am cut!" A "greaser" had knifed him in the side.

My revolver was out in a moment, and seeing an ugly yellow belly sneaking for the door, I sprang upon the *banqueta*, fired over the heads of the crowd and shot the bravo in the back; with a yell he fell dead. The women disappeared through back doors, while the men drew their knives and made a rush for us, but we had gained a good position behind the bar. Two more shots laid out two more of them and they fell back and crowded together at the further end of the hall.

We gathered from their chattering that they had sent for firearms, so our only chance was to work quickly. I loaded the three empty chambers of my revolver, the only pistol in the party, while Moore, who was bleeding profusely, and Jones broke up a huge oaken settle, and made clubs of the legs. Then swinging the body part we let it go when at its greatest momentum; it flew across the room and struck the mob with the force of a battering ram, bringing at least half of them to the floor. With loud yells we charged them with clubs and they fled through a rear door.

After the victory our first act was to strengthen our position; the doors were secured by the heavy bars, and the settle and tables piled against them. We put out the candles and felt quite safe as it was a stone house, the windows well protected by iron *rejas* like a prison. Seated in the angle of the room by Moore, we awaited events. We could hear the low muttering of the mob outside, and suddenly a volley of pistol balls was poured into the room through the open *reja*, but we were protected by being out of the line of fire. It was now near midnight, and I felt satisfied that we could hold out until daylight, when Ellen, alarmed at my absence, would report it, and a patrol would be sent into town to hunt us up.

Shots continued to be fired through the different windows, when on a sudden all sound ceased except a rushing noise as of a mob in flight. Soon the regular tramp of soldiers sounded on the stone pavement; a sharp command in Spanish, and the ring of muskets told of the arrival of a patrol. At a loud rap on the door followed by the command to open I asked who was there. "*La patrolla*" came the answer.

It would have been madness to resist soldiers, so we pulled away the barricade, unbarred the door, and there entered a lieutenant, carrying a lantern, and half a dozen soldiers. We were made prisoners, other soldiers came in, and the dead "greasers" examined. I gleaned from the remarks of the lieutenant that he was much pleased at something, and that we were all right. "*Carajo! Shingara! esto hombre esta ensebado,*" he exclaimed as he kicked over the *ladron* I first shot. Then he informed us that he would protect us to camp, and for our own safety we had better keep quiet about the affray.

Moore was got up and could with little assistance walk very well—his cut, though long, was not very deep—and having secured several bottles of "pass whiskey" we left the house, and with an escort of a Sergeant and six soldiers, we took our way through the now silent streets for camp. Nothing was seen of the mob, the moon had risen, bathing one side of the street in a flood of light, while on the other the grotesque shadows of the quaint Moorish buildings gave a weird aspect to the scene. We had now reached a long street that led direct to camp, and the guard left us after cautioning us again to keep silent on the adventures of the night.

What followed, I must confess I am not very clear about. We had drunk freely in the dance hall, and now we seated ourselves on the sidewalk, on the moonlit side, and refreshed ourselves again from the aguardiente del Paso, Moore taking his share. We drank the health of the courteous officer, and the patrol, drank confusion to all ladrones, and my health was drunk, for my good shooting, and then I was called on for a song, the "Battle of Buena Vista," four hundred verses, composed by our poet, Happy Jack, Co. A, 1st Dragoons. The first verse is as follows:

It was on the 22nd, the day it being clear,

We espied the advancing Army of Mexican Lancers,

At two o'clock they fired a shot when we returned the same

"Dam ye eyes," Old Zack cries, for now commence the game.

[Chorus:]

So cheer up my lively lads, for it never shall be said

That the First Dragoons was ever yet afraid.

I had commenced on the second verse when we suddenly received a shower of rocks from the dark side of the street, then were rushed by a crowd. I received a blow in the head, as if from a sledge hammer, and my face was covered with blood; black faces and glittering knives were all around me. I felt faint and thought my time was come, but the idea of being hacked to pieces gave me the desperation of madness. Giving them the contents of four of the chambers of my revolver, I dashed through the crowd, with a yell more savage than their own, using my pistol as a club. Moore and Jones were bounding down the street like deer, well ahead of me. I was no longer weak and faint, I seemed to fly, and reached the bank of the river a hundred yards ahead of my pursuers.

Here I found Moore lying in a faint; Jones was not in sight. My danger and bloodletting had fully sobered me, and I realized the condition of things at a glance. I could easily reach Camp alone; our white tents shone in the moonlight, almost within stone throw. But my duty was plain—to save the Sergeant or go under with him. I raised him onto my back, and with his arms around my neck I gathered his legs under my arms and waded into the river, which was over two feet deep and twenty yards wide. Stones flew around us, one hit Moore in the back with a sickening thud, bringing me to my knees; I arose, staggered and fell into the cool water. I knew the devils were on me but I could do no more, when there reached me a woman's voice crying out, "Courage Jack! I am here, courage!" Then round oaths in good English and several shots followed, and I was pulled out of the river onto the bank, and found myself supported in the arms of Miss Ellen, with a number of Dragoons around me.

I was assisted to my tent where a Surgeon found my scalp badly bruised and cut, but my thick skull still sound. Moore who was a great favorite with the officers was taken to the hospital tent. Next day Major Rucker called on me and gave me a regular d——g and swore as only Black Dan could swear, that it was all my fault, and if Moore died, he would have me hung! There is gratitude for you!

Jones, finding that Moore could go no further than the river, and hearing my shots, had concluded that I had gone up, so he had put for camp and found Ellen at the guard house, anxious for my safety. She and the guard doubled quick to the river, and arrived just in time.

Rucker investigated the affair, and Colonel Justiniani, the Mexican commander, informed him that an officer commanding a patrol reported that in endeavoring to arrest a band of *ladrones*, he had met with resistance, and the patrol had killed five of them, one of whom was a famous assassin, one Ramires, known as *El escorpion*, for whose head there was a reward of one thousand dollars. This reward had been paid to the valorous lieutenant. No wonder he wanted us to keep silent!

XXXVIII

THE MARRIAGE OF SCOTCH ELLEN

ELLEN for some days had been blue and gloomy, and refused all explanation, and to my repeated inquiry of what was the matter would reply "nothing." We went one day on a long walk up the river, and at length after much urging she confessed her troubles. She had received an offer of marriage! One McPherson, a countryman of hers, also a Wagon Master with the train going to Santa Fe, had been for some time smitten with her charms and now that he was about to be separated, he had spoken out, and in spite of the position his lady love occupied, had made her an honorable offer of his heart, hand and blankets! Ellen said that if I offered the least objection to the match, she would refuse the offer, and go with me to California, but that she was convinced that I never would marry her and as she now had a chance to become an honest woman, she did not think it right for her to throw it away.

I was raving at first, and thought of calling the Scotch poacher to account, but my better nature prevailed, for I knew that the marriage was the best thing for the poor girl's happiness. Ellen was too good a woman for such a fate as would fall to her if she continued to follow the fortunes of so reckless a rover as Peloncillo Jack, Esq. That evening I sent for the would-be Benedict and we three talked the matter over and I gave my free consent to their unity.

The marriage proved quite an epoch in camp; it took place at Headquarters on the last day of our encampment in Chihuahua. A *cura* of the city tied the knot assisted by Lieutenant Wilson, who to make all sure, performed it over again reading the service from an Episcopal prayer book, I gave the bride away! Mrs. Chapman and Mrs. De Lancey were present, and appeared much impressed with the solemnity of the ceremony. Colonel Washington, Majors Graham and Rucker gave the fair bride a chaste salute and the happy couple departed, hand in hand, to the bridegroom's home, i.e., his tent.

I returned to my once happy, but now solitary abode, and felt desolate enough. Our horses no longer munched barley from the same trough, her brass bound trunk was no longer in its accustomed place against the tent pole, the bed, robbed of half its blankets, looked shrunken and mean, her jaunty riding hat no longer hung from its nail, and the whiskey keg was gone! When too late, I was sorry that I had let her go, and found I was not quite so much of a saint as I thought.

XXXIX

A RANGER'S LIFE IN SONORA

NEXT day the entire command marched sixteen miles and encamped at Sacramento, the scene of battle between Colonel Doniphan and a much superior force of Chihuahuans. In the morning Lieutenant Colonel Washington, with Kilburn's Battery, the First Dragoons and Troop H of the 2nd Dragoons started for Sante Fe via El Paso, while the remainder under Major L.P. Graham moved off on a road to the left for California.

Most of the country to the Northwest of Chihuahua was at this time practically unknown to the rest of the world. The citizens of Chihuahua gave us vague traditions of great cities in the far north, inhabited by *white* Indians, called Pintos, of rivers that run over beds of gold pebbles, of beautiful women who fought mounted and ate their prisoners—in short the most fabulous stories were told us. I must confess that I rather took stock in these romances, for a warm imagination had prepared me to expect many strange and startling adventures in the unknown land.

It was in the month of September when we left Sacramento, the air was clear and bracing, and we were yet in a cultivated country, but in one where every house was fortified, and numerous wooden crosses by the wayside marked the scene of murder by the dread Apaches.

Our march so far had been a success, and the command was in as good a condition as when we left Monterey, but now the total incompetency of Major Graham for a separate command was made manifest to the most obtuse intellect. The marches were ill timed, without proper care for grass and water, and in a country of plenty our animals suffered for forage. We lay by at all Haciendas, especially if the *mujeres* was *mucha bonita*, consuming our provisions and even selling them to the "greasers." Lack of discipline in the Dragoons and worse in the Quartermaster Department threatened the worst results to the expedition. Major Rucker and Captain Chapman done their duty nobly, but with a drunken, ignorant commander who seemed to delight in acts of petty tyranny little could be done.

After several days' march from Sacramento we reached a branch of the Rio Yaqui, the banks of which for miles were covered with peach trees, full of ripe delicious fruit. A large well-armed party from New Mexico was encamped here engaged in collecting and drying the fruit for the Santa Fe market. We remained here two days, and found a great plenty of sweet pumpkins, corn, and barley, with ruins of ranches and Haciendas scattered up and down the valley, while wild cattle was plenty and so fat as to appear all body.

With the party from New Mexico was a man of remarkable size and strength. Madame Sarah Borginnis-Davis, the "Great Western," saw this Hercules while he was bathing and conceived a violent passion for his gigantic proportions. She sought an interview and with blushes "told her love." The Samson, nothing loth, became the willing captive to this modern Delilah, who straightway kicked Davis out of her affections and tent, and established her elephantine lover in full possession without further ceremony.

Our route after we left the Peach Orchard on the Rio Yaqui was over a barren desert of sand and rocks, mountains and deep precipitous valleys. The vegetation was remarkable; many new species of the cactus family appeared, among them' the gigantic *petahaya*, a monster cactus rising in a single fluted column to the height of forty to sixty feet. Sometimes they display four or more arms, that rise from the sides with great regularity and present the appearance of a gigantic candelabra. They bear a fruit something like a prickly pear of a sickly sweetish taste. This strange vegetable grows on rocks and in sandy places where even "gammer" grass cannot be found.

Since we left Chihuahua, I had found my position anything but a pleasant one. One thing—since I had parted with Ellen, I drank to excess. I always had a supply along in a wagon, but I had never allowed drink to interfere with my duty. But now everything went wrong. The air was so warm and dry that it took all the life out of the command, men and animals seemed to lose all of their vitality and dry up, wagons fell to pieces, tires came off, spokes came out, constant halting to repair broken-down wagons soured the disposition of all, while Major Graham—Old Pidgeon Toes—cursed all and everything, I coming in for more than my share of the general abuse.

One day one of my wagons broke down, and while I was repairing it the confounded Major must ride up. As usual he d——d and swore at me, said he would disrate me and make me drive a team. I very imprudently replied "that as he had the power he might do as he d——d please." The Major's natural red face now glowed like a furnace, and swearing to hang me, he told his orderly to bring me along a prisoner. I made no resistance and rode along in silence until we reach the guard, when my horse and revolver was taken from me and I was obliged to "frog it."

I walked for days but this kind of marching was not very hard as the command did not average over fifteen miles per day, and the guard was from my old Squadron who permitted me to ride when the Major was out of sight.

One day near Tucson we emerged from a wilderness of mesquite and cottonwoods into an open space where arising from the huts of an Indian village was one of the grandest church edifices of Northern Mexico, the Mission of San Xavier del Bac, built in 1668. The village was inhabited by a tribe of Indians known as the Papagoes, with no white men or Mexicans nearer than Tucson. The buildings are in an excellent condition, with a number of fine paintings and images well preserved. The Mission appears to be unknown in Mexico, and is certainly a most remarkable edifice standing as it does in the midst of a desert, the home of wild savage Apaches.

I was sketching the place from my guard house (a scaffold used by the Papagoes to dry pumpkin on) when Graham rode up and saw me. "What in H——l have you got there?" was his polite inquiry. I respectfully replied, "My sketch book. Major." "Sketch book! You d——d hound, what in H——l do you know about sketching?" and riding up he snatched the book from my hands, and after glancing at its contents threw it in my face. Then turning to the Sergeant of the Guard he said, "Tie Peloncillo Jack up for two hours, and then put handcuffs on him, and see if he can sketch then!"

I was accordingly tied up. Graham's tent was in plain sight, and he rode up to it and dismounting took up a position where he could watch me. What dignity! A Major of the U.S.

Dragoons, and commander of an important expedition, tormenting a poor boy, a citizen at that; and watching his guard to see if his brutal orders were carried out! Yet the man was brave; he led the charge at the battle of Resaca de la Palma, for which May received the credit.

When my two hours were up, I was cut down and ironed, but the pair was so large that I could slip them off and on, with the greatest ease. Next day we made a short march to Tucson, when again in spite of Graham and Handcuffs, I sketched the old mined Presidio, but he saw me and I got another damning and was tied up again.

This Tucson is a very hot place, and being tied up in the sun I was in a fair way of becoming *tasajo* (jerked beef). I could feel my brains "sizzling" and my skin was commencing to crack, when a strange white man strode up to the "guard house, and after taking in the situation at a glance, drew a Bowie Knife and coolly cut me down. He was seized by the guard and in spite of a desperate resistance was tied up himself.

He was a small, dried up, wiry man, dressed in a half Indian, half Mexican costume and armed with a heavy Kentucky rifle, revolver and a huge Bowie Knife. His actions and language was strange and highly ludicrous; he would howl like a coyote, bellow like a bull, crow like a cock, bray until all the mules joined in the chorus, and intermingle all this with strange oaths and expressions in a mixture of Spanish, English and Chinook. "Hy'er, usted d——d Porkeaters," he said, "yer got hold of the wrong hombre! Carajo! I am that old Buffalo, Tom Hitchcock, crying to be tied up like a Buffalo calf! (bellowing like a Buffalo Bull). H——l fire! shooty me! what will Glanton say?" He ended with the prolonged howl of a Prairie Wolf, and then broke down crying like a child.

I was tied up alongside of him, and the name he mentioned recalled to my memory the tragic scene I had witnessed in the Bexar Exchange, San Antonio, Texas. I engaged him in conversation, and learned he belonged to a band of Indian hunters employed by Don D. José Urrea, Governor of Sonora. The band was known as the "Scalp Hunters" and was commanded by John Glanton of Texas, the desperado of the Bexar Exchange.

We were cut down by order of Lieutenant Coutts, officer of the day, and the Free Ranger was taken before Major Graham, who interrogated him as to his business in Tucson, the route between the place and the Rio Gila, and obtained about as much information from "Crying Tom" as he would from a mule. Hitchcock was returned to the Guard House and I informed him that I had made up my mind to escape and join Glanton's company. He with much bluntness advised me to "join Satan and go to H——l at once" but finding I was in earnest, he promised to help me all he could.

A plan was agreed on, and I laid down to sleep, but my mind was too active to rest, the step I was about to take, to separate myself from all civilization and friends, to join a band of outlaws, for such the Scalp Hunters was considered, even by the half savage frontiersmen, was an act to make one think and reflect. In the morning Tom Hitchcock was released and his arms restored to him, and with a significant look at me the ranger departed *crying*.

During our march this day, a "solitary horseman" was seen hanging on our rear, and was pronounced by the officers an Apache scout, but I knew it was my lachrymal outlaw, Crying Tom Hitchcock. Finding water a little after noon we went into camp, when I saw the figure of the horseman in bold relief against the sky. He was standing by a lofty *petahaya* that grew on a rocky mesa, overlooking the camp. I waved a handkerchief three times (the signal agreed on), then came the answer, the cry of a Coyote, and the horseman disappeared. I sent for Captain Chapman, and making a plausible excuse, I asked him for my pay for two months, seventy-five ($75.00) dollars. I had at this time over four hundred dollars of my own, so I had plenty.

I now took one of the guard into my confidence (Happy Jack of Company A); he was under an obligation to me, and was glad to assist me in anything that lay in his power. After dark I succeeded in eluding the Sentinel, and with my blankets, sketch book, &c, reached a solitary alamo, and was soon joined by Happy Jack with my horse, revolver and knife. Besides my regular kit, I found two holster pistols in the holsters and a long-range Hall Rifle, with plenty of ammunition. Without questioning the right of Happy Jack to make the donation I accepted the gifts in the same liberal spirit that they were given in, and with a hearty pressure of the hand, but a sinking heart, I bid my old comrade good-by. Mounting, I turned my back on the Camp and rode forth in the dark desert, friendless and alone.

I reached the mesa, dismounted and with much difficulty led my horse up, and seated myself near the huge cactus where I last saw Hitchcock. I looked back on the Camp in the valley; the fires flaring up brightly among the cottonwoods, lighted up the white covered wagons and disclosed the forms of men as they passed in front of the blaze. A deep silence prevailed, only broken by the occasional bray of a mule, and the prolonged melancholy cry of a Coyote from the plain. How I regretted the step I had taken. Who was Glanton, or Hitchcock? What would be my fate with such desperados? Would I ever see Boston and home again? These and similar thoughts flittered through my brains until I quite broke down and cried like a child. Come to the test, I found I was not so much of the heroic mould as I imagined and would have been glad to be back in the Guard House and march to California in irons—anywhere but in this terrible desert solitude!

I was aroused from my gloomy thoughts by a heavy hand on my shoulder, and the howl of a coyote in my ear. Springing up I confronted the eccentric ranger, who said, "What, crying? This old Buffalo don't allow anyone to cry but himself. Yer a fine colt to hitch to John Glanton yer are! Carajo! ye' ain't worth shucks."

In his presence all my feelings of despondence fled. I was ready for adventure. We started from the mesa and took the trail back for Tucson. About an hour's march beyond the place we turned off the trail to our left, and passed up a canyon for some distance. Tom dismounted and led the way into the intense darkness that shut us in like a wall. We moved on for more than an hour in silence when the Ranger halted and said, "We'll rest here tonight, *Muchacho.*" After a hearty meal of *pinola* and *tasajo* Tom carefully put out the fire, and we lay down well wrapt up in our blankets and I was soon sound asleep.

When I awoke it was in the gray of morning and Tom was up and breakfast ready. We had passed the night in a wild gorge of what he called the Sierra Chiricahua, a retired place well known to Glanton's band of Scalp Hunters. Saddling up, we retraced our steps on foot until we struck a trail that ascended the side of the canyon in a zigzag manner; up this we climbed with much difficulty, and it was two hours before we reached a level place to rest ourselves and our weary animals.

Though it was now the middle of October, and the clouds hanging around the peaks of the mountains gave notice that the rainy season would soon commence, yet the sun's rays were hot and overpowering. The scene was drear and desolate; rocks piled on rocks showed the most irregular and grotesque forms, some black and charred as by the action of volcanic fires, others composed of marl and sandstone had the appearance of ancient castles, with towers, battlements and fortified walls. Below us lay San Xavier and Tucson, looking like toy houses, while away off to the north, a long cloud of dust and little white specks showed the position of the Graham Expedition.

We rode now in an easterly direction, my hitherto taciturn guide became more loquacious and gave me an insight into the wild, lawless life led by the Indian Hunters of Sonora. Glanton was paid fifty ($50.00) dollars for every Apache scalp brought in; he had recently returned from an unsuccessful hunt in the Navajos' country where in an encounter with the Navajos he had lost eleven men, and not a scalp to show for it. He was now encamped at the Presidio of Frontreras, and hearing of a large body of Americans on the road north of Chihuahua, he had dispatched several of his men to intercept the command at different points to obtain recruits if possible. Crying Tom, not relishing his treatment in camp, was glad to get off with a whole skin and my humble self.

We pushed on as rapidly as the nature of the ground would permit. The heat was fearful, and our suffering animals were kept up under the application of our heavy spurs. We descended to a table land or elevated plain on which the *petahaya* grew in abundance. The ranger cut one down with his knife and with my assistance cut off the thorny fluted outside; the succulent inside we gave to our horses who fed on it with much relish. We had crossed halfway over the plain when Crying Tom pointed out in the distance to our right what at first appeared to me nothing but a long line of yuccas or Spanish Bayonets. But I soon saw they had motion and made out a long column of horsemen in single file. Apaches on the war trail. Soon they collected in little squads and then started across the plain direct for us. I became alarmed, and half turned my horse to fly, but my companion not only

331

showed no signs of fear, but appeared delighted! and as they came yelling across the plain, brandishing their long lances, and rattling their bull hide shields, Tom yelled and shouted and slapped himself.

I told the ranger that I thought I might fetch one with my rifle, but he d—d me for a fool. However I dismounted and using my saddle for a rest, I drew a bead on a big chap and fired, when the huge savage sprang with a yell to the ground. His companions used their quirts freely on their ponies until out of range. Hitchcock sprang off, and embraced me with odd expressions of delight, hugged and kissed the (to him) miraculous rifle, and pronounced it a "Big Medicine" that "shoot a heap."

The wounded warrior presented a ghastly sight, he tried to call his pony to him, but the affrightened animal stood at a distance, snorting in terror. The savage then gave a wild startling yell, and by his hands alone, dragged himself to the brink of the deep barranca, then singing his death chant and waving his hand in defiance towards us he plunged into the awful abyss.

"Cincuenta pesos gone to h——l, muchacho," cried Tom. "The doggone mean red nigger done that thar, to cheat us out of his har!"

We moved on in silence for somehow my agency in the death of the warrior affected me greatly; I felt as if I had committed a murder. Conscience said. You were safe, he never harmed you, and he was on his own soil, yet you killed him.

Crossing the plain we entered a ravine that ascended the gloomy mountain; we toiled on for hours up its narrow bed, with walls of rock rising on each side shutting us in from all view outside. We crossed the summit at sunset and began to descend, the light began to fade out, the canyon became dark and forbidding and soon all was gloom and the darkness of a dungeon prevailed. My strange companion who led the way disappeared! The sound of his horse's hoofs on the rocky bed of the canyon ceased, all was still.

I was beginning to feel alarmed at the desertion of the ranger when a wild shriek of laughter, which seemed to burst forth from the solid rock above my head, was caught up and repeated from a thousand points, then fierce whoops burst forth mingled with stunning reports of fire arms and wild yells. That I was in the midst of a terrific combat in which hundreds were engaged I had not the least doubt, and my safety was my first consideration. I sprang off, and feeling a huge boulder in the intense blackness, I pulled my footsore steed behind it, and made ready for a struggle. No one assailed me, the noise of the conflict seemed to die away up the mountain with an occasional loud report as of artillery. I was stupefied at the strangeness of this mysterious battle in the darkness, when suddenly the rocky walls were lit up by a bright light held by a wild looking figure. I drew a bead, and was about to fire when I recognized my quondam companion. Tom cried out, "Muchacho, yer welcome to Tom Hitchcock's rancho El Fonda del Cieneguilla. Entra! entra! hombre, tote yer caballo into my casa!"

By the light of his mesquite torch I saw a narrow opening in the wall, rising up in rough, irregular steps. My tired animal at first refused to climb, but with Tom's assistance we arrived in safety at a large cave fifty feet above the bed of the ravine. I was full of curiosity to know more of this magician of a Ranger, who kept a hotel in the wild desert. Tom replenished the fire, produced from a nook in the wall a *Coffee Pot! a Frying Pan! Jerked Beef* and a large leather bag of *pinola*. We made an excellent supper and then my magician took from his mysterious cupboard one of those double headed gourds used for canteens by the "greasers," and to my delight I found it contained Pass Whiskey, the pure *aguardiente* of El Paso. Then this good Genie brought out a crock or *ollo* and a bag of beans or *frijoles* and soon the crock was on the fire to be in readiness for the morning's repast. A spring of clear cold water ran through the back part of the cavern, in fact nothing appeared wanting to make us comfortable.

The cave was admirably adapted for concealment and defense. It contained numerous winding galleries and compartments running through the cliff, a hundred feet above the bottom of the ravine, and was often used by Glanton's men, who kept provisions and fuel stored here. It possessed a remarkable echo, a specimen of which had so alarmed me. A single rifle shot, sundry whoops and yells, had the effect of a severe conflict in which hundreds were engaged. Tom also told of mysterious noises, groaning and sighing, with occasional heavy reports, which he credited to some supernatural agency, though he said that "Judge" Holden (one of Glanton's men) said they were caused by the wind, and called the Earth's Colic. These strange sounds combined with the echo had a powerful influence on the savage hordes, who always avoided the canyon, though it was the best pass through the Sierra for hundreds of miles.

We slept safe and sound, though the dying Indian troubled me in my dreams. In the morning when all was yet dark in our rocky world, we ate our breakfast, saddled up and after carefully removing all traces of our visit, we led our rested steeds down the steps and left Hitchcock's ranch. As we moved down the pass we tried the powder of the echo and I am satisfied it repeated over twenty times! At one place away up on the side appeared walls built by the hand of man, or what I judged to be such from my point of observation. The whole place is worthy of a scientific exploration, and no doubt many interesting discoveries would be made. The rocks are marl, sandstone and limestone.

XL

GLANTON'S GANG

TWENTY miles from the canyon we came to a mule trail that crossed the ravine, and ascended the right hand bank on foot. We came out on a broad plateau and after an hour's sharp trot, came in sight of some distant buildings on a hill, mud hovels, the tower of a church and a Presidio. This was the town of Frontreras. Leaving the trail, we directed our course towards a small grove of cottonwoods on the bank of a small stream.

Here under the shade trees, engaged in sleeping, playing cards, cleaning arms or grooming horses, were some forty wild brigand-like men who welcomed my companion with rough greetings. To my great joy, my old acquaintances Ben Tobin, Doc Irving and Sam Tate of McCulloch's Rangers came forward and bid Peloncillo Jack welcome to Glanton's bivouac. A rough looking, short thick-set man came forward and saluted Hitchcock and myself in the following choice language. "What in h——l have you got thar, Tom? Whar were ye spawned, stranger, and whar do ye tie up?"

I recognized in this frontier Chesterfield the John Glanton of the San Antonio Bexar Exchange tragedy, and was about to answer him when he extended his hand as if to shake hands with me. I reached out mine, when the ruffian with a hoarse

335

laugh seized me by the nose, giving it a severe twist. Surprised and indignant at such unwarranted treatment, the moment he let go, without thinking of the consequence, I struck him with all my might in the face, sending him to grass. My safety was now the question. Springing onto my horse, I drew my revolver, but fortunately before I could fire I was lassoed and dragged to the ground, and tied to a tree.

Glanton arose with the blood streaming from his face, staggered up to me and presented a cocked revolver to my head. Though I expected instant death I looked the brute calmly in the eyes while I silently prayed to my Heavenly Father for forgiveness. For full one minute he glared into my eyes, with the cold tube pressed against my forehead, and then lowering his pistol, he grasped my hand and shaking it warmly said, "Real grit, stranger, ye'll pass, ye strike like the kick of a burro." I found I had passed a successful ordeal, and was thus initiated into Glanton's Band. There was Sonorans, Cherokee and Delaware Indians, French Canadians, Texans, Irishmen, a Negro and a full blooded Comanche in this band of Scalp Hunters, with a miscellaneous collection of weapons, and equipment and a diversity of costume seldom seen in a regular organized body of volunteers for Indian warfare.

John Glanton was born in South Carolina, but when a mere youth his parents moved to Texas and joined the settlement of Stephen Austin. Nothing remarkable distinguished Glanton in his youth from the other young men of the settlement, without it was a deep religious feeling and a strict moral conduct. A young orphan girl, whose parents had been killed by the Lipans, gained the affections of the young South Carolinian; his love was returned, the marriage day was set, though his affianced was only seventeen. Glanton had built a log hut for his bride on the bank of the beautiful Guadalupe, and one day while most of the male settlers was at Austin's house discussing the threatening attitude of Mexico, a band of

Lipan warriors charged on the outskirts of Gonzales, killing and scalping the old women and young children, and carrying away the girls, Glanton's betrothed among the latter. The alarm was given and instant pursuit made by the frenzied frontiersmen. The next day the savages were overtaken and suffered a severe defeat at the hands of the outraged Texans, but the prize for which they fought, the poor girls, were tomahawked and scalped while the fight was raging.

From this tragic scene Glanton returned a changed man. He would often absent himself from the village and when he returned he invariably brought fresh scalps. During the war of Texas independence Glanton was a "free scout" attached to Fannin's command, and was one of the few who escaped from the massacre at Goliad. He always "raised the hair" of his slain, and rumor gave him the credit of being the owner of a mule load of these barbarous trophies, smoke-dried in his lonely hut on the Guadalupe. He drank deeply and sought the companionship of the most hardened desperados of the frontier; in all Indian fights he was the devil incarnate.

During the civil wars between the Regulators and Moderators, Glanton would join neither party, but with the utmost impartiality picked a quarrel with some famous fighter of one or the other party and "rubbed him out." Any other man in Texas would have been lynched, but his terrible loss, his services in the Mexican and Indian wars, made him respected by the masses and gave him strong friends of men in power. He was outlawed by Houston, but this did not affect him in the least. During the late war between the United States and Mexico, he was a "free Ranger" hanging around our army without belonging to it, often going out with scouting parties but always independent of all authority.

At the close of the Mexican war, hearing that the governor of Sonora was offering dollars for every Apache scalp brought in, he organized a motley band of adventurers and entered the service of his old enemy General D. Jose Urrea, the Butcher of Fannin's command. Urrea gladly gave all encouragement to the "Scalp Hunters" and seemed equally pleased when Ranger or Indian went under. He offered an additional bounty of one thousand dollars for the hair of the famous Apache Chief, Santana. Glanton had made two raids in the Indian country, with but small profit, and had met with considerable loss. There was in camp drying thirty-seven of those disgusting articles of trade, Apache scalps, cut with the *right ear* on, to prevent fraud, as some Indians have two circles to their hair.

This was the band of cutthroats that I had joined and such was John Glanton, the Captain of the Scalp Hunters of Sonora.

XLI

LIFE WITH THE SCALP HUNTERS

NEXT day after my arrival at Frontreras, Glanton with ten men started for La Villa de Mapimi to obtain the bounty on the scalps. During their absence we had rather a gay time, attending Fandangos in town, and receiving calls of the poblanas of the place in camp.

The second in command, now left in charge of the camp, was a man of gigantic size called "Judge" Holden of Texas. Who or what he was no one knew but a cooler blooded villain never went unhung; he stood six feet six in his moccasins, had a large fleshy frame, a dull tallow colored face destitute of hair and all expression. His desires was blood and women, and terrible stories were circulated in camp of horrid crimes committed by him when bearing another name, in the Cherokee nation and Texas; and before we left Frontreras a little girl of ten years was found in the chapperal, foully violated and murdered. The mark of a huge hand on her little throat pointed him out as the ravisher as no other man had such a hand, but though all suspected, no one charged him with the crime.

Holden was by far the best educated man in northern Mexico; he conversed with all in their own language, spoke in several Indian lingos, at a fandango would take the Harp or Guitar from the hands of the musicians and charm all with his wonderful performance, and out-waltz any *poblana* of the ball. He was "plum center" with rifle or revolver, a daring horseman, acquainted with the nature of all the strange plants and their botanical names, great in Geology and Mineralogy, in short another Admirable Crichton, and with all an arrant coward. Not but that he possessed enough courage to fight Indians and Mexicans or anyone where he had the advantage in strength, skill and weapons, but where the combat would be equal, he would avoid it if possible. I hated him at first sight, and he knew it, yet nothing could be more gentle and kind than his deportment towards me; he would often seek conversation with me and speak of Massachusetts and to my astonishment I found he knew more about Boston than I did.

At the end of five days Glanton returned without money, three of the party wounded, and all as mad as hornets. Their story was as follows: The second night after they left us, they discovered a camp of Sonorans, and judging that they must have goods of value along they resolved to plunder them, disguising themselves as Indians. At midnight they charged the camp with frightful yells; the surprised Sonorans made but little resistance and fled, leaving their camp to the supposed Apaches. Glanton found some forty mules and burros with pack saddles, blankets, provisions, &c, but no money, and five women. Three Mexicans were killed—they were scalped—as well as three of the women, who being old and ugly were knocked on the head. The murderers, turning loose the stock, withdrew, carrying away the best of the blankets and two young Señoritas. Traveling all night they reached a retired place that they considered safe from pursuit. Here they spent the day in a brutal saturnalia, the two girls being subjected to gratify the lust of the gang. At dark they in turn were surprised by a large body of Sonorans who took them for Apaches. The unfortunate girls were brained at once to prevent all unpleasant discovery, and then with the fierce war whoop of the Tontos they charged their assailants with Indian lances, with so much fury that they gained a free passage. Glanton, not deeming it safe to venture into Mapimi, returned to Frontreras with eight additional scalps and three men wounded.

A stormy council of war was held. Glanton said that the Señoritas had stated that their party was on its way to upper California where gold had been found in immense quantity. Similar rumors of gold had been reaching Frontreras, so we now decided to go gold hunting. Hitchcock alone doubted our success in California—he thought that Major Graham's command would gather all the gold before we could reach the placers—and volunteered to venture into Mapimi and cash the hair, the bounty amounting to over two thousand dollars.

Glanton gave the required permission and with Long Webster and Charley McIntosh, a Cherokee half breed, Tom left with the scalps, both Indian and "greaser." We gave out that we were all going to Mapimi, and passed through Frontreras together making a great display of the raised hair and Indian lances. When five miles from the Presidio, Hitchcock and his two companions, after being instructed to meet up at the end of eight days at a place well known to the band, Ojo del Conejo, or Rabbit Spring, kept on to the south. The rest in Indian file climbed the mesa on our left and pushed on over the parched-up plain. We passed a few miserable herdsmen's huts, the inhabitants fleeing in affright, taking us for Apaches. To impress this belief more forcibly on their minds, we gave them a specimen of savage war whoops, and towards night, coming onto a drove of fat beeves, we killed several and sent the rest scampering away with arrows sticking in their flanks; this with the remains of a poor *vaquero* who was slain and scalped by "Judge" Holden was sufficient to convince all Arizuma (Arizona) that the fell Apaches were out on the war path in force.

We passed the night at a deserted Hacienda, feasting on the juicy beef and smoking the rest to pack along. Next day we reached the rendezvous at Rabbit Spring. The place had been recently visited by numerous horsemen, the ground around the spring was trod into mire, there were fresh horse chips, remains of cattle, and other signs of late visitors. An arrow sticking in a lofty *petahaya* near by informed the experienced eyes of our mountain men that the horsemen were Maricopas. Scouts were dispatched on all sides, hunting parties sent out, a camp was formed in a gulch near the spring, and every precaution taken to insure our safety and comfort until the return of Hitchcock. Our scouts reported that the Indian trail led towards New Mexico, the hunters returned with cattle and sheep, so we lived right royally.

In seven days our hair traders returned, their venture had been a decided success. Glanton's little affair had after all helped them, as the Sonorans continued to believe that the attack had been made by Apaches. Urrea's agent paid them the cash, the Mexican scalps passing for good Indian without question. Hitchcock brought a supply of pass whiskey, ammunition and *pinola*.

That night a regular orgy was held in camp. Glanton proved that he was well fitted to be the master spirit of the fiendish band. Drinking deeply, he swore with the most fearful oaths that we were all sinners bound to eternal Perdition, that it was his mission to save us. He then knelt down and in well chosen words prayed with all the fervor of a hard shell Baptist for the salvation of all. Suddenly he sprang up and drawing his revolver opened fire on us right and left. One of the Canadians received a shot in the leg, as a gentle reminder to flee from the

342

wrath to come. Judge Holden seized the madman in his powerful arms, laid him down and soothed him as a mother would a fretful child, and Glanton soon sank into a drunken sleep.

Next morning we started for El Dorado or the mystic city of Cibola. Tradition represented this city as situated in a deep valley surrounded by lofty mountains. It was inhabited by a race of white Indians called Pintos and there was believed to be an abundance of gold and silver in the place. To find this great city, to sack and plunder it, appeared to the crazed brains of Glanton a matter of easy accomplishment. All believed in the legend, and all swore to follow Glanton to the death.

We travelled for several days over a barren desert, destitute of all animal life, but the home of the great *petahaya* and giant Cactus. On the third day a strange object miles away attracted our notice. It appeared like a tent, but what was a tent pitched in the desert for? We started for it and after three hours' ride reached a sad scene: a broken wagon, skeletons of cattle and horses, the remains of an American emigrant man on the ground, while in the wagon was the bodies of a woman, a little girl and boy, all killed by arrows and scalped. Singular to relate the wagon was not plundered. We searched the baggage to find some clue to the mystery, but the only scrap of writing found was on the flyleaf of a small Mormon Bible which was as follows: "To Ollis, from her defender Hickman."

One of our men. Mountain Jim, who had been examining the arrows, said, "This is the work of white men. No doggone red niggers carry so many kind of arrows and leave them behind." The wagon was fired and the bodies consumed on this strange funeral pyre.

We continued our weary aimless march, and at the close of the day found water and gammer grass in an arroyo, to the great relief of our suffering animals. Next day after climbing a rugged cerro, Glanton, who was at the head of the column, cried out, "El Dorado, at last by God!" We all hurried to the front where a most extraordinary spectacle greeted us. From the other side of an extensive plain rose the houses, towers, domes and walls of a vast city! What appeared to be fortified walls ran for miles, and lofty battlements stood out in bold relief. The city had a strange weird aspect, as of something unreal and unnatural.

We sat in silence gazing on this realization of our hopes, when the mocking laughter of Judge Holden broke the spell. "So, Glanton, this is El Dorado, is it? The city of gold and fair women! I wish you joy of the discovery—a city of sandstone built by dame nature!"

It was too true. The grand city in our front, the legendary Cibola of the Spaniards, the city of white Indians of the trappers' tales, was one of those curious freaks of nature, common in New Mexico: strange shaped columns of sandstone, wrought by the action of the rain on the hills during ages. Though we all were used to such sandstone formations yet we had never met with any equal to this. Nature had carved out here a city whose towers and columns would cause the cyclopic ruins of Thebes and Luxor to appear like children's toys in contrast. As we neared the silent streets of the place, the beautifully proportioned Moorish domes, the light symmetrical towers, became gradually piles of sandstone and marl. Looking back, the summit of the hill from which we first espied this El Dorado appeared crowned with a frowning fortress with plumed warriors on its walls! The illusion was perfect, yet it was only walls of marl with yuccas and cactus growing behind them.

Judge Holden mounted a rock for a rostrum and gave us a scientific lecture on Geology. The Scalp Hunters, grouped in easy attitudes, listened to the "Literati" with marked attention. The whole formed an assemblage worthy of the pencil of Salvator Rosa. Holden's lecture no doubt was very learned, but hardly true, for one statement he made was "that *millions* of years had witnessed the operation producing the result around us," which Glanton with recollections of the Bible teaching his young mind had undergone said "was a d——d lie."

Next morning we moved out of the enchanted city, our rout being towards the north. Indian signs were plenty today, a column of smoke rose straight in the air from a rock crowned mesa that we had just passed. It was answered by another and still others, away off to the north, until over twenty of these signals were in sight. We had come to hunt Redskins, but it seemed as if we might be hunted ourselves. No Indian had been seen, but evidently the Apache nation was aroused for the signals covered hundreds of miles.

A ride of forty miles brought us to gammer grass and water. Our mountain men pronounced the stream the Little Colorado. During the night all was quiet. Some of the hunters had the good luck to kill a large brown Bear, which was very acceptable, for we had had no fresh meat since we left Rabbit Spring. All the next day mounted Indians was seen in the distance but we moved on without being molested. This night, after a march of at least fifty miles, we were compelled to halt in the plain without water. Next day we moved on over the hot arid desert when about noon we descended into an arroyo, hoping to find water. No Indians or smoke had been seen that day, but of a sudden a volley of arrows fell among us and the Apaches' war whoop sounded on all sides.

Though unexpected, the attack found us not unprepared. It was scarce the work of a minute for our entire party to be well covered behind the huge rocks, and our animals safely secured in the ravine. The only person visible to me was Ben Tobin, who shared with me the huge boulder behind which I crouched. Soon the crack of a rifle, succeeded by a wild cry, told us that our comrades were on the alert and a Redskin hit. I incautiously raised up to look, to see if I could see an Indian, when three arrows whizzed by my head, one carrying away in my hat, with a hole in it more suitable for ventilation than ornamental purpose.

Tobin called my notice to a movement on a mesa that rose some four hundred yards from us on our right. The headdress of a warrior was seen behind a clump of yuccas as he reconnoitered the arroyo. As if satisfied that he was out of range he left his covert and came forward to the very edge of the cliff, and presented in bold relief against the sky as graceful a warlike figure as ever an ancient Greek warrior did. Lying flat down I got his range, when he gave a shrill cry and I let him have it; his cry changed into a yell and springing clear of the rock he fell a corpse at the foot of the mesa.

Then yells arose on all sides, arrows flew in clouds, and a crowd of painted, yelling and leaping devils closed in on us from all quarters.

The next few minutes seemed hours to me. There was no mistake I was badly scared, and without knowing what I was about laid about me like mad, out-yelling the Redskins themselves. All was confusion, rifles and pistols cracked and the hoarse shouts of the rangers gave token that all were engaged. In five minutes the horrible melee was over and all that could of the enemy fled. Glanton and five others were with us in the last rush, and while I expected to get H—l for being afraid, to my surprise I received their rough compliments for doing grandly, and I found myself quite a hero. Five Apaches lay in sight besides the one at the foot of the hill.

Glanton pointed out a grove of Pecan and cabbage trees some two miles further down on the bank of the arroyo, and said we must gain that place or all of our animals would die of thirst. He gave his orders, the rangers crawled away to give the details to the rest. Soon one of the pack mules, loosened on purpose, dashed down the ravine towards the grove. This was the signal to go, and the next moment all were in the saddle, and amidst a shower of arrows and to our astonishment shots from firearms, we charged on the skulking foes in our front and made for the refuge. When we left our covert, we could realize the extent of our danger. Indians on foot swarmed all around, throwing in their arrows like hailstones and we saw several armed with escopettes. Their ponies were brought up and now the mounted yelling fiends were on us again.

"Ride like devils for the timber," cried Glanton, and ride we did. I was soon out of the thickest of the conflict and with nine others gained the grove unharmed. Out on the plain a cloud of dust, shouts, savage yells and the reports of firearms told how desperate was the situation of our comrades. Our impulse was to go back to their assistance but our orders were to hold the grove. We sprang off, secured our horses, tied lassos all around our shelter, and secured our pack mules as they came running in, the smell of water being their guide. Glanton made a desperate dash for our position, and with thirteen others cut their way through and reached the grove. Holden and Long Webster came in on foot, their horses being killed.

We had now breathing time to look about us. Fourteen of our party was missing and of the twenty-four present, seven were wounded, four quite seriously. Twelve of our pack animals were gone, but fortunately our provision and ammunition mules had come in safe. All hands went to work with a will. Doc Irving attended to the wounded, trees were cut down and formed into barricades, our suffering animals watered from the spring of excellent water that gushed from under the roots of

a gigantic Pecan tree, and picketed out to graze on the gammer grass, and taken altogether our affairs were not so bad after all.

The Apaches were having a "big talk" about a half a mile from our position; one old shriveled-up buck was making a violent speech, judging from his actions, and soon a cordon of warriors was thrown around our position. Our mountain men and Indian fighters were in high glee, for they said that there was no other water for seventy miles, and in consequence the savages would soon be compelled to vamoose. But they would not go without another trial; the mules that they had captured from us were brought into line and fastened together by lariats, then a crowd of Redskins dismounted and under the cover of this moving breastwork advanced on us.

Glanton ordered us to hold our fire until he gave the word. When they came within two hundred yards and arrows struck the trees, he shot down the right flank mule which made the left mule wheel around, exposing the storming column to our rifles. A deadly volley was poured in, and then twelve of us sprang on our horses and charged on them before they could regain their ponies. The result was most glorious, we regained the grove without loss, while seventeen Indians lay on the plain and several warriors had to be helped into the saddle. The Apaches had enough, their sentinels withdrew, and the entire party disappeared among the yuccas and rocks to the south. All of our mules were re-captured but two, and we caught several Indian ponies.

Though the enemy had retreated, our situation was one of great danger. Our band reduced to twenty-four, and only fourteen of them fit for duty, hundreds of miles from any settlement, encumbered with our wounded, and liable to be attacked at any moment by fresh bands of hostile Indians—all this was sufficient to daunt the boldest and most experienced Indian trailer. John Glanton was a man of prompt action and remorseless in carrying out his decision. He ordered Holden and Irving to examine all of the wounded and report all that were unable to ride. He then called us together in a distant part of the grove, where we received the report of the ministers of fate, who gave the names of *four* who could not travel any further at present.

Glanton made a short but forceable speech, the drift of it was "that *mercy*, and our safety demanded the death of these four, and that the laws of the desert sanction it." I was horrified and expressed myself freely, but the execution was ordered. All were compelled to draw lots to decide what four should commit the murders. Twenty Apache arrows were placed in a coyote skin quiver, four of them being marked at the point. Thank God I drew a blank!

The poor fellows had watched our proceedings with anxious eyes. One was a young Kentuckian, Dick Shelby, two were Delawares, the other a Sonoran. Sam Tate chew the one marked for Shelby, Long Webster that of the Mexican, and a Delaware Indian volunteered to dispatch the two of his tribe.

They were informed of their fate, and the best of care given them during the entire night. All were busy, the worst of the mules were killed and jerked, their hides made into moccasins, leggings &c, bags of mesquite beans gathered and after a few hours' sleep, all that could move were ready to start at early dawn. We moved off in silence, the executioners standing beside the victims with Apache war clubs in hand. As we cleared the grove, Glanton fired his pistol, when we all heard the dull crushing sound that told us the deed was done. All felt sad and guilty.

XLII

THE GREAT CANYON OF THE COLORADO

WE marched due north all day after the terrible sacrifice on the altar of necessity in the grove. Little conversation was held, we moved on in silence, moody and suspicious of each other. Our wounded suffered dreadfully but with the lesson of the "lottery of death" before them, they endured their agony without complaint. Dr. Irving done wonders; he gathered a species of the cactus, cut away the outside and thorns, made a pulp of the soft part and poulticed their wounds with it. This reduced the inflammation and had a wonderful cooling effect. A young Mexican, Manuel Reis, who had no less than six arrow wounds in his body, begged of me not to let him be killed as the men in the grove were. I firmly pledged myself to protect him. I sounded three of the men and they declared that they were heartily sick of this butchering of comrades, and would allow no more of it.

With but two hours' rest at noon we pushed on all day and halted for the night in a strange old ruin, with no water to be found. All we had in our gourds was gone, the wounded men having received the most of it. Two of the poor fellows died during the night, which was one of extreme misery to all. Late in the afternoon the next day a solitary Cabbage Palm pointed out water, and we remained here all next day. A bear and a Big Horn was added to our commissary department, and our animals regained their strength.

Glanton was of the opinion that the barranca in which we found the water ran into the Rio Colorado, and that we had better follow it down the junction, and then follow that river down to the Pima village on the Gala river. The old mountain men objected and said that the route was impassable because of the deep canyons and barrancas that intersected it. But Holden joined with Glanton, so bidding with reluctance good-by to this oasis, we started down the winding bed of the ravine. As we advanced the rocky walls rose higher and higher until we seemed shut out from the world.

The little rivulet that trickled over the stony bed, sometimes disappearing for miles and then again forming deep pools full of fish of the trout species, was a source of great delight and comfort to us, which only those who have experienced a similar trip over the arid wastes of the alkaline deserts of the west can appreciate. At our noon-day halt we drank, bathed, washed our animals, and anyone seeing us would have thought we had no other object in view but to indulge in its benefits. Hitchcock shook his head and growled at the delay and asked where we would be if rain fell in the country above us. Several clamored to return, but Glanton swore he would shoot the first man who made the attempt; this stopped all complaints and repacking we continued on our way.

Judge Holden rode with me and stated that he knew that we would be obliged to retrace our steps, but that Glanton's plan gave him an opportunity of seeing the greatest natural wonder of the world, the unexplored Great Canyon of the Colorado, reported by hunters as a "cut through the plain from one to five miles in depth, and extending for some three hundred miles." As we rode along Holden, in spite of my repugnance of the man, interested me greatly by his description of the great cut and how it might have been formed. He also was fluent regarding the ancient races of Indians that at a remote period covered the desert with fields of corn, wheat, barley and melons, and built large cities with canals bringing water from rivers hundreds of miles distant. To my question "how he knew all this," this encyclopaedian Scalp Hunter replied, "Nature, these rocks, this little broken piece of clay (holding up a little fragment of painted pottery such are found all over the desert), the ruins scattered all over the land, all tell me the story of the past."

We passed the night at a pool of water. I thought of rain, as it was now late in November, and looked at driftwood lodged in crevices full fifty feet above our heads, with a shudder. Next day about ten in the forenoon a shout from the men on the advance caused us to all hurry ahead, when we found ourselves standing on the brink of a chasm that cleft the earth to an unknown depth at our feet. The Great Canyon of the Colorado at last! We dismounted and lying on the rocky bed of the canyon, we looked down the awful gulf under us. Away down, far, far below, we could see a bright silver ribbon, the water of the great river of the West, here imprisoned between walls whose height and vast extent seemed to shut it out forever from the light of day. The depth of the canyon we had no means of determining, But Holden, Doc Irving and Ben Tobin agreed in giving it a depth of *three thousand* feet, or not quite two thirds of a mile, while the mountain men swore that it was good three miles. I believe the first estimate is rather over than under, for judging from the banks of the barranca that we were in, which rose not over six hundred feet above us, the opening below did not appear over three times deeper. But at any rate it is the greatest wonder I ever saw. In the rainy season, when a torrent fifty feet deep rushes down the barranca and leaps over this sheer precipice of so frightful a depth, what a grand and stupendous cataract it must be!

This thought struck us all, and after many a hard word with Glanton for getting us in such a position of danger, we started back up the barranca. I am satisfied that we were the first white men who ever saw the Great Canyon from this point. What is very singular in regard to it is that the cut is not through mountains, but through a level plain, with mountains rising above it from three to twelve thousand feet.

In two days' march, without any incident, we reached our former stopping place, the spring of the lone Cabbage Palm. We reached it none too soon, for that night the storm of rain burst over the desert with great fury. The rain fell heavy all the next day but we resumed our march, our animals receiving new life from the torrents of water that pounded down on the thirsty earth.

Five days of hard marching brought us to the Gila river opposite a village of Pima Indians. We built rafts of dry cottonwood and prepared to cross. Glanton, savage and surly, swore he would assault the place, and give no quarter to man, woman or child. Holden supported him, but Hitchcock, Tobin and all of the mountain men not only opposed this cruel massacre but swore it should not take place. Two of our men had been at the village before and spoke in strong terms of the kind and peaceful character of the inhabitants. Glanton finally put it to vote and all but three voted against the slaughter.

A party of Indians came down on the other bank and hailed us in Spanish, offering their assistance, and soon crossed over by swimming. They had stout, short figures, with their hair cut square across the forehead and hanging down the back or done up in a strange sort of club. They appeared very friendly and glad to see us, and with their assistance we safely crossed the now swollen Gila and marched to their village. We obtained from a chief a small supply of flour, beans and pumpkins. the old fellow excusing himself for not furnishing more, as the *camisas colorado* (Graham's command) had consumed everything that they had for sale.

I was struck with the graceful proportions of the young Pima girls—regular bronze Venuses—but with the exception of their eyes, their features were rather repulsive than otherwise. The women dressed in a skirt of cotton cloth or strips of the inner bark of the cottonwood, they wore padding on the hips and behind under their skirts, in fact regular bustles. The men went almost naked, though a few had on shirts obtained from Graham's command; they had an odd fashion of filling their hair full of mud from the Gila, and then twisting it up into a helmet-like form and letting it dry. This served a three-fold purpose; it was an effectual protection from the clubs of their natural enemies the Yumas of the Colorado, it increased the growth of hair, and was sure death to the *piojos* who became prisoners in this singular adobe prison. From cotton of their own raising they weave blankets in the most primitive manner, four sticks being all they require for the loom. Their fields are irrigated by a system of canals from the Gila, the women doing the work of the fields while the men take care of the children and do the weaving.

We remained here two days and in company with Judge Holden, Doc Irving, Tobin and three others, with several *Pimas* for guides we visited some remarkable ruins, about twelve miles up the river. These were the remains of three houses. Our guides said that Montezuma built them. They were made of mud with coarse gravel mixed in, forming a kind of concrete. I sketched them from different points, much to the wonder of our guides. In all directions I found what must have been the sites of houses or corrals, oblong circles of stones, while the ground was covered with broken pottery and we found three stones similar to those used by the Mexican women in grinding corn.

On our return we found Glanton raving drunk from fermented juice of the *agave*, obtained from some Coco-Maricopas who lived in another village close by. To prevent trouble Glanton was lassoed and bound fast for the night. Next day I believe I was waited on by the entire village to be sketched, our guides of the day before having well advertised my great abilities as an artist. The girls gathered around me forming beautiful groups of living statuary; they seemed shy and modest, but full of fun and like all the sex overflowing with curiosity. They laughed and chattered like magpies, their beadlike eyes sparkling with merriment. I gave away several drawings to the belles, who returned the compliment by bringing me huge watermelons, and one gave me a cotton sash such as the "bucks" wear on their heads, woven with bright red and blue lines.

While I was sketching an uproar arose in the village caused by Holden's seizing hold of one of the girls and proceeding to take gross liberties with her person. A dozen cocked rifles brought to bear on him drove the brute from his prey, but the whole village was in ferment, and it seemed as if we stood a chance of being wiped out. However, Holden made some explanation to the crowd in Spanish that appeased them.

On the third day we bid good-by to these half civilized savages and started down the Gila for the Colorado. After a five days' march we reached the bluffs at the junction of the two rivers in good condition. Indians showed themselves and at first appeared hostile, but soon flocked around us with offers to ferry us across the Colorado. They belonged to a tribe known as Yumas and were in stature superior to the Pimas. We rested at their village for two days, recruiting ourselves and animals for the hardships to be encountered in crossing the great Colorado Desert, where for one hundred and thirty miles, according to the Indians, all was sand, with no water to be found.

The ferry was about four miles below the junction of the two rivers and consisted of two boats made from wagon bodies which I recognized as having been part of the equipment of Graham's command—the letters U.S. were still visible. I told Glanton of this, when a dirty old chief pulled out of a skin pouch a greasy bit of paper, with the well known (to me at least) signature L.P. Graham, making a present of the pontoon boat to the head chief of the tribe, for services rendered to his command in crossing. The other boat they said they found on the desert, and that there were many more there.

Glanton and Holden, after we made camp, had a long conference together, and from Holden's earnest manner I was sure some new devilish scheme was on foot. Next morning Glanton unfolded his plans. He told us that this ferry was our "El Dorado, our gold mine," the gate to California, and he proposed to seize it, kill the Indians if they objected, capture the young girls for wives &c. A few of us opposed the diabolical scheme, but the measure was carried by an overwhelming majority and the plan organized to make it a success.

During the day our camp swarmed with Yumas, and at a signal from Glanton the two boats and nine of the prettiest girls were secured. The Indians being unarmed fled without resistance,

361

and Glanton's *coup d'etat* was a decided success. The poor captive girls, who seemed to expect death, were tied hand and foot and placed under a guard, and all the rest went to work to build a fort on the summit of an isolated hill near the ferry. The ground was covered with loose stones of irregular shape, and with men working for their lives it did not require much time to erect a circular wall, capable of holding our entire party and well constructed for defense against any weapons such as the Yumas possessed. We named it Fort Defiance.

Indians hovered around the camp all night and next day many warriors appeared above and below our fortification and about noon four of them advanced towards us waving their hands and crying out, "*Amigo, amigo.*" Glanton and three others, laying aside all arms but their revolvers, which they concealed under their *serapes*, went out to meet them. The Yumas demanded the return of the Boats, the girls, and our departure. To this Glanton replied that he should keep all he had taken, and if they did not supply him with beans and bunch grass he would destroy their village and kill all. Their answer was to produce short heavy clubs, and with loud cries they rushed on Glanton's party who at once dropped four of them with the Colts. By force of habit the savages' hair was raised and brought in. The Yumas, seeing this, retired with many howls to the deep shade of the willow thicket that covered the bank. So matters remained for several days, no Indians appearing to trouble us, and all hands kept busy strengthening our camp, and ferrying over numerous parties of Mexicans on their way to California. Glanton, leaving the gang in charge of Holden, left for the California settlements with three of our party to buy beef, taking with them over a thousand dollars. Indians only appeared at a distance, and business at the ferry was brisk and highly lucrative, as we demanded and received four dollars per head for all crossings, and one dollar a head for all animals, we swimming them alongside the boats to which they were made fast by lassos.

Our honorable captain returned alone after ten days' absence with no beef, no money, but two animals, one a mule loaded with whiskey, a few pounds of coffee, sugar and ship's biscuit. He was quite sober, but cross and surly. He said his companions had deserted him and gone to the gold mines, that he had got into trouble in San Diego with some soldiers, had killed two, and was fortunate in getting away with a whole skin. He also informed us that a party of Sonorans were two days back on the desert, on their way home from the mines, that he had travelled with them to a place called Vallecita, and that they had plenty of gold in their possession. Glanton proposed in a cool businesslike way for his band of cutthroats to wipe out the entire party.

An indignant refusal from all the band but the two principals admonished him that he had gone too far, and he passed it off as a joke. That night another disgusting orgy was indulged in by Glanton and most of his band, which now numbered only fifteen. I had become so thoroughly horrified with the hellish deeds of my companions that dread feelings akin to the nightmare took possession of me, making my days miserable, and my nights a series of fearful dreams I sounded Ben Tobin, Hitchcock and Long Webster on the subject of quitting the gang and going to the mines in California. They were as disgusted as myself, and we agreed to start whenever a favorable opportunity presented itself, and formed our plans accordingly.

One morning about two days later Tobin, Hitchcock and Webster volunteered to go to the river bottom to cut firewood—each day three men were detailed for this duty—while I was to guard the animals grazing on the brush-like grass near by. Hitchcock had secured thirteen *onzas* or doubloons, we had secreted in the timber some jerked mule meat, and two gourds of whiskey. As per arrangement we four met about ten in the forenoon, behind a huge sand drift about a mile from Fort Defiance, I mounted on Soldan, the others on the best mules of the band. With the statement of Glanton and the Sonorans in regard to the desert fresh in our minds, we let our animals drink their fill at a gully, while we filled our blankets with the screw shaped bean of the mesquite bush.

We were just ready to take the plain trail of the emigrants through the cottonwoods to the sandy plain that stretched between us and California, when savage yells with three shots reached our ears from the direction of the fort. We rode down to the river again, and Fort Defiance was in plain sight; the bluff on which it was built was covered with howling Indians.

"Glanton rubbed out, by G———d!" was Crying Tomb's eulogy on his old commander, as we rode back through the timbered bottom, somehow feeling sad and blaming ourselves for deserting in the hour of danger and death. But Tobin, the renegade priest, the profane, the wicked reckless ranger, raised his sombrero and said. "It's the hand of God! To Him, and you, Peloncillo Jack, His blind instrument, we owe our lives. Ho for the desert, for California, and Gold!"

We toiled through loose drift sand for some time, and then the trail left the cottonwoods and struck boldly out on the great desert, the "*Jornado del Muerto*." (Journey of Death.) We moved on some twenty miles and came to a clump of mesquite bushes in a sink of the plain. A well had been dug here, but it was now filled with sand. Three dilapidated government wagons had been abandoned near by with several dead mules, dried to mummies. A tail board made fast to the bows of one of the wagons bore the following legend, cut with a knife; COOK'S WELLS, WATER 10 FT. D. H. RUCKER.

My old commander's card! Out here in the California Desert! How the name brought up all the romance of my soldier life in the Dragoons, of Monterey, Buena Vista, of her, the incomparable, the sainted Carmeleita. How wretched, how wicked I felt, as the visions of my wild irregular life passed with panoramic distinctness before me, raised by the name of my friend and commander!

A deep draught at the whiskey drove away such unpleasant thoughts. Seeing no water could be obtained for want of digging tools, we moved off on the well-defined trail. Tobin, looking back towards the Colorado, suddenly halted and with an exclamation of astonishment caused the rest to look in the same direction. Away off towards the dark belt of timber that marked the course of the river, we could see several figures of men, coming our way. Even at the distance they were from us we could plainly make out that one of them was a white man, who was fleeing for his life from savages. Without a word our blanket of mesquite beans was thrown to the ground, the spurs drove into our animals, and away we went to the rescue.

As I neared the scene I recognized the gigantic form of Judge Holden, who had been brought to bay by about a dozen yelling Yumas, who appeared to be armed only with their short clubs. Holden was resting, leaning on his heavy rifle, which he had been using as a war club, with effect, for one savage lay brained at his feet, while the rest were seated on their haunches around him, like a pack of prairie wolves mound a fagged Buffalo Bull. Neither Holden or the bucks showed the least sign of being aware of my approach until I raised the old yell of the Dragoons, when the Yumas, with their strange sharp war cry like the bark of a Coyote, started off on a run. I charged on one who wore a shirt that I recognized as belonging to a Mexican of our party, and rode him down, but my gallant steed stumbled on him, throwing me over his head.

I was not hurt and was on my feet at once, just as Holden dashed out the brains of the red devil with the butt of his rifle. "Just in time, Jack!" he said, "I owe you one," and held out his huge hand. I replied "No thanks, the service is of no value," and did not take the extended hand. My *tres companeros* now came up and Long Webster dismounted and gave his mule to the Judge, and we resumed our way.

We passed by Cooks Wells and continued our course until late in the afternoon, when we rested for two hours. We traveled several hours this night on foot, leading our animals. There was no mistaking the trail—deserted wagons and skeletons of horses and mules marked every rod of ground. This was a black day with us. We all became cross and distrustful of each other, as yet I don't think any of us suffered much from hunger or thirst. At midday we gave the animals the last of the beans and finished our jerked "muley," when Holden volunteered, if I would let him have my horse, to push on to the settlements, obtain a supply of meat and water and return. I saw through the scoundrel's design, and refused, but an hour later when he was riding Soldan, he whipped him into a run and was off.

I was plodding along with the rest, carrying my rifle, when a shout from the treacherous villain made me realize my loss, and his base ingratitude. I threw up my rifle, but he had gained too great a distance for a sure shot. When some six hundred yards off he held up and cried out to us, "You cursed robber's and murderers, I go to denounce you in the settlements! You shall hang in California!" and with another yell of triumph dashed off. He did not get far, for Soldan stumbled, throwing his rider, and before he could recover himself, we were on him with our rifles bearing on his villainous heart.

The Judge tried to turn it off as a joke, but we kept an ominous silence. I was left with him, while the other three retired and consulted. They soon returned, and informed him of his fate—to be tied fast with a lariat, and left. Heaven! How he begged and pleaded! But in vain; he was soon made fast to a half-buried wagon body, his arms secured behind him, and then as we departed his entreaties changed into curses and ravings.

We rode on in moody silence for several miles, when we halted and looked back. We could see him in the distance—a small dark spot on the desert. I could not stand it. "He is a white man, and no doggone 'greaser' or buck, and I'll be d—d if he shall go under in that fashion!" I cried out, and without waiting for answer I started back.

It took me a good hour to reach the miserable wretch, and as I dismounted, drew my Bowie Knife and advanced on him, judging my motive by his own black heart, he begged me not to kill him, to let him live, even to linger and die of starvation! What a cowardly heart the bully had! I cut the rawhide thongs without a word and rode off.

My companions had kept on, and as I reached the rise where I had left them, I could just discern them some six miles away. Looking back, I was surprised to see Holden, not over a mile in my rear. Poor Soldan showed much distress, and while I favored him all I could, I was compelled to urge him along at a trot, under spur. At dark none were in sight, I was alone once more in the desert, hungry, thirsty and weary. I broke down completely and found myself blubbering like a child. I had fancied myself a man, when I was nothing but a boy.

When I dismounted, Soldan, more weak and used-up than his master, stretched himself with a groan on the sand. Wrapping myself up in my blanket, I lay down between my old companion's legs, and with my head resting on his flank, fell asleep. I awoke with a start, chilled to the bone, sore, stiff and hungry. It was yet dark, no signs of day in the east, the sky appeared black, and seemed to close in and shut down on me, while the stars seemed little cuts in the black cover, through which a light beyond was seen. I aroused my weary companion, and cold and shivering, with the bridle over my arm, led the way guided by the North Star and the debris of former caravans. I walked on for hours, with nothing living in sight. The sun had come up, of a dull brassy color, the sky was like bronze.

Away to the north the black mountains of California seem to recede as I advanced. I knew I must reach them before I could obtain water; what little sugar I had left I gave to Soldan, who showed much weakness, his two falls having evidently strained him. At noon we halted for two hours, then once more resumed our solitary way. I was getting weak, my heavy arms weighed me down like lead, I had drawn my waist belt tighter and tighter, until I was shaped like a wasp. On we went for hours, but the black mountains seemed as far off as ever. Long into the dark night we stumbled on, until we sank exhausted on the sand. I slept but little this night, and at daylight it was difficult to get Soldan to his feet. He carried my arms, and I had to partially pull him along. All day we kept on, lying down now and then, and then staggering on, trying to gain on those craggy peaks which always fled before us.

Towards night Soldan stopped and refused to go any further; he groaned and seemed in much distress, and when I threw off the saddle he fell to the ground. I raised his head in my lap, crying as if my heart would break. I knew it was my duty to shoot him and put an end to his sufferings, but my heart failed me. Spreading over him my blanket, I loaded myself down with my arms, and went on my solitary way towards those distant peaks. The sun went down, darkness shut down around me, yet I staggered on. My tongue was dry, and my mouth felt as if full of ashes, yet I somehow never lost heart, or hope. I prayed silently to my Heavenly Father for strength to enable me to reach water. Finally I fell down and lay like a corpse until morning.

Next day the sun was high overhead when I was saluted with a cry like a Coyote's and two Indians came in sight from behind a sand drift. Weak and raving as I was, I managed to draw my revolver, when they threw up their arms and cried out "*amigo, amigo!*" and held up a double-headed gourd. They gave me a long drink which tasted reekingly of sulphur.

Using signs I made them understand that my horse might he saved, and one of them went back to look. The other guided me on for several hours until we came to their village. To my great delight I found my three comrades sitting in front of a campfire and getting my supper: broiled mule meat, acorn bread and real pure coffee! They told me the place was called Vallecita, or little valley, the first water after leaving the Rio Colorado, one hundred and twenty five miles away. They had arrived some twelve hours ahead of me and sent the "Diggers" back to my rescue.

Next day, to my great joy, the second Indian came in leading Soldan, who he found following up the trail. Hitchcock, who acted as interpreter, engaged two of the bucks to go back for my saddle, promising them and the man who saved my horse my old ragged red shirt! and this without consulting me. It was all the shirt I had.

We concluded to remain here several days to recruit our animals. Two of the Indians agreed to go ahead to the Spanish settlements to purchase a beef for us with a doubloon we gave them for that purpose. They were *Cristianos* and appeared trusty as Indians go. Our animals seemed to relish the coarse wiry grass, and the stinking water, and we turned them out to graze without a guard.

On my second night here we received quite a fright. It was towards morning when a shout from Ben Tobin awoke us, and the sight that greeted us caused us to seize our arms. Seated cross-legged by the fire, broiling raw meat, was the gaunt specter of the Judge! The old scoundrel acted as cool as if nothing unpleasant had ever happened! On being interrogated, we found to our great indignation that when he reached Vallecita, guided by the light of our fire, he had in the dark stumbled onto our animals, killed one of the mules (Ben Tobin's) and cut out a chunk, which he was now eating. On the desert when he was about dead, some Indians had come across him and given him some water and parched acorns. They must have been the ones going after my saddle.

We held a hurried counsel of war. At first we decided to shoot the miscreant, but on second sober thought we let him off and were soon roasting tough chunks of Tobin's mule and cracking jokes at that worthy's expense. Next day we gave the mule's offals to our Indian friends, who held a grand pow wow and ate up everything.

On the third day, there being no sign of the Indians we sent for beef, we decided to start for the settlements, informing Holden that he could not go with us, but must remain one day after we left. After a tedious march of six hours over a barren rocky country, and some miles of it through a narrow pass, we reached the Indian *rancheria*, of San Phillippe, where we found grass and water. Here our Indians met us with two beeves instead of one, and we found they had paid only four dollars for both. We killed one, made a good meal of its lean stringy meat, cut off some of the best pieces to pack along, gave the rest to the Indians and the live one to its driver for his trouble.

POSTSCRIPT

It is on this rather abrupt note that Chamberlain's *My Confession* comes to a close.

However, the historical record offers a few clues as to his whereabouts in the aftermath. On May 9th, 1850, three Americans claiming to be members of Glanton's gang presented themselves before the Alcalde of Los Angeles, telling a story of their narrow escape from Indians on the Colorado in April. Their names were Marcus L. Webster, William Carr, and Joseph A. Anderson. Webster is named in *My Confession*; the other two are presumably aliases for Chamberlain and another scalp-hunter. The local militia was roused by their story, and established an army post at the ford, near the original site of Glanton's Fort Defiance.

After this, Chamberlain's exact whereabouts are unclear for a period of three years. He lived in California—apparently quite satisfied with the climate—and was known to have participated in William Walker's 1853 filibustering expedition to Baja, California. Afterwards, he sailed home to New England, taking the "scenic route" around the world.

Despite returning to the relative domesticity of Boston, Chamberlain did not remain tranquil for long, nor did he give up his romantic streak. However, he did finally settle down, marrying Mary Keith in 1855. He would stay with Mary for the rest of his life, having three daughters: Tranceita, Delorious, and of course, Carmeleita. In typical Chamberlain fashion, he worked various jobs, though only his time as a teamster and eventually a policeman are recorded. It was during this time (1855-1861) that Chamberlain began work on his memoirs.

When the first shots of the Civil War were fired in 1861, Chamberlain wasted no time in volunteering for his home state. Once again joining a rowdy group of volunteers, this time he was elected first lieutenant—a rank from which he quickly rose. After four years of combat, he rose to the rank of general in the Union Army. In 1863, at Kelly's Ford in Virginia, he was seriously wounded by a bullet which passed through his face and stopped between his shoulders, which placed him out of action for the rest of the war. By the close of the conflict, Chamberlain had risen from a first lieutenant to a brevet brigadier general. However, the action of the Civil War also had the effect of stopping his writing—hence *My Confession*'s abrupt close.

After the war, Chamberlain became politically active, receiving an appointment as the deputy quartermaster general of Massachusetts. Following this, Chamberlain began his final career, as the warden of state prisons in Massachusetts and Connecticut. During his two decades as warden, he was known as humane and understanding, despite (or perhaps due to) his own violent, swashbuckling background.

After his retirement in 1893, Chamberlain led a quiet family life at home, a manor which he dubbed "Maple Hall". He passed of old age on November 10th, 1908.

The historian Roger Butterfield noted that "The Boston newspapers remarked at the time that he was 'known throughout the circles of the Grand Army of the Republic as the 'veteran of veterans' of Massachusetts…He had fourteen horses shot in battle and was wounded seven times…In all he participated in more than 100 battles…'"

It was a life of adventure, danger, and intrigue equaled by few.

Chamberlain with his family

Made in the USA
Middletown, DE
05 October 2023

40312072R00227